THE CHURCH
BEFORE THE COVENANTS

For Anna

THE CHURCH BEFORE THE COVENANTS

The Church of Scotland 1596–1638

by

Walter Roland Foster
*The General Theological Seminary
New York*

SCOTTISH ACADEMIC PRESS
EDINBURGH AND LONDON

Published by
SCOTTISH ACADEMIC PRESS LTD.,
25 Perth Street, Edinburth EH3 5DW

Distributed by
Chatto and Windus Ltd.,
40 William IV Street,
London W.C.2

First published 1975
© 1975 Scottish Academic Press

All rights reserved. No part of this publication may be reproduced, stored in a retrieval system, or transmitted, in any form, or by any means, electronic, mechanical, photo-copying or otherwise, without the prior permission of Scottish Academic Press Ltd.

SBN 7011 2129 7

Printed in Great Britain by
Cox & Wyman Ltd., London, Fakenham and Reading

Contents

1. Introduction: From Reformation to Revolution, 1560–1638 ... 1
2. Notional or Real Bishops ... 6
3. The Bishops of Scotland, 1611–1638 ... 32
4. Kirk Sessions ... 66
5. The Brethren of the Presbytery ... 85
6. The Senior Courts of the Church ... 111
7. Admission to the Ministry ... 133
8. A Constant Platt Achieved: Provision for the Ministry ... 156
9. Parish Life in Scotland ... 173
10. Conclusions ... 199
    Bibliography ... 207
    Index ... 215

List of Abbreviations

A.P.S.	*Acts of the Parliaments of Scotland*
B.U.K,	*Acts and Proceedings of the General Assemblies.*
Calderwood	David Calderwood, *The History of the Kirk of Scotland.*
Fasti	Hew Scott, *Fasti Ecclesiae Scoticanae.*
K.S.	Kirk Session
O.L.	*Original Letters Relating to the Ecclesiastical Affairs of Scotland.*
Presb.	Presbytery
R.M.S.	*Registrum Magni Sigilli Regum Scotorum.*
R.P.C.	*Register of the Privy Council of Scotland.*
R.S.S.	Registrum Secreti Sigilli.
Reg. Assig. Stipends	Register of Assignation and Modification of Stipends.
Reg. Pres.	Register of Presentations to Benefices

Preface

For an American to have spent three years in the delightful and beautiful city of Edinburgh was itself one of the joys of working on this study. My interest has been to examine the ordinary, working records of the kirk as a way of understanding its actual operation and life during a particularly important period in the reformation. That church often contrasted sharply both with contemporary estimates of what should happen or was happening and with later estimates of what did happen. In fact, the church that is revealed by its own records was remarkably creative and effective. Major advances toward meeting the goals of the kirk were made in many ways and in many areas of the country.

The graciousness and courtesy that my family and I found in Scotland remain as a very happy memory. I am especially indebted to Professor Gordon Donaldson, whose knowledge of the sources was matched only by his encouragement, counsel, and direction. The staff of the Scottish Record Office of HM General Register House in Edinburgh could not have been more helpful in making records available and providing much assistance in the deciphering of difficult texts. My thanks are also due to the staffs of the Library of the University of Edinburgh and the National Library of Scotland. The Presbytery of Stirling and Dunblane kindly made available the seventeenth-century records of the presbytery of Dunblane. W. H. Makey, City Archivist of Edinburgh, helped to clarify some important points about the membership of kirk sessions, and Dr Ian B. Cowan kindly reviewed and commented on one chapter. I am indebted to the Overseas Department of the Episcopal Church of America for a grant which made our years in Edinburgh possible.

Acknowledgements are due to the following for permission to include copyright material: the Scottish Church History Society, the Saint Andrew Press, the S. C. M. Press, the Oxford University Press, and Oliver and Boyd.

Above all, my wife and family, who cheerfully moved to another country where we found a home and who endured and encouraged the arduousness of seventeenth-century research, made this book possible.

RF

CHAPTER ONE

From Reformation to Revolution, 1560-1638

The events of 1560 were hardly the beginning of the Scottish Reformation – as early as 1525 parliament had to forbid the importation of Lutheran literature – yet 1560 was a crucial turning point in the formation of the reformed kirk. In May 1559 John Knox returned to Scotland and by October of that year the 'Lords of the Congregation' had formally suspended the French regent, Mary of Guise. By the summer of 1560 they, with the help of the English, had driven out the French. In August 1560 an irregular parliament repudiated the authority of the pope, adopted a reformed Confession of Faith and forbade celebration of the Latin Mass. A 'book of reformation' known to later students as the first Book of Discipline was prepared during the final months of 1560.

These were momentous events, and if the future of the reformed church seemed precarious and uncertain in 1560, yet by 1638 many of the promises and policies proclaimed in the Book of Discipline, sometimes triumphantly and sometimes hesitatingly, had become firmly and securely established.

A casual glance at the eighty-year period from the reformation of 1560 to the revolution of 1638 suggests a time of violent changes. A queen deposed and the trappings of her Catholic religion, including episcopacy or prelacy, repudiated; a flourishing and triumphant presbyterianism established only to be sabotaged by a disingenuous king with the help of complacent, Erastian churchmen; the establishment of a new episcopacy; a subservient church which at last recovered its reformed freedom in the revolution of 1638 – these are some of the themes of an old tradition of Scottish historiography. And an uncritical reading of some of the great seventeenth-century church histories – especially David Calderwood's massive eight-volume *History of the Kirk of Scotland* – will confirm the view.

Fortunately, the surviving church documents of the period are extremely rich; and closer examination of the evidence soon reveals a pattern that was at once more complex and more realistic. The overwhelming impression is one of continuity and development. Of course there was change, debate and conflict. Frequently the reformed Christians of Scotland disagreed about the meaning of their commitment to a reformed faith. Yet there remained a surprising amount of unanimity about fundamental matters of faith and worship, and the lines of continuity between the implicit as well as explicit claims of the first Book of Discipline and the established reformed kirk before the revolution of 1638 are clear enough.

The most obvious mark of continuity throughout this eighty-year period was an almost unchallenged commitment to a reformed theology. By 1560 the lines of reformed orthodoxy were clear enough, and Scotland contributed little that was original to the development of Calvinist and reformed thought. The strength of solid Calvinism formally expressed in the Confession of 1560 remained throughout the entire Reformation period. Although Scotland played no official part in the proceedings of the Synod of Dort (1618), yet the uncompromising canons of that synod were at once accepted and the synod's reputation remained high throughout the seventeenth century.[1] Calvinism was reaffirmed during the Interregnum and continued through the Restoration period as well.

Arminianism did have some slight influence in Scotland in the early seventeenth century. It was feared, along with popery, and frequently condemned; but most of the charges could only be vaguely established. Even the Aberdeen Doctors, one creative theological school which developed at Aberdeen in the decade before 1638, could not successfully be accused of Arminianism. 'Their Calvinism was definite enough though not satisfactory to an extremist such as Rutherford.'[2]

In the books read by bursars or students for the ministry in the universities, in the voluminous sermons published throughout the period, and in the trials of expectants or candidates for ordination, the virtually unchallenged commitment to reformed orthodoxy remained as one striking sign of continuity.

[1] G. D. Henderson, *Religious Life in Seventeenth Century Scotland*, 84, 94; W. R. Foster, *Bishop and Presbytery*, 156.
[2] Henderson, 50.

The story of Scottich worship after 1560 is also one of slow development rather than violent change. Scots and English reformers alike were influenced by continental developments, and both the English Book of Common Prayer and the Book of Common Order, a book of Geneva were known in Scotland. Numerous editions of the latter established the normal standard of worship; and the great Sunday service, with its pattern of confession, psalms, Scripture, sermon, intercession, thanksgiving and blessing, remained the norm.

It is true that James VI tried to re-establish greater conformity between the worship of the two kingdoms by introducing Five Articles which were eventually passed by an assembly at Perth in 1617. The one requiring communicants to neel to receive communion created much controversy for a few years and did alter that part of the service in a significant part of Scotland. However, communion was at best an annual service for most parishes; and none of the Perth Articles would have affected the regular weekly worship of the church even if they had been enforced. Charles I went even further in his effort to introduce a Scottish Book of Common Prayer in 1637. Although that book contained a number of concessions to Scottish practice, its introduction into an explosive and revolutionary situation provided at least the occasion for revolutionary forces to consolidate. Its impact on the actual worship of the kirk was minimal.

Scottish worship was not static, and the monarch did succeed in introducing small changes, such as the observance of the anniversary of the Gowrie conspiracy and the Gunpowder Plot, or the celebration of communion at 'Pasch' or Easter. However, the overall pattern of daily and weekly worship as well as the administration of the Lord's Supper remained remarkably constant throughout the period.

Questions of polity and government produced more controversy and change. Here again Scotland developed little that was original in terms of a theological understanding of polity. The creative and original contribution of the kirk was the adaptation of reformed concepts of polity into a comprehensive and remarkably efficient system which recognised the needs of many different groups and classes within Scotland and which developed a system of good order and supervision that might well be envied by churchmen south of the Border. In many ways the greatest interest of the period lies in investigating these developments in government and order.

Certainly seventeenth-century churchmen saw questions of government and polity as the most controversial of their day. David Calderwood's voluminous history returns again and again to these questions. Perhaps the greatest architect of Scottish presbyterianism was Andrew Melville – scholar, systematic thinker, a university figure. It has been well said that 'the John Knox of mythology is very largely compounded of the Andrew Melville of history, for it was Melville and not Knox who was the originator of Scottish presbyterianism.'[3] Melville wrote little, but all of the themes for which he is best known – the life-long character of lay elders, the 'parity' of ministers, the authority of the presbytery, the right of the church to all ecclesiastical temporalities and spiritualities, the supremacy of church officials over those of the civil government, including the king – all deal with issues of government and polity.

Even in questions of government, much persisted throughout the period, and a close examination of the evidence suggests a pattern of slow evolution and gradual modification. The foundation stone of Scottish church government was the kirk session. Developing early in the reformation, the kirk session continued throughout and invariably was supported and encouraged by all serious churchmen. Presbyteries were a second-generation development; but after some initial hesitation in the 1580s, when presbyteries began to be organised, they too won the support and backing of all responsible churchmen, including bishops. The basic officers of the church were the lay elder and the minister. Andrew Melville's doctrinaire concept of the elder remained stillborn, but the offices of elder and minister as they had developed before Melville remained unchallenged and flourishing throughout the entire period. Episcopacy underwent more fluctuations, but even here – if we think of episcopacy in terms of 'oversight' and not in terms of medieval prelacy – the tradition of the supervision of each portion of the church by one churchman was remarkably continuous.

The overwhelming impression of numerous kirk session, presbytery, synod, and assembly records is not that of a thousand parishes which for eighty years hotly debated the question of

[3] Gordon Donaldson, *Scotland: Church and Nation through Sixteen Centuries*, 71.

episcopacy. More pressing was the need to curb immorality, preserve the sanctity of the Sabbath, see that the pure Word of God was preached and the great sacraments of Baptism and Lord's Supper duly and godly administered, fight the remnants of Roman Catholicism on the one hand and of superstition on the other, restore the material fabric of both church and manse, establish and strengthen schools, maintain the high standards in both living and learning that were expected of ministers, and secure to those ministers a decent and acceptable income. In eighty years the reformed Christians of Scotland made remarkable progress in meeting those needs.

Professor Gordon Donaldson's study of *The Scottish Reformation* concentrated on questions of government and order in the sixteenth-century period. My own *Bishop and Presbytery* looked at similar questions in the Restoration period from 1660 to 1688. This present study is an effort to fill a gap and deal in like manner with the structures of government, order and life which flourished during a particularly important phase, the early seventeenth century. The period from 1596 to 1638 forms a natural unit during which a synthesis began to emerge and some of the problems and issues raised by the reformation found at least an acceptable solution. It is to that period that this study is devoted. Episcopacy, kirk sessions, presbyteries, synods and assemblies, ministers, finance, church life – these are the topics which reveal both the limitations and the successes of the church before the covenants.

CHAPTER TWO

Notional or Real Bishops

Few probably realised it at the time, but 1596 was in many ways a major turning point for both church and nation in Scotland. The Scots had not enjoyed an extended period of stable government since the death of James V in 1542. For half a century after that, Scotland had been troubled by conflicts during regencies, the tumultuous reign of Mary Stewart and the long minority of James VI. However, by 1596 James was thirty years old and had been an anointed king for twenty-nine years. He could remember neither father nor mother, and his early life was dominated by strict and thorough Calvinist tutors. About 1582, at the age of sixteen, he had begun to take an active part in the government of Scotland, but his early attempts to establish secure rule and authority were not too encouraging. He was kidnapped in 1582, and a second attempt almost succeeded in 1592; more than once he was forced to sacrifice favourite friends and advisers (Esmé Stewart, Duke of Lennox, in 1582 and James Stewart, Earl of Arran, in 1585). But, as he approached thirty, James became more skilled in using his limited resources, chiefly his wits and his royal status. The increasing effectiveness and stability of his monarchy was one important reason why the next generation of Scots (from c. 1596 to c. 1638) enjoyed a greater measure of peace and prosperity than the Scottish people had known for decades. 'Under his peace, lairds and burgesses had become wealthier, life was less precarious for the poor, inroads had been made on the political influence of the nobility, there were everywhere signs of vitality'.[1]

The year 1596 was also a turning point for the reformed Church of Scotland. By that year the Reformation in Scotland was more than a generation old and its fundamental convictions on matters of faith and worship were never again to be seriously challenged. John Knox had died in 1572, and Andrew Melville was now at the

[1] Gordon Donaldson, *Scotland: James V to James VII*, 295.

NOTIONAL OR REAL BISHOPS

height of his power and influence. The Reformation in Scotland had not at first been a revolution, for the old ecclesiastical structure had not been completely swept away. Rather the transition from a medieval to a reformed kirk had involved an almost infinite series of adjustments and had raised numerous problems which were still far from solved in 1596. The complex and potentially explosive question of church finances – involving the disposal of monastic lands, perhaps also of episcopal lands, and the intricate question of teinds (or tithes) – affected the interests of king and nobility as well as those of churchmen. The development of a reformed and educated ministry as well as the need to provide adequate recompense for that ministry occupied the attention of reformers again and again. The reformation of discipline, the establishment of schools and the reduction of the people of a thousand parishes to the discipline of a reformed kirk were far from complete. The work, even the authority, of general assemblies, and their relationship to parliament and to the crown, were still unsettled issues. The kind of ecclesiastical supervision or oversight that the reformed church would adopt to direct and guide kirk sessions, to supervise the examination and ordination of ministers, and to extend the discipline and doctrine of the church into unreformed areas was also unsettled.[2]

Yet the control and direction which King James exercised after 1596 affected the church as well as the civil government. From that point the monarch was increasingly a potent factor in ecclesiastical decisions, and, considering the achievements of the Jacobean church, the term 'godly monarch' is not entirely inappropriate.

By 1596 the question of ecclesiastical supervision or oversight had been a matter of keen debate in Scotland for twenty years. In the first Book of Discipline (1560) the early reformers had proposed a system of ten superintendents who would roughly succeed to the

[2] Recent secondary studies of the sixteenth-century Reformation include Gordon Donaldson, *The Scottish Reformation* (Cambridge, 1960), and Duncan Shaw, *The General Assemblies of the Church of Scotland, 1560–1600* (St Andrew Press, 1964). The most important seventeenth-century account, strongly anti-episcopal in outlook, but containing many primary documents, is David Calderwood, *History of the Kirk of Scotland* (8 vols., Wodrow Society, 1842–9). A shorter account by his contemporary which presents the episcopal point of view is John Spottiswood, *History of the Church of Scotland* (3 vols., Spottiswood Society, 1851).

duties and jurisdiction of bishops. This system had been implemented in part with the nomination of five superintendents, among them John Erskine of Dun in Angus and John Winram in Fife, whose vigorous and effective ministry for a generation was an important precedent for the revival of a reformed episcopate in the seventeenth century. Although no further superintendents were appointed, later general assemblies appointed commissioners or temporary visitors to exercise oversight similar to that of superintendents.

A significant step in the development of this tradition of church oversight was taken at an extraordinary general assembly which met at Leith in January 1571-2. As part of a compromise worked out with the regent, the Earl of Mar, the assembly authorised the establishment of a system of reformed or godly bishops. In a long and detailed act, the assembly ordered 'the names and titillis of Archebischoppis and Bischoppis ... to stand and continew in tyme cuming'; it provided for 'personis qualifeit to be nominat within the space of yeir and day' after the occurrence of a vacancy; and it ordered the new bishops to 'exerce na farther iurisdictioun in spirituall functioun nor the superintendentis hes and presently exerces'. The new bishops were to be nominated by the crown, elected by cathedral chapters (or rejected if they were not qualified), and confirmed by the king and his regent.[3] Between 1572 and 1577 bishops were nominated and inaugurated in most of the ancient dioceses, and in spite of some friction the system of superintendents and bishops began to coalesce. The compromise seems to have been generally satisfactory to contemporaries. John Knox, in a letter to the general assembly of 1572, urged 'that all bishoprics vacand may be presented ... according to the order takin in Leith'. Indeed, as Professor Donaldson roundly puts it, 'the great reformer's farewell advice to the Church of Scotland was that it should have bishops'.[4]

The compromise reached by 1572 was, however, soon challenged by a rising presbyterian party whose chief spokesmen were Theodore Beza in Geneva, Thomas Cartwright and Walter Travers in England, and Andrew Melville in Scotland. Melville returned to Scotland in 1574 after some years in Geneva and was soon able to inspire a party of younger men from his position of leadership

[3] *B.U.K.* I, 203-36 (Calderwood, III, 170-96).
[4] Calderwood, III, 766; Donaldson, *Scottish Reformation*, 170.

in the university of Glasgow and later in the university of St Andrews. The new leaders saw even 'godly bishops' as (in Beza's famous term) *pseudepiscopos (Papatus reliquias)*[5] and asserted as a theological principle the doctrine of equality or parity of ministry.

Extant evidence is scarce, but evidently the issue was at first intensely debated in general assemblies between 1575 and 1580. The second Book of Discipline, adopted by the General Assembly of 1577, argued that 'it aggreit not with the woorde, that Bishoppis sould be pasturis of pasturis, pasturis of mony flokkis', and in 1580 an assembly 'in ane voyce ... finds and declares the samein pretendid office [of bishop] ... unlaufull in the selfe, as haveand neither fundament, ground, nor warrant within the Word of God'.[6] At about the same time the first presbyteries began to be organised, and by 1596 the earlier reformed system of oversight by bishops or superintendents had been in large part replaced by the establishment and spread of presbyteries. After 1586 jurisdiction over presentations to benefices and discipline itself were gradually transferred from bishops and superintendents to presbyteries. Episcopal prestige received another blow in 1587 when a parliamentary Act of Annexation deprived bishops of their temporalities or lands.

Yet in 1596 episcopacy had not yet disappeared entirely. Bishops were found as lords of the articles in the parliaments of 1593 and 1594, and both of these parliaments passed acts 'in favour of the bischop of Abirdene ... for recompence of the temporalities of the bischoiprik'. In 1595 a presentation was directed to the bishop or commissioner of Argyll.[7] But this was all little more than a façade, and the status of episcopacy in 1596 was neatly indicated by George Gladstanes, later Archbishop of St Andrews, who wrote in another context that now Scotland had more 'notionall than reall Bishopes'.[8] And another archbishop, John Spottiswood, whose father had been superintendent of Lothian, described the remnants of Scottish episcopacy in 1600. Episcopal revenues and lands had been almost entirely taken over by the nobility except in two dioceses.

[5] Beza, *Epistolae*, LXXIX.
[6] *B.U.K.* II, 506, 453 (Calderwood, III, 548, 469).
[7] *A.P.S.* IV, 7, 32–3, 56, 77; R.S.S. LXVII, 184.
[8] *O.L.* I, 54.

Aberdeen and Argyle had their own incumbents at the time, both actual preachers; St Andrews and Glasgow were in the hands of the Duke of Lennox; Murray possessed by the Lord Spynie; Orkney by the Earl of Orkney; Dunkeld, Brechin and Dunblane had their own titulars, but these were not ordinary preachers; Galloway and the Isles were so dilapidated as scarce they were remembered to have been. Only in Ross and Caithness some provision was left.[9]

More important than the faint and occasional vestiges of episcopacy was the fact that even after presbyteries developed, the reformed kirk continued to find the work of overseers of some kind extremely useful. In 1593 a general assembly decided that presbyteries 'throughout the haill realme' needed to be visited and their work and records examined. That assembly and subsequent ones regularly appointed 'Commissioners and Visitors of the Kirk', giving them authority over large areas of Scotland and power to 'viset and try the doctrine, lyfe, and conversation, deligence and fidelitie of the Pastouris'.[10] Instructions to commissioners by the general assembly of 1596 were a remarkable precedent for the pattern which bishops were to follow fifteen years later. Commissioners were ordered to try pastors 'within the Presbytries, where they are established already' with the assistance of 'such brethren of the Presbytrie . . . as they think most zealous, sincere, and best affected'.[11] The authority of these temporary commissioners was considerable. In 1593 Mr Robert Pont, the distinguished minister of St Cuthbert's, Edinburgh, and visitor of Orkney and Shetland, was commended for having shown 'great deligence usit be him . . . and specially in deposing of the persounds not making residence'.[12]

Another way in which the theoretical parity of ministers was in practice infringed was the appointment by some general assemblies of interim commissions to meet in Edinburgh for the purpose of providing direction and leadership between meetings of assemblies.

[9] Spottiswood, *History*, III, 82.
[10] *B.U.K.* III, 800–801 (Calderwood, V, 246). For commissions in 1595 see *B.U.K.* III, 848–9 (Calderwood, V, 371–3).
[11] *B.U.K.* III, 862–3 (Calderwood, V, 419). For the later pattern of visitations by bishops and the brethren of the presbytery, see below, 49–52, 105–6.
[12] *B.U.K.* III, 812.

The assembly of 1588 'appointed certan Commissioners and brethren to meet every week [in Edinburgh] to consult upon affaires pertaining to the weill of the Kirk in so dangerous a time', and subsequent appointments, either for general affairs or specific projects, were made as well.[13] During the tense final months of 1596 some of the commissioners lived in Edinburgh and met daily. This commission has been described as a 'council of war' for the presbyterian party. A record of their vigorous and ultimately unsuccessful opposition to the king is preserved in the minutes of their meetings.[14]

Ultimately, however, a pro-episcopal policy could only be successful because Scotsmen themselves were divided over the question of church polity. There was a considerable body of conservative opinion to which James could and did appeal. It is difficult to estimate the extent of this opinion, but there are many signs of its existence. Approval by the general assembly of 1586 of a compromise plan which retained a moderate episcopacy as well as presbyteries indicated that support for episcopacy was still substantial at that date.[15] Veteran reformers such as John Craig, Erskine of Dun and David Lindsay continued to support a moderate episcopal policy, and their influence was far from negligible. The north in general was well-known for its conservative views, and the revival of episcopacy was supported there. The idea that James could impose episcopacy upon an unwilling and altogether resistant church is based upon a most unrealistic estimate of James's actual power.

Although James lacked the means (and probably the inclination) to be an absolutist monarch, his rôle in the restoration of episcopacy was decisive. Nor could there be any doubt about his views on church government. In 1599 he described the doctrine of parity as 'the mother of confusion and enemie to Unity' and urged the advancement of:

> godlie, learnid, & modest men of the ministrie, quhom of god be praised thair lakis not a reasonable number, & be thair praeferrement to bishoprikkes & benefices ... ye shall not onlie banishe thair paritie, quhilke can not agree with a monarchie, but ye also

[13] *B.U.K.* II, 742, III, 814, 849–51 (Calderwood, V, 3–4, 247, 374–5).
[14] Calderwood, V, 477–521; W. L. Mathieson, *Politics and Religion*, I, 274. Cf. Edinburgh Presb. 28 December 1596.
[15] *B.U.K.* II, 664–84 (Calderwood, IV, 567–83).

sall reestablishe the aulde institution of three estates in parliament.[16]

It seems likely that these views were reached by James well before 1599, nor was his preference for episcopal authority difficult to understand. Bishops dependent upon the crown would make the doctrine of royal supremacy a reality, and a strong clerical or first estate might well serve as a counterweight to the nobility as well. Accordingly, between 1596 and 1610 James pursued a pro-episcopal policy with obstinate tenacity of purpose and with a remarkable dexterity and variety of methods. There can be little doubt that the programme to revive episcopacy was planned and directed by the king himself.

The turning point came in 1596. The Melvillian party overreached themselves in that year, and gave the king the opportunity to organise an effective response. In March 1595–96 a general assembly in Edinburgh not only included in its list of sins of the nation 'His Majestie . . . blotted with banning and swearing' and the queen for 'not repairing to the Word and Sacraments, nightwaking, balling, &c' but also 'proceeded to discuss arrangements for the training of a militia in every parish and for its equipment with suitable armour to be purchased from abroad'.[17] In September Andrew Melville lectured 'God's silly vassal' on his subordination to those 'whome Chryst hes callit and commandit to watch over his Kirk'.[18] About the same time Mr David Black of St Andrews refused to appear before the privy council to answer charges of having declared in a sermon that 'all kings are devil's children' and (perhaps more serious for James's English plans) that Queen Elizabeth was 'an atheist and that the religion that was professed there was but a show of religion guided and directed by bishop's injunctions'.[19] In November commissioners of the assembly at Edinburgh sent representatives to the privy council to 'admonish

[16] *Basilicon Doron*, I, 79–80.
[17] Calderwood, V, 408–9, cf. 459; R. S. Rait, *The Parliaments of Scotland*, 17; *B.U.K.* III, 860 (Calderwood, V, 400).
[18] James Melville, *Diary*, 370—1; 'Again, I mon tell yow, thair is two Kings and two Kingdomes in Scotland. Thair is Chryst Jesus the King, and his Kingdome the Kirk whase subject King James the Saxt is, and of whase kingdome nocht a king, nor a lord, nor a heid, bot a member'.
[19] *R.P.C.* V, 326–7; 334–6, 340–2; *Calendar of Scottish Papers*, XII, No. 288.

[them] of their duetie'. It is hardly surprising that the English ambassador should have described some of the ministers as 'preachers of the blessed Word and some of them thought to be more insolent than their calling will afford'.[20]

The next few weeks saw a tense struggle between the commissioners and James over the case of Mr Black, popish plots, public criticism of the king and council, and the whole 'questioun ... anent the limits of the two jurisdictions, civill and spirituall'.[21] On 17 December a riot took place in Edinburgh while the king and some of the nobility were meeting in the tolbooth and the ministers and people were in a neighbouring church.

> In the meane tyme, there ariseth a rumour in the toun, that the king had givin no good answere to the kirk; and in the Tolbuith, that the toun was in armes. ... A messinger of Satan ... came to the kirk doore, and cryed, 'Fy! save yourselves;' and ranne to the streets, crying, 'Armour! armour!' The people ryse in armour. Some runne one way, some another. ... In this hurlie-burlie, two or three came to the Tolbuith doores, which were closed, and called for some of the Octavians [members of the Privy Council] abusers of the king ... that they might take order with them.[22]

Order was soon restored, but the king chose to blame the ministers and people of Edinburgh for the tumult. The commissioners of the assembly left Edinburgh; the ministers of Edinburgh were warded in the castle; and the town council, thoroughly frightened, was willing to accept almost any requirement to regain James' favour.[23]

The whole incident does not appear to be especially important, but it was a significant turning point. Thereafter James appears to have permanently seized the initiative from the ministers and commissioners. Within a few months he opened his campaign for the revival of episcopacy, a campaign which was not complete until 1610. James Melville, nephew of Andrew Melville, recognized the importance of the incident when he wrote of 'the xvij day of

---

[20] Calderwood, V, 461; *Calendar of Scottish Papers*, XII, No. 452.
[21] *Ibid*. V, 461–510.
[22] *Ibid*. V, 511.
[23] *Edinburgh Burgh Records*, VI, 174.

December [1596], that accursed wrakfull day to the Kirk and Comounweill of Scotland'.[24]

In February 1596–97 James summoned a general assembly to meet at Perth. He encouraged greater representation from the conservative north, a section of the church which had hardly been represented at all in assemblies of the previous decade. David Calderwood, an historian from the presbyterian party, wrote in dismay, 'the ministers of the North conveened in suche numbers as were not wount to be seene at anie tyme before, and everie one of them great courteours'. The assembly appears to have been respectful but not subservient. James's greatest victory was an acknowledgement from the ministers that their meeting was in fact a general assembly.

When the mater was putt in voting, the ministers of Angus and the North sweyed muche. Eight presbytereis refused to allow that meeting for an Assemblie: ellevin approved it, under the name of EXTRAORDINAR.[25]

It was an important precedent. James had reestablished his right to summon a general assembly and to determine its place of meeting. He was to use this advantage again and again to strengthen the conservative party.

In May 1597 James summoned another assembly to meet at Dundee. It was, as Calderwood noted, 'of this new fashioun', which primarily meant that the north was adequately represented and that the king and his advisers were active, even aggressive, agents. James appears to have won most of his points at the Dundee assembly. His candidate for moderator was elected, presbyteries were ordered 'to meedle with nothing in thair judicatour ... but controversie proper to the Ecclesiastick judgment', and – most important of all – most of the commissioners chosen by this general assembly were ministers sympathetic to royal views on church polity.[26]

[24] James Melville, *Diary*, 372. There is a convenient summary by A. Ian Dunlop, 'The Polity of the Scottish Church, 1600–1637', *Records of the Scottish Church History Society*, XII, 161–5. However, James began to manipulate the date and place of General Assemblies in February 1596–97, not in 1601. See below, 121.
[25] Calderwood, VI, 606–7; cf. Gordon Donaldson, 'Scotland's Conservative North in the Sixteenth and Seventeenth Centuries'.
[26] *B.U.K.* III, 813–30 (Calderwood, V, 628–47).

NOTIONAL OR REAL BISHOPS 15

Although commissioners of assembly were a familiar institution the choice of commissioners at Dundee gave that body a wholly new outlook. Of the first fourteen commissioners appointed, of whom seven were a quorum, five were destined to become bishops.[27] James Melville was at first willing to serve as a commissioner, but within a year he had 'smeld out the purpose of erectioun of Bischopes againe' and resigned.[28] Subsequent assemblies saw the appointment of more men who were soon to be bishops: four at Dundee in March 1597–98,[29] four at Montrose in 1600[30] and one at Holyrood in 1602.[31] It is little wonder that Calderwood described the commissioners after 1597 'as a wedge taikin out of the kirk, to rent her with her owne forces and the verie needle which drew in the thread of bishops'.[32]

James's next step was to revive a civil or parliamentary episcopacy. Since 1580 churchmen and assemblies had debated the question of the best way the church could be represented in parliament and have its voice heard there.[33] The government's solution of this issue was a traditional one. Ministers of the kirk were to be chosen

[27] George Gladstanes, Bishop of Caithness in 1600; David Lindsay, Bishop of Ross in 1600; Alexander Douglas, Bishop of Moray in 1602; James Nicolson, Bishop of Dunkeld in 1607; William Cowper, Bishop of Galloway in 1612. (*B.U.K.* III, 928 [Calderwood, V, 645]).

[28] Melville, *Diary*, 433–4. At least by June 1598 the presbyterian party realised what was happening. In that month Alexander Douglas warned James that some of the commissioners 'specialie thay of Sanctandrois' intended either to boycott meetings 'or els gif thay keip dyett ... to sett thame selffis altogider aganis your Majesties intentioun' (*Warrender Papers*, II, 356–7).

[29] Peter Blackburn, Bishop of Aberdeen in 1600; Andrew Knox, Bishop of the Isles in 1605; Gavin Hamilton, Bishop of Galloway in 1605; Alexander Lindsay, Bishop of Dunkeld in 1607 (*B.U.K.* III, 943 [Calderwood, V, 692]).

[30] John Spottiswood, Archbishop of Glasgow in 1603; Alexander Forbes, Bishop of Caithness in 1604; James Law, Bishop of Orkney in 1605; Andrew Lamb, Bishop of Brechin in 1607 (*B.U.K.* III, 959 [Calderwood, VI, 21]).

[31] Andrew Boyd, Bishop of Argyll in 1613. The commissioners now included four bishops and seven men who would become bishops (*B.U.K.* III, 996 [Calderwood, VI, 177]).

[32] Calderwood, V, 644.

[33] Melville, *Diary*, 118–9; Calderwood, IV, 260–1, V, 430–1; *B.U.K.* II, 527, 787 (Calderwood, III, 578, V, 157): cf. G. Donaldson, *Scotland: James V to James VII*, 201–2.

as bishops of the ancient dioceses to sit in parliament as the first or clerical estate. The policy was embodied in an act of parliament in December 1597 – an act which was to be cited in presentations to bishoprics for many years. It ordered that 'sick Pastoures and ministers ... as at ony time his Majestie sall please to provide to the office ... of ane Bishop, Abbot, or uther Prelate, sall at all time hereafter have vote in Parliament', and further required that bishoprics 'salbe onelie disponed be his Majestie to actual Preachers and Ministers in the Kirk'. The act provided only for the civil duties of bishops and acknowledged that 'bishoprikis in thair spirituall policie and government' could only be determined by the king and general assembly.[34]

James tried unsuccessfully to secure confirmation of this solution from two general assemblies. An assembly in March 1597–98 merely agreed that 'the Ministrie [should] have vote in Parliament', and an assembly at Montrose in 1600 proposed an alternative to the king's episcopal policy by sanctioning the appointment of ministers as parliamentary commissioners.[35] Thwarted by two assemblies, James threatened to appoint bishops simply by letters patent. However, presentations when they began were not simply civil decisions. In September 1600 the presentation of Mr Peter Blackburn, minister of Aberdeen, was directed to 'the ministeris of the generall assemblie and thair commissioneris' who were charged 'to try and examinat the learning, etc.' of Mr Blackburn.[36] On 15 October, at a meeting of commissioners from synods, 'the king, with his commissioners, and the ministers there conveened, nominated and choosed three bishops ... and appointed them to vote at the nixt parliament in name of the kirk'; and royal presentations (including a confirmation of Blackburn's earlier one) were issued on 5 November.[37]

Later controversialists were often to see episcopacy in simple right or wrong terms. For some the issue may not have seemed quite so clear at the time. Peter Blackburn was reported to have told Mr Patrick Simpson, minister of Stirling, that the king 'had

[34] *A.P.S.* IV, 130–1.
[35] *B.U.K.* III, 945–6, 954–6 (Calderwood, V, 696, VI, 17–20).
[36] Reg. Pres. III, 37.
[37] Calderwood, VI, 96; Reg. Pres. III, 39. The three were David Lindsay, Bishop of Ross, Peter Blackburn, Bishop of Aberdeen, and George Gladstanes, Bishop of Caithness (Calderwood, VI, 96).

offered the bishoprick of Aberdeen to him, assureing him if he would not take it for his awin benefite and the benefite of his brethren, to provyde them better, he would dispone it to a courteour'. Two prominent members of the presbyterian party, Robert Bruce and Andrew Melville, advised 'him to take the benefice, and let the Generall Assemblie provyde kirks therewith'; and the presbytery of Stirling likewise advised him to accept the appointment and at the next general assembly 'lay the benefice down at their feet'. However, James 'stayed any resolution of that kynd to be put in execution'.[38]

No further presentations to bishoprics were made until November 1602. An assembly at Holyrood in that month gave implicit approval to James's earlier presentations when it 'thocht expedient to adjoyne and nominat uthers . . . to be adjoynit to these, quhilk were nominat be Commissioners of Provinces conveinit at Halierudehous, the 15 of October 1600'. Twenty-five ministers were nominated 'out of the quhilk number his [Majestie] sould make choise of such as he sould present to the benefices vacand', and at the end of the month a fourth bishop was appointed.[39] Thereafter, presentations were regularly made, until by 1608 all sees were filled with men who were 'actual Preachers and Ministers in the Kirk'.

In addition to reuniting the active ministry and parliamentary episcopacy, James worked to restore the estates and income of the bishoprics. Temporalities or lands of bishops had been annexed to the crown by the act of annexation of 1587. The act exempted only episcopal spiritualities (teinds or tithes) and the principal castles and 'yairdis' of bishoprics.[40] Restoration of episcopal temporalities had long been a goal of James,[41] and crown presentations soon reflected this policy. Appointments in 1600 or 1602 did not mention temporalities, but the first appointment which James signed 'at Hamptoun Court' showed his determination to take full advantage of the exceptions allowed by the act of

[38] Row, History, 204.
[39] B.U.K. III, 1000 (Calderwood, VI, 179). Alexander Douglas, minister at Elgin, was presented to the bishopric of Moray on 30 November 1602 (Reg. Pres. III, 65–6).
[40] A.P.S. III, 433.
[41] Basilikon Doron, I, 79.

annexation. On 20 July 1603 John Spottiswood was presented to the Archbishopric of Glasgow with:

> all maner places castellis touris fortalices housses bigingis orcheardis yeardis and dowcottis as weill within the wallis and precinct of the bischopis place ... as els quhair ... notwithstanding the act of annexatioun.[42]

A presentation of Gladstanes to St Andrews in October 1604 was even more ample, as was that of Alexander Forbes to Caithness the following month.[43] However, in December 1604 the bishop of Ross was confirmed in his benefice by a presentation using language which certainly envisaged the restoration of temporalities. The bishop was presented to all:

> touris, fortalices [etc.] ... togedder with all and haill the superioritie and Lordschip of regalitie thairof ... notwithstanding of the act of annexatioun.[44]

A presentation of Andrew Knox to the Isles on 12 February 1605 used similar language. And the presentations of James Law to Orkney on 28 February 1605 and of Gavin Hamilton to Galloway a week later left no doubt about the intentions of the king. Both men were presented to all the privileges of their bishoprics 'alsweill of the temporalitie as spiritualitie'.[45]

The whole policy was appropriately concluded with an act of parliament in 1606 which annulled 'the forsaid act of annexatioun of the temporalities of benefices'[46] and which restored to all bishoprics what had already been recovered in some. Although purely civil and financial in its effect, the 1606 act was an important step in the restoration to bishops of material power and prestige – adjuncts which were universally regarded in the seventeenth century as a necessary part of episcopacy.

---

[42] Reg. Pres. III, 77–8.
[43] Reg. Pres. III, 92, 98–9.
[44] Reg. Pres. III, 96–7.
[45] Reg. Pres. III, 97–8, 107–8. In February 1606; five months before parliament met, a ratification of Alexander Douglas to Moray had presented him to the 'spiritualitie as temporality' of the bishopric (Reg. Pres. III, 112). The language of these three presentations was the same as that used in 1607, after the act of restitution (e.g., Reg. Pres. IV, 4–5, 12–13, 16).
[46] *A.P.S.* IV, 281–4.

NOTIONAL OR REAL BISHOPS

The episcopacy which James had revived was an almost purely civil office, and the new bishops had no significant authority or status in the kirk. They had received no authority from a general assembly and apparently made little effort to exercise anything like episcopal functions. Not many records from this period have survived, but even in the presbyteries of Ellon and Aberdeen, where the episcopal tradition was stronger than in many areas, the bishop of Aberdeen in 1606 was little more than a prominent minister of the church.

There was one remarkable attempt to exercise episcopal oversight in the church in 1601 when Bishop Blackburn of Aberdeen tried to intervene in a disciplinary case. The results must not have been very encouraging for the proponents of episcopacy. The case began when Janet Stuart challenged the proclamation of banns of marriage of Walter Wood to a third party, claiming that he had made a prior promise to marry her. The presbytery of Ellon summoned Janet to prove her charge. However, she:

> comperit not ... but a letter [was] sent be the bishop off Aberdene shawing that he was informit off a promese mad to the said Janet be the said Walter and theirupon that the proclamaation of banns suld stay. It being testified by famous witnes the same day that the said Janet was infamous and had na certain residence that a letter suld be sent ... to the bishop informing him forder in the mater and of her non comperence, ... that in caise he had any forder he wald inform the presbitery and until that tyme that the proclamatioun off banns suld proceid.[47]

Nothing further was heard of the case, and it was many years before the bishop of Aberdeen made any similar attempt to regulate presbyterial discipline. Thereafter Peter Blackburn appeared occasionally in the minutes of Ellon presbytery, but no more frequently, and with no greater prominence, than other distinguished ministers. Sometimes he assisted in difficult visitations, but other ministers assisted as regularly.[48]

Most presbytery registers have no occasion to mention any bishop at this time. Indeed, until 1606 most bishops continued to

---

[47] Ellon Presb. 16 December 1601.
[48] See for example, two difficult visitations at Slains and Udny in 1605. Blackburn was one of the commissioners present at Udny, but other ministers were sent to Slains. (Ellon Presb. 23 and 30 May 1605).

hold parochial charges and to attend presbytery meetings as ordinary members of that body. This was certainly the position of Blackburn, bishop and minister of Aberdeen, and of Andrew Knox, bishop of the Isles and minister of Paisley. Alexander Douglas continued to moderate the kirk session of Elgin after he became bishop of Moray; and George Graham, Bishop of Dunblane in 1603, was still listed as minister of Scone, and drawing the stipend thereof, in 1607 and 1608.[49]

By 1606, however, James was determined to give the developing Scottish episcopate greater authority within the church. In the same year that his parliament restored episcopal temporalities, he successfully pressured a general assembly at Linlithgow into giving bishops certain rights within the church, Bishops were now to be 'constant moderators', that is permanent moderators of the presbyteries where they resided and – at least as the assembly minutes were altered by James – of synods as well. The latter looked very much like diocesan episcopacy and there was considerable resistance during the next eighteen months. However, by July 1608 presbyteries and synods seem to have accepted their constant moderators.[50]

Opponents of episcopacy argued that bishops were accepted as constant moderators because they were able to manipulate the stipends received by ministers. A contemporary historian, John Row, wrote that in 1607 'the King appoynting that the modification of ministers stipends should be in the hands of Bishops, ... many poore, many corrupt and ill-principled ministers begouth to acknowledge them'. A year later Calderwood reported that 'the modificatioun of ministers' stipends for this year was committed whollie to the bishops. By augmentatioun they allured, by diminutioun they weakenned and discouraged, a number of the ministrie'.[51]

There is little doubt that bishops did attempt to manipulate stipends. However, their ability to weaken and discourage by diminution was evidently limited. In a letter to James, the arch-

[49] Aberdeen Presb., Paisley Presb., Elgin K. S. *passim*, Reg. Assig. Stipends, Scone (Perth), 1607, 1608.
[50] For synods and Presbyteries, see below 91–3, 113–14. The assembly of 1606 is discussed below, 122–3.
[51] Row, *History*, 245; Calderwood, VI, 705 (cf. 688); Melville, *Diary*, 749–50. Manipulation of stipends was a frequent device to encourage ministers to conform. See, for example in 1584, *R.P.C.* III, 701–4, or in 1596, *Calendar of Scottish Papers*, XII, No. 320.

NOTIONAL OR REAL BISHOPS

bishop of St Andrews acknowledged that he had tried to do so, but 'albeit a great nomber hes nocht receaved any testimoniall of us as your Maiestie directed, yit they tak up thair stipendis peciablie'.[52] The archbishop's complaint is further borne out by the Register of Assignation and Modification of Stipends. Only portions of the register have survived, but figures for stipends for most presbyteries for the years 1599, 1601, 1607 and 1608 are extant. An examination of the stipends of fourteen ministers, all of whom had in one way or another opposed royal policy and been warded in their parishes as a consequence, shows little significant change in their assigned or modified stipends. Six stipends dropped slightly, one rose considerably, and seven remained the same.[53] Even in the case of well-known opponents, bishops seem to have had little success in reducing stipends.

Of greater significance was the influence of bishops in raising stipends. Parliament in 1606 had appointed an important Commission for Modification of Stipends, composed of noblemen, bishops and ministers. The achievements of this important commission, on which bishops took an active and leading part, are recorded in many charters and presentations.[54] Within a few years it must have become apparent to some that reformed bishops could be valuable agents in improving the efficiency and well-being of the kirk.

By the end of 1608 controversy appeared to be dying down.

[52] *O.L.* I, 130.
[53] The stipends of David Calderwood (Crailing), John Carmichael (Kilconquher), William Hog (Ayton), Tobias Ramsey (Foulden), William Row (Forgandenny), and John Smyth (Maxton) dropped from an average of 389 merks in the 1599–1601 period to an average of 323 merks in 1608. The stipend of Robert Wallace (Tranent) rose from 195 merks in 1601 to 500 merks in 1608. The stipends of John Cunningham (Dalry), John Dykes (Newburn), James Greig (Loudoun), John Hepburne (Cranshaws), Nathan Inglis (Craigie), George Johnston (Ancrum), and James Martin (Peterhead) averaged 351 merks in the 1599–1601 period and remained the same in 1608. These figures are compiled from the Reg. Assig. Stipends, 1599–1601, 1607–08, and a full table is in my thesis, 'Episcopal Administration in Scotland, 1600–38', Appendix A. Not all of the reductions were necessarily due to episcopal interference. The remaining records are too scanty to permit comparison of figures on other warded ministers. For ministers' stipends in general at this period, see below, Chapter Eight.
[54] *A.P.S.* IV, 299–300. For the work of this commission, see 159–61.

At a general assembly in July of that year, a bishop was elected moderator for the first time since 1575.[55] The assembly itself had little to say about episcopacy, although it did continue a full bench of bishops as commissioners of assembly. One act requested bishops and other commissioners 'to apprehend traffiqueing Papists, Jesuites and Seminarie Priests that does haunt within thair bounds'.[56]

In 1609 Calderwood wrote, 'As they [the bishops] growed in greatnesse ... numbers of the ministrie fell to them', and another leader of the presbyterian party was equally discouraged. In a letter to James Melville, John Carmichael wrote, 'Manie tyme my heart is cast doun and freatteth, to see the universall defectioun of al. There is no man now to speeke a word in seasoun',[57] that is, against episcopacy. And there was good reason for their pessimism. In October 1608 the presbytery of Jedburgh, a centre of resistance to episcopacy, submitted peacefully enough to an episcopal visitation. The presbytery clerk wrote, 'Thair wes no tyrall that day becaus Mr James Law [Bishop of Orkney] had tryed them and had the tryall in his owne scrolls'.[58] Open resistance, at least, was at an end.

Parliament in 1609 passed a series of acts favouring episcopacy, the most important of which was an act for the restoration of the bishops' consistorial jurisdiction.[59] Commissary courts had been set up for confirmation of wills and had jurisdiction over marriage and divorce cases, small debt cases, and suits concerning teinds, testaments, and slander; these courts were also courts of record. The four commissaries of Edinburgh were a court of appeal from other commissaries on certain matters. The right of the lords of session (the judges of the central civil court) to appoint commissaries was ratified by letters patent in 1581 and by parliament in

[55] At the assembly at Edinburgh on 7 March 1574–75 James Boyd, Archbishop of Glasgow, was moderator. At the Assembly at Linlithgow on 26 July 1608 James Law, Bishop of Orkney, was moderator. In 1608 the choice of Law 'passit hardlie aneuch, for he caryit it be thrie onlie fra Mr Patrick Symsone' (*B.U.K.* I, 314, III, 1046 [Calderwood, III, 339, VI, 751]; O.L. I, 145).
[56] *B.U.K.* III, 1053 (Calderwood, VI, 765).
[57] Calderwood, VII, 46–7.
[58] Jedburgh Presb. 5 October, 1608. For earlier resistance by the Presbytery of Jedburgh, see below, 92–3.
[59] *A.P.S.* IV, 430–1. Cf. Gordon Donaldson, 'The Church Courts', *Introduction to Scottish Legal History* (Stair Society).

1592. The act of 1609 restored to bishops the right to appoint commissaries, their deputies, and other officers of the court. However, it did not revive the pre-Reformation right of appeal to archiepiscopal courts, but retained the practice of appeals to four commissaries of Edinburgh, who were to be appointed by the two archbishops. Furthermore, the act provided for a system of appeals from the commissaries of Edinburgh to the court of session. The procedure and jurisdiction of commissary courts were not altered by the act, but the right of bishops to appoint the officers of those courts was another significant step in the restoration of episcopal authority.

It was also in 1609 that Archbishop Spottiswood received a royal warrant to visit the Borders to 'tak ordour with the repairing of the kirkis ... for planting of the same with ministeris, and for uniting of kirks togidder'. In the course of his visitation he also apprehended two notorious Roman Catholic leaders and seized some vestments and other sacred articles.[60]

The same year Bishop Andrew Knox made an even more extraordinary and successful expedition to the Isles. The previous year the bishop had accompanied Lord Ochiltree on a military expedition to the Isles which had secured the submission of many of the leading chiefs. In July 1609, however, the bishop himself was the head of a more peaceful expedition. The mission culminated in a court held at Iona by 'ane Reverend Father in God, Andro, Bischop of the Illis', in whose presence many of the chiefs agreed on a series of statutes and entered into a solemn bond. The statutes of Iona did not 'attempt to alter the social structure of the clans; instead, abuses were to be checked and there was to be reformation through religion and education'.[61] The following year Bishop Knox received a commission of justiciary over the Isles, and he established his headquarters at the castle of Dunivaig in Islay. The editor of the Privy Council Register concluded:

> [By 1613] it is pretty evident that the Council had retained the chiefs of the Icolmkill contract satisfactorily within their grasp, and that, though there may have been no very great progress in the work of introducing into the Western Islands the social and

[60] *R.P.C.* VIII, 266–7, 564–5, 584–5, 301. The bishop of Galloway received a similar commission in January, 1610 (*R.P.C.* VIII, 616, 433).
[61] *Source Book of Scottish History*, III, 265.

economic reforms promised in the Statutes of Icolmkill, Bishop Knox's stewardship of these Islands had been very prudent and successful.[62]

By the end of 1609 the archbishop of Glasgow wrote that 'the king by his letters was now daily urging the Bishops to take upon them the administration of all Church affairs'; and the prelate concluded, 'an Assembly to this effect was appointed to hold at Glasgow'.[63] The Glasgow assembly which met in June 1610 was only the most notable of a series of events in that year which sought to establish episcopal authority on a secure and permanent basis. On 30 January Archbishop Spottiswood was made an additional judge of the court of session.[64] On 15 February the establishment of two courts of high commission was publicly proclaimed.[65] The work of these courts will be considered later; but their establishment gave the bishops, and especially the two archbishops, positions of power and authority. About the same time presentations to benefices ceased to be sent to presbyteries and were directed to bishops instead. Although most presentations before 1610 were directed to presbyteries, some presentations continued to mention bishops, commissioners, superintendents, or the commissioners of the general assembly. Between 1597 and 1609 eight presentations mentioned bishops,[66] four were directed to the commissioners of the general assembly,[67] twenty-four were directed to either commissioners or presbyteries,[68] and sixteen mentioned only commissioners or superintendents.[69] Although it

[62] *R.P.C.* IX, 27, 30–1, xxxii. The bishop was less successful in 1614 when the castle of Dunivaig was captured by the MacDonalds. Knox led an expedition against the rebels but was cut off, had his own boats burned and was forced to leave his son as a hostage. The castle was eventually recaptured by the laird of Caddell, and sometime between 1614 and 1618 Bishop Knox left for Ireland. (*R.P.C.* X, 264, 267, 279n. xxxvi–xxxix; *O.L.* II, 272–5; *Memoirs of the Maxwells*, II, 73–4).
[63] Spottiswood, *History*, III, 205.
[64] Brunton and Haig, *Senators of the College of Justice*, 251.
[65] Calderwood, VII, 57–62. Also see below, 47–9.
[66] Reg. Pres. III, 51, 104²; IV, 10–11, 14, 27, 31.
[67] Reg. Pres. III, 53, 93; IV, 14, 34.
[68] Reg. Pres. III, 11, 15, 25, 31, 33–4, 51, 54, 74, 91, 104, 108, 109, 110, 119, 126; IV, 10, 18, 31, 32, 33, 49.
[69] Reg. Pres. III, 9, 12, 26, 31, 36, 41, 43–4, 46, 47, 52, 57, 59, 67, 69, 96, 100.

might not be surprising to find presentations directed to 'the bischop of Argyll or commissioneris over the kirkis thairof', or to 'the Bischop or Commissioner of the dyocie of Cathnes and presbiterie of Sutherland',[70] it is more surprising to find commissioners mentioned in Lanark, Duns, Glasgow, Jedburgh, Brechin, Stirling, and East Lothian.[71] However, a radical change occurred in January 1610, months before the Glasgow assembly. On 2 January a presentation was directed to 'the moderator and presbiterie of Hadingtoun'. On 20 January five presentations were recorded: one to 'the moderatour and presbiterie of Aberbrothok [Arbroath]', three to 'the archbischope of Sanctandrois or the presbiterie of Sanctandrois', and one to 'the archbishop of St Androis'. The next presentation, on 3 March, was directed to 'the maist reverend father in God, George, archbischope of Sanctandrois', [72] and thereafter all presentations without exception were directed to bishops and archbishops. The transfer of crown presentations from presbyteries to bishops was far more abrupt and universal than was the reverse trend in the 1580s.

Long before the Glasgow assembly ever met, it is clear that much had been done to restore 'reall bischopes'. A leader of the anti-episcopal party summarised the status of bishops immediately before the assembly:

> When the bishops became lords in parliament, counsell, checker, sessioun, lords of temporall lands and regaliteis, patrons of benefices, commissioners in the king's high commissioun, and consequentlie, great and terrible to the ministrie, ... then was it thought fitt tyme to convocat a Generall Assemblie.[73]

And even this list failed to mention that bishops now possessed commissariot jurisdiction and were receiving presentations to benefices. A local example of the kind of jurisdiction bishops were exercising in the months before the Glasgow assembly was a letter which the presbytery of Ellon received on 31 January 'fra Mr Peter Blackburn, bischop of Aberdene, in favor of the commiss[ary],

---

[70] Reg. Pres. III, 51; IV, 10–11.

[71] Reg. Pres. III, 9, 11, 12, 15, 25, 41, 43–4, 52, 59, 67, 74, 91.

[72] Reg. Pres. IV, 36, 39, 37, 41, 37. The same presentation of Mr James Fardin to Ferry-Port-on-Craig had been directed on 1 November 1609 to 'the presbiterie of Sanctandrois' (ibid, 34, 42–3).

[73] Calderwood, VII, 90.

beiring in effect that the ministrie haid not hertofoir gevin up the names of the defuncts of the severall paroches', and the presbytery ordered names to be brought at the next meting.[74]

However, the Glasgow assembly which met in June 1610 was a decisive turning point for Jacobean episcopacy; and the conclusions of that assembly, duly modified by parliament two years later, established the limits of ecclesiastical jurisdiction within which episcopacy was to operate until 1638. The assembly granted to bishops four broad types of jurisdiction.[75]

First, bishops were to preside over presbyteries or to appoint moderators of presbyteries. Bishops were to be moderators of synods as well, and parliament added that a bishop could appoint a minister to be moderator of a synod if he were absent.

Second, bishops were given considerable authority over the discipline of laymen by virtue of their right to approve, or withhold, the final sentence of excommunication. Bishops were also responsible for the discipline of ministers, being given the right to try and to depose ministers, 'associating to himselfe the Ministrie of these bounds quher the delinquent served', that is, the presbytery. Parliament added that the same procedure was to be used in suspending ministers.

Third, the rights of bishops to make regular visitations of their dioceses were restored, although if necessary each bishop was allowed 'to appoint some worthie man to be visitour in his place'.

Fourth, presentations to benefices were to be directed to bishops, who were to give collation; and, after examination of the presentee by 'the Ministers of these bounds quher he is to serve', the bishop, 'being assisted be such of the Ministrie of the bounds quher he is to serve as he will assume to himselfe', was 'to perfyte the haill act of ordinatioun'. Parliament also confirmed the rights of patrons to have 'any qualifeit Minister' admitted whom they might present.

The most important modification introduced by parliament was its refusal to ratify the assembly's act that 'Bischops salbe subject, in all things, . . .to the censures of the Generall Assemblie'.

Although there were Reformation precedents for the conclusions of the Glasgow assembly, yet the achievements of the past twelve years were remarkable enough. Primarily, they were due to the

[74] Ellon Presb. 31 Jan. 1610.
[75] *B.U.K.* III, 1096–98 (Calderwood, VII, 99–103); *A.P.S.* IV, 469–70.

persistence and determination of the king and to the growing power of the crown, which made it possible for James to exert so decisive an influence. But James was also able to retain the support of the nobility, or at least forestall their active opposition to his ecclesiastical policies. By 1597 the presbyterian leaders had lost almost all support from the nobility. In that year an anonymous letter to James by a member of the Melvillian party complained of:

> your Majestie's nobilitie . . . of whom, some are enemeis, some professors, some neutralls. The enemeis yitt are about you; . . . the professors, some ly by, some kythe [i.e., manifest] themselves. As for neutralls, a small part of preferment will make them plaine enemeis.[76]

Clearly the author believed that he could appeal to only a small number of the nobility.

A report to Elizabeth in 1597 showed just how little support the presbyterian leaders did have. There were in Scotland, she was told, 'a number of professors of the Word such as noblemen, gentlemen, burgesses and townsmen, whereof never one will assist their ministry against the King so long as he remains, . . . [even] if it were but by outward show, professor of their religion'. And the report concluded that 'the present estate of that realm is such that never a nobleman will countenance the ministry, such excepted as has private quarrels to debate'.[77]

Nor could the newer nobility created after 1600, most of whom were endowed with abbey lands, be expected to support a Melvillian policy which sought to recover those lands for the use of the church. Lack of support from the nobility was fatal to the cause of the presbyterian leaders. A slightly later contemporary wrote that by 1597 assistance from the nobility was disappearing, 'and without them it was well known they [i.e., the presbyterian leaders] could effectuate nothing'.[78]

Although the nobility might not support radical presbyterianism, yet their support for episcopacy was by no means certain. An observer in 1598 saw the real problem.

> In case the ministers should yield freely unto the King for the setting up again of bishops, in my opinion the greatest ple

[76] Calderwood, V, 549.
[77] *Calendar of Scottish Papers*, XII, No. 452.
[78] Guthrie, *Memoirs*, 7.

[plea] would be between the King and nobility who have the bishops' lands in their hands and will be [loth?] to leave them.[79] The prediction was accurate, and at first the government met opposition when it attempted to restore episcopal lands in the parliament of 1606. However, the act for the 'Restitution of the estate of bishops' passed with much less difficulty than was expected,[80] undoubtedly because James was also willing to allow the erection of numerous abbey lands into temporal lordships, thereby giving hereditary rights to noblemen who had previously held their lands only as commendators.[81] After this compromise, there was almost unqualified support from the nobility, not only in the parliament of 1612, but also in the general assemblies of 1608 and 1610.[82]

The attitude of ministers was less unanimous. Some ministers resolutely opposed attempts to revive episcopacy. However, the opinion of the ministers as a whole is more difficult to determine. A report to Lord Burghley in May 1597 probably expressed a widely held position. A rumour had been circuling that the king would not restore three ministers of Edinburgh who had been suspended after the tumult there. 'This kind of proceedings... is not generally approved by the ministers in this realm. Nevertheless, it is reccived with hope that the peace in the Church shall be best preserved and established by the same'.[83]

As has been seen, James' policy was more sympathetically received in the north, and greater representation by northern commissioners at the assemblies after 1596 affected the decisions of that body. However, by a variety of methods, including bribery and threats, James was able to build up a substantial body of support from ministers over the entire country. Bribery was certainly used at the Glasgow assembly of 1610 and commissioners from presbyteries were nominated as well;[84] but these practices alone

---

[79] *Calendar of Scottish Papers*, XIII (Pt. 1), No. 135.
[80] Melrose Papers, I, 16–17.
[81] *A.P.S.* IV, 281–84. In the parliament of 1606 there were eleven erections from former abbey lands as well as confirmations of earlier erections (*A.P.S.* IV, 321–362).
[82] Calderwood, VI, 751; VII, 104, 107.
[83] *Calendar of Scottish Papers*, XIII (Pt. 1), No. 177. The three ministers were eventually restored.
[84] See below, 123–4.

are probably not sufficient to explain the overwhelming majority who voted for the acts favouring episcopacy. Of 126 ministers present at the assembly, 'only five of the whole number voted against the Conclusions'.[85]

Regardless of private opinions which ministers may have held, James's policy was at least acceptable to the vast majority; and most of them continued as ministers of the church. Archbishop Gladstanes may have been too sanguine when he wrote in 1610 that 'the great multitude of the Ministerie ar desyrous that Presbitries sall stand, bot directed and gouerned be the Bischops'.[86] However, most of the ministers were at least willing to serve in a church governed by presbyteries and bishops. Presbytery records make it clear that most ministers continued in their parishes without interruption. The point had not yet been reached in Scottish history when changes in ecclesiastical polity would be accompanied by numerous deprivations.

The events of 1610 were brought to an appropriate conclusion when, on 21 October, John Spottiswood (Glasgow), Gavin Hamilton (Galloway) and Andrew Lamb (Brechin) were consecrated by the bishops of London, Ely and Bath.[87] Neither of the English archbishops took part in the consecration, to avoid any appearance of 'a sort of subjection to the church of England'; and the Scottish bishops were not first ordained presbyters by English bishops, because, as the archbishop of Canterbury argued, 'there was no necessity, seeing where bishops could not be had, the ordination given by the presbyters must be esteemed lawful; otherwise that it might be doubted if there were any lawful vocation in most of the reformed Churches'.[88]

[85] Calderwood, VII, 104–7; VIII, 72.
[86] *O.L.* I, 245.
[87] Spottiswood, *History*, III, 209. Peter Heylyn (born 1600) wrote that Dr Neale, Bishop of Rochester, also participated in the consecration (*Aerius Redivivus* [1670], 387). Cf. Balfour, *Works*, II, 35–6, for a third list.
[88] Spottiswood, *History*, III, 209. According to Peter Heylyn, however, Bancroft's reason was an appeal to the catholic practice of consecration *per saltum*. The archbishop argued that 'Episcopal Consecrations might be given without it [i.e. ordination to the priesthood] as might have been exemplified in the cases of Ambrose and Nectarius; of which, the first was made Archbishop of Millain; and the other Patriarch of Constantinople, without receiving any intermediate Orders, whether of

No discussion of Scottish episcopacy in the early seventeenth century would be complete without a thorough recognition of the royal absolutism under which it existed. This was one point at least upon which members of all parties could agree. A protestation against episcopacy in 1606 declared that the bishops:

> have their lordship and living, their honour and estimatioun ... of the king. ... The king may sett them up and cast them doun, give them and take from them, putt them in and out at his pleasure. And, therefore, they must be at his directioun, to doe what liketh him. ... But with other estats he cannot doe so, they having ... heritable standing in their roomes by the fundamental lawes.[89]

In 1612 the archbishop of St Andrews wrote to the king that 'no Estate can say that they are your Maiesties creatures as we [the bishops] may say, so there is none whose standing is so slipperie when your Maiestie shall frowne, as we, for at your Maiesties nodd we either most stand or fall'.[90] Nor were these sentiments merely theoretical. In 1607 the bishop of Aberdeen violated an act of the general assembly by installing a minister in Aberdeen without obtaining royal approval, and the bishop was threatened with imprisonment by the king.[91] Two years later Archbishop Gladstanes, who had irritated James over some customs duties, was warned that 'howevir we haif bene cairfull to ... establishe the estate of bischoppis, ... yitt wes it never our intentioun to communicat with theme ony pairt of oure royall pouer, prerogative, or previledge'.[92] It is significant that parliament refused to ratify the 1610 act that 'Bishops salbe subject, in all things ... to the censures of the Generall Assemblie'. Bishops were not to be subject to general assemblies, they were to be subject to the crown. According to James 'the bishops must rule the ministers, and the king rule both, in matters indifferent and not repugnant to the

---

[89] Calderwood, VI, 530–1.
[90] O.L. I, 295.
[91] R.P.C. VII, 411, 532; O.L. I, 103–4; cf. B.U.K. III, 896.
[92] R.P.C, VIII, 604–5.

Priest, Deacon, or any other (if there were any other) at that time in the Church'. (Aerius Redivivus, 387–8; cf. Leonel L. Mitchell, 'Episcopal Ordinations in the Church of Scotland, 1610–1688', 143–4.) At least Spottiswood's version is the record of one who was there at the time.

Word of God'.[93] And although Charles often preferred to rebuke Scottish bishops through letters sent by the archbishop of Canterbury,[94] he had no less exalted a view of his royal prerogative.

Whatever may be thought of royal supremacy today, it was not regarded as a liability by many in the early seventeenth century. Shakespeare's Richard II expressed a widely held conviction in Scotland as well as in England.

Not all the water in the rough rude sea
Can wash the balm off from an anointed King.
The breath of worldly men cannot depose
The deputy elected by the Lord.[95]

And Archbishop Spottiswood expressed the same conviction more plainly. 'It is nowhere permitted to subjects to call their princes in question, or to make insurrections against them, God having reserved the punishment of princes to himself'.[96]

The revival of episcopacy between 1597 and 1610 may be compared with the reintroduction of episcopacy in 1661-2. Although there was support for bishops at the Restoration, episcopacy was restored purely on the authority of crown and parliament. No attempt was made to secure even the pretence of approval by a general assembly. 'The ancient government of the church by archbishops and bishops' was restored swiftly and completely.[97] At the beginning of the century, however, restoration of episcopacy was a much longer process and was completed with at least the nominal approval of general assemblies. James might have manipulated assemblies, but he never ignored them completely.

The sixteenth-century Reformation had seen the development of two rival systems of ecclesiastical oversight – bishops, commissioners and superintendents on the one hand, presbyteries on the other. By 1610 both of these systems were widespread and flourishing. The revival of episcopacy was not accompanied by the suppression of presbyteries,[98] and in subsequent decades a serious attempt was made to integrate two systems which have too often been regarded as mutually incompatible.

[93] Spottiswood, *History*, III, 241.
[94] Robert Baillie, *Letters and Journals*, I, 431-6.
[95] *Richard II*, III, 2.
[96] Spottiswood, *History*, I, 302.
[97] W. R. Foster, *Bishop and Presbytery*, 4.
[98] See below, Chapter Five.

CHAPTER THREE

The Bishops of Scotland, 1611-1638

I

BISHOPS AND THE STATE

After 1610 bishops continued to be officers of the state as well as officers of the church. Often it was not easy to draw a distinction between the two. As civil officers they held posts of importance, though not of first rank, in the government. All bishops were members of parliament, and they attended that body as well as less formal conventions of estates called by James and Charles.[1]

Even more important was the membership of some bishops on the committee of the articles. By 1612 that committee in effect controlled parliament. No measure could be introduced which had not passed the articles, and parliament became little more than a 'registrar of conclusions reached elsewhere'.[2] About one-fifth of the regular members of this crucial committee were bishops. By 1621, and perhaps earlier, the crown was able to use episcopal membership to control the choice of other members. 'The bishops selected eight nobles, who in turn chose eight bishops, and those sixteen then chose the barons and burgesses'. The same method was used in 1633.[3] Since bishops could always find eight noblemen who supported the king, and the nobility could hardly find a bishop who did not, this method of election gave bishops a vital part in the maintenance of royal authority over parliament. It was therefore likely that any attempt to reject royal control would also mean a rejection of the bishops who helped to maintain it.

Even more important to the regular government of Scotland was the privy council. After 1610 there were always three to six bishops

[1] *A.P.S.* IV, 466, 524, 581, 592; V, 7, 166.
[2] *Source Book of Scottish History*, III, 234-5.
[3] G. Donaldson, *Scotland: James V to James VII*, 284-5; cf. Calderwood, VII, 490; *A.P.S.* V, 9.

on the council, although only the two archbishops were at all active, and even they were not among those who attended frequently.[4] Bishops were sometimes given routine administrative tasks, but at no time before 1635 did they take a prominent part in the council business.[5]

Sometimes bishops were able to use their civil authority to secure better order in the church. In 1616 John Spottiswood, the new Archbishop of St Andrews, sent a strong letter to John Grant of Freuchie, the laird of Grant. After noting the 'desolatioun of the kirkis of Strathspey', he condemned the laird's:

> wickit cours, I mean of abstractinge the rentis of the kirk from the right use and applying them to your privat. *It is someqhat tolesable qhair a part is bestowit upon Godis ministeris, so muche as may gif them mantenance to attend thair callingis*; but to withhold the qhole and gif no portioun for intertayning the exercisis of Godis worschip in a kirk and settled estate, is planly unsufferable.

He urged the laird to provide for a minister with the advice of the bishop of Moray and some ministers, and he concluded with a threat:

> If this sal take no more effect ... you sall then hold me excusit if, according to the power gifin me by God and his Majestie, I keip a more strict and rigorous dealinge with yow, and cal yow quair yow must bothe answer and mak redresse.[6]

Probably the most important civil duty of bishops before 1625 was their work on the commissions for plantation of kirks in 1617 and again in 1621. The work of these important commissions will be considered later; they did much to improve inadequate stipends, and bishops had a prominent part in their activities.[7]

One striking exception to the modest civil status of bishops was the authority of the bishop of Orkney and Shetland. An unusual situation there enabled that bishop to exercise extraordinary civil

---

[4] *R.P.C.* IX, vi–vii, 237–8; X, 319, 381; XI, cl, 438; XIII, 406, xi.

[5] E.g. *R.P.C.* IX, 503–4; XIII, 219–23; I (Second Series), liii–liv; II (Second Series), 54; V (Second Series), 107.

[6] William Fraser, *The Chiefs of Grant*, II, 41. The proposal in italics represented a common compromise. (Italics added.)

[7] See below, 161–4.

power. In November 1608 Bishop Law sent a complaint to James that the people of Orkney and Shetland were 'manifoldlie and greviouslie oppressed' by Earl Patrick Stewart. The next year the earl was summoned to Edinburgh and warded in the castle there. In January 1610 James sent 'ane ample and large commissioun' to Law to go to 'the boundis of his diocey, that als weele he may tak ordour for a goode reule in the Churche thair as for the quietnes of the cuntrey itselff'. In June 1611 a proclamation announced that 'James, Bishop of Orkney, and Sir John Arnot of Birswark, Knight, were constituted His Majesty's Sherifs and Commissioners' in Orkney and Shetland. A year later a court was held by 'ane reverend father in God, James, bischop of Orknay, his majesteis commissioner, schiref and justice'. In October the lands of the earl of Orkney were permanently annexed to the crown and Law was given 'ane large and ample commissioun to . . . uplift his Majesteis haill dewteis . . . [and] lykwise to administrat, use, and exerce the officeis of schirefship, justiciarie, and fowdrie [i.e. chief magistrate in the Norse system] of the said Erldome'. Subsequent courts were held in Orkney and Shetland by the bishop or his deputy throughout 1612 and 1613.[8]

Meanwhile, Robert Stewart, a natural son of Earl Patrick, attempted a revolt; and in 1614 the Earl of Caithness led a successful expedition to suppress the revolt. In the attack upon the rebels, the bishop of Orkney was clearly the right-hand man of the earl. The bishop wrote letters seconding the earl's requests for more funds and describing the progress of the final siege. He took an active part in negotiating the surrender of the rebels and in paying and disbanding the army after the battle was over. It was, as Lord Binning wrote, the 'expedition of the Earle of Caithnes and Bischop of Orknayes'. At one point 'the Earle of Cathynes went about to demolish and throw down the church [the Cathedral], bot he was with great difficultie hindered by the Bishope of Orkney, who did not suffer him to throw it doune'.[9]

In 1614 the episcopal lands of his bishopric were redivided, and thereafter the bishop had complete jurisdiction in civil affairs

---

[8] *O.L.* I, 167–9; *R.P.C.* VIII, 406, 408, 413, 615, IX, 480; J. B. Craven, *History of the Church in Orkney, 1558–1662*, 94; R. S. Barclay, *The Court Book of Orkney and Shetland*, 17.

[9] *Melrose Papers*, I, 145–7, 151–4; *O.L.* II, 270–2, 378–82; J. B. Craven, *History of the Church in Orkney, 1558–1662*, 100.

over those lands. A month after the rebellion was settled, Law began to hold courts again.[10] His successor, George Graham, was translated from Dunblane in August 1615; and the next summer a court was held 'in presence of George, bishop of Orknay, schiref principall of the bischoprik thairof'. Occasionally the bishop's deputy held court, but between 1618 and 1636 most of the courts were held 'in presence of ane Reverend father in God George, bischop of Orknay and Zetland'.[11]

The situation in Orkney was unique, and most bishops had a far more modest rôle in the government during the reign of James VI. However, James's successor had more exalted ideas about the civil status of bishops ,and a series of directives tried to implement a new policy. In March 1626 Charles ordered the establishment of a commission on the exchequer which consolidated all previous revenue offices in one new body. Archbishop Spottiswood was made president of the commission. At the same time the king ordered a reorganisation of the commission on grievances. Spottiswood was made president of this commission also. In June Patrick Lindsay, Bishop of Ross, was appointed a judge of the court of session. And in July Charles 'commandes that the Archbischope of St Andrewes . . . may haue the place of praecedencey befor the Lord Chanceler of Scotland'.[12]

None of these appointments was very effective. The commission on the exchequer was apparently inactive. As for the reorganised commission on grievances:

> the wyssest and best-sighted . . . did see that this new commissional courte wes nothing els bot the star chamber courte of England under ane other name, come doune heir to play the tyrant. . . . Bot after muche debait betuix the nobility then at courte and his Maiesty . . . it evanished in itselffe.

In 1628 Bishop Lindsay was superseded on the court of session, and Spottiswood was never able to have a 'place of praecedencey' before Lord Chancellor Hay. In 1633 Charles requested the

---

[10] Court Book of the Bishopric of Orkney, 1614–38, 20 Nov. 1614, and subsequent entries.
[11] Court Book of the Bishopric of Orkney, 1614–38, 26 July 1616 and subsequent entries.
[12] *R.P.C.* I, liii–liv, 263–7; Brunton and Haig, *Senators of the College of Justice*, 276; Balfour, *Works*, II, 141.

Chancellor to take second place on the day of his coronation. The chancellor's reply was ominous enough:

> Since it was his royall will he should enioy it [i.e. the chancellorship] with the knowen praeuilidges of the same, neuer a ston'd preist in Scotland should sett a foote befor him so long as his blood wes hotte.[13]

Although episcopal appointments in 1626 had little permanent significance, except as an indication of Charles's intentions, the appointment of bishops to the commission on teinds in January 1627 was a very different matter.[14] This important commission was responsible for putting into operation Charles's plan to settle the teind issue and to provide an adequate endowment for the church. Nine of the sixty-six members of the commission were bishops. Almost at once trouble began between the bishops and the nobility. Even that staunch supporter of royal policy, the Earl of Melrose, wrote in March of the 'ignorance and impertinences' uttered on the commission by the Bishop of Ross; and the earl added, 'It is still beleeued by many that their [i.e. the bishops'] cheif aym is to destroy the erections [of church lands into hereditary lordships] grantit by blissed King James'.[15] Charles probably never intended to suppress erections granted by his father. However, the erections were fundamental to the alliance James had established between the nobility and the bishops;[16] and even a rumour that bishops hoped to destroy the erections was serious indeed. A few weeks later the earl returned to the same theme. His charges were less sweeping but much more specific. The clergy, he wrote, plan to 'encrease the burdings of noblemen and gentlemen' by dividing parishes and appointing new 'liberall stipends . . . to ministers, readers, clerks, schooles, and musiciouns'. He concluded that they will create 'passionat contention, stirre vp dislikes, and . . . dissolue the commission'.[17]

Nor did relations between the bishops and the nobility improve. Henry Guthrie, who was a contemporary, wrote that in 1633

[13] Balfour, *Works*, II, 131, 141–2; Brunton and Haig, *Senators of the College of Justice*, 276.
[14] *R.P.C.* I, clxxxi–clxxxiv, 509–11. For the work of this Commission, see below, 166.
[15] *Memorials of the Earls of Haddington*, II, 149.
[16] See above, 27–8.
[17] *Memorials of the Earls of Haddington*, II, 151–2.

that which advantaged them [a reviving presbyterian party] more, was the turning of certain noblemen to their side; for besides that the generality of the nobility was male contented, there were by this time observed to be advowed owners of their interest, in Fife the earl of Rothes and lord Lindsay, in Lothian the earls of Lothian and Balmerino, and in the west the earls of Cassils and Eglinton, and lord Loudon, which accession rendered them very considerable.[18]

And a protest to the king in 1634 by 'a great number of the nobility and other commissioners' made its anti-episcopal sentiments plain enough. Among other grievances, the authors protested against the use of bishops to control the lords of the articles, especially because the bishops:

cull and single out such noblemen either popishly affected in religion or of little experience in our laws, as having had their breeding abroad, and so none of the ablest to be upon our Articles, but fittest only for the clergy's mystical ends.[19]

James's episcopal policy had succeeded in part because he won support from the nobility. Anti-episcopal sentiments from the nobility threatened the entire episcopal settlement.

Charles's next step – placing bishops in high civil posts – was hardly designed to placate the nobility. In 1633 Bishop Maxwell of Ross was made a judge of the court of session, and two years later Archbishop Spottiswood became 'High Chanceller of this Kingdome'.[20] This was the first time since the Reformation that a bishop had become the highest officer of state in Scotland. The number of bishops on the privy council was also rising. Council membership included six bishops between 1625 and 1631. In 1631 the number rose to seven, in 1636 to nine, and in 1637 to ten.[21] More significant was an increase in the frequency with which bishops attended meetings of the council. The following table shows the dramatic increase in episcopal attendance around 1633.

[18] Guthrie, *Memoirs*, 10.
[19] *Source Book of Scottish History*, III, 81.
[20] Brunton and Haig, *Senators of the College of Justice*, 293; *R.P.C.* V, 452–3.
[21] *R.P.C.* IV, viii, 209; V, vi; VI, 253, 359, 549.

	Aug. 1630 to Dec. 1632	Jan. 1633 to Mar. 1635	Apr. 1635 to Dec. 1637
David Lindsay (Edinburgh)	—	32	142
Patrick Lindsay (Ross and Glasgow)	27	88	135
John Maxwell (Ross)	—	49	87
John Spottiswood (St Andrews)	25	48	186
Walter Whitford[22] (Brechin)	—	—	81

In 1636 the bishop of Ross was apparently expecting to be the next treasurer of Scotland, although manoeuvres by the nobility prevented that appointment.[23] Extravagant rumours were being spread about the intentions of bishops. In 1635 Sir William Brereton wrote on his visit to Scotland:

> The clergy of late extend their authority and revenues ... I was informed by some intelligent gentlemen, it is here thought and conceived that they will recover so much of that land and revenues belonging formerly to the Abbeys, as that they will in a short time possess themselves of the third part of the kingdom.[24]

Two years later another contemporary wrote, 'Last year [1636], our Bishops guided all our estate, and became verie terrible to our whole countrie: They are now a little lower'.[25] They were to become lower still. Although the Prayer Book of 1637 was enjoined by act of council, the primary responsibility for introducing both the Prayer Book and the Canons remained with the bishops. Presbyteries received letters from their bishops requiring each minister to purchase and use two service books.[26] Even after the

---

[22] *R.P.C.* IV, 811, 813; V, 717, 732, 818, 821; VI, 733, 762, 776, 852, 855.
[13] Robert Baillie, *Letters and Journals*, I, 7; cf. Guthrie, *Memoirs*, 14.
[24] Brereton, *Travels*, 100; cf. Row, *History*, 389.
[25] Robert Baillie, *Letters and Journals*, I, 6.
[26] *R.P.C.* VI, 336, 352–3, 448–9; Robert Baillie, *Letters and Journals*, I, 18–19, 442–3.

riot in Edinburgh in July 1637 some bishops continued to urge the use of the service book.[27]

The attempt to impose the service book was the last effective action of bishops in Scotland. Opposition to the Liturgy soon turned to bishops – first as authors of the book and later to episcopacy itself.[28] In March 1638 David Mitchell, a minister of Edinburgh and a staunch supporter of episcopacy, wrote, 'Thair is nothing expected but civill warr. Thair is no meiting of counsell. The Chancellar [Archbishop Spottiswood] may not attend it with saftie nor any bischope. The verie name is more odious among young and old than the divell'.[29]

The rejection of episcopacy by the Glasgow Assembly of 1638 was part of a much larger movement. A powerful opposition had formed and opposed many of the policies of Charles I. Bishops of 'His Majesty's foundation' had no place in a revolutionary Scotland, and the Glasgow assembly succeeded in expunging bishops completely from the life of the Church of Scotland for the first time in more than a thousand years.

II
BISHOPS AND THE CHURCH

With the revival of episcopacy, the thirteen medieval dioceses of Scotland became once again basic ecclesiastical units of the nation. The dioceses of Aberdeen, Brechin, Caithness, Dunblane, Dunkeld, Moray, Orkney, Ross and St Andrews formed the province of St Andrews; and the dioceses of Argyll, Galloway, Glasgow and the Isles formed the province of Glasgow. 'The

[27] Robert Baillie, *Letters and Journals*, I, 19–20, 41. The 'Canterburian bishops' were especially persistent. In November, 1637 'the Bishope of Brechine [Walter Whitford] went on to reid the new service buiks, all the people fell upon hime'. As late as March, 1638 Bishop Maxwell of Ross 'stayes at home and keipes up the service buik in his cathedral but I feare sall not be able long' (Breadalbane Letters, 703, 718).
[28] Robert Baillie, *Letters and Journals*, I, 35, 36, 82–3, 456; Wariston, *Diary*, I, 332. In May, 1638 Johnston wrote, 'The Lord hes led us hitherto by the hand fra step to step ... and, instead of thos cautions and limitations of praelats nou conteined in our articles, suffer us not to settle til we speak plaine treuth according to the will of God, that is the utter overthrou and ruyne of Episcopacie, that great grandmother of al our corruptions' (*ibid*. 347).
[29] Breadalbane Letters, 718.

Metropolitane of North-Britane',[30] as the archbishop of St Andrews once called himself, was primate. The first Book of Discipline had proposed to remedy the irrational boundaries and eliminate the detached portions of medieval dioceses by redividing the country into ten districts for superintendents;[31] but the proposal was never put into operation, and the convention of Leith in 1572 decided that 'the boundes of the Dioceis [are not to be] confoundit; but to stand and continew'. And subsequent attempts to reform diocesan boundaries did not succeed.[32]

One change did take place in 1633 when the diocese of Edinburgh was erected from the southern portion of the huge diocese of St Andrews. The establishment of an additional diocese south of the Forth would no doubt improve the efficiency of church administration; but the almost bankrupt city fathers of Edinburgh, who had to refurnish the church of St Giles as a cathedral and to build a new parish church, the Tron, must have found it difficult to see the advantages of a new diocese.[33]

Elaborate machinery for appointment of bishops had been agreed upon in 1572,[34] but this machinery was not revived in 1600, and bishops were at first appointed upon simple crown presentation followed by a charter under the great seal. In 1617 parliament reorganized the entire procedure for election of bishops, bringing it much closer into line with the arrangements made in 1572.

The first step was to reaffirm the rights of cathedral chapters. Chapters had never been completely extinguished, for the dignities and canonries continued to exist although after the annexation of episcopal temporalities in 1587 chapters had little to do.[35] When episcopal temporalities were restored in 1606, chapters again

[30] *O.L.* I, 53.
[31] Knox, *History of the Reformation*, II (Dickinson), 292. Comparative maps of the two schemes are in G. Donaldson, *Scottish Reformation*, 112-3.
[32] *B.U.K.* I, 209 (Calderwood, III, 172); Spottiswood, *History*, III, 210; W. Fraser, *Memoirs of the Maxwells*. II, 56. In 1636 the presbytery of Kirkcaldy still had to request permission from the bishop of Dunkeld to visit two of its parishes in the heart of Fife – Leslie and Auchtertool (*Kirkcaldy Presb.* 113).
[33] *Source Book of Scottish History*, III, 84–6.
[34] *B.U.K.* I, 217–221 (Calderwood, III, 181–5).
[35] *R.M.S. 1580–93*, 1922, 2180. I am indebted to Professor Donaldson for the references in this footnote and the next.

became important legal bodies, granting charters of lands and tacks of teinds.[36] By 1614 efforts were being made to restrict chapters to ministers. And the 1617 parliament took the further important step of restoring temporalities to chapters, although many reservations were made in favour of existing possessors.[37]

The same parliament revived the procedure agreed upon in 1572 for the election of bishops.[38] After a royal mandate authorising an election had been issued, a bishop was to be elected by the dean and chapter of his diocese. At the same time the chapter was to receive the name of the royal nominee, 'he alwayis being ane actuall minister of the Kirk'. Unlike the 1572 act whereby the chapter could find the nominee 'not qualifeit in the haill or part of the qualities requirit in a bischop', the 1617 act required the chapter to 'chuse the persoun quhome his maiestie pleased to nominat and recommend'. After election, royal assent under the great seal admitted the candidate to the spirituality of his benefice, and a royal mandate was issued to consecrate the nominee 'be the rites and ordoure accustumed'. A final presentation to the temporalities of the see, issued under the great seal, was followed by the new bishop's act of homage. Archbishops were to be elected by the bishops of a province and certain selected ministers. The first election to take place under the new act was that of Patrick Forbes to Aberdeen, and subsequent elections followed the same procedure.[39]

The election of David Lindsay by the dean and chapter of Brechin in 1619 shows the care with which elections were conducted. Notice of the election was announced to 'the chapter and all that pretend to have voice in the said election to be present on the fyift of October in the Chapter House'. On the day of the election, summons was again given at the door of the church to 'ony persone or persons whiche of right or custome used in this Cathedrall Churche at ony tyme bygone may, will, or ought to be

---

[36] *R.M.S. 1609–20*, 33, 68, 174, 195, 269, 298, 329, 334, 395, 409, 587, 621, 658, 677, 875, 890, 932, 1025, 1121, 1150, 1154, 1242–3, 1249, 1290, 1331, 1333–4, 1387, 1455, 1509, 1584, 1589, 1602, 1525, 1742–3, 1753, 1842, 1855, 2136.
[37] Fife Synod, 168; *A.P.S.* IV, 529–30.
[38] *A.P.S.* IV, 529.
[39] Reg. Pres. V, 8–9. Cf. Snow, *Times, Life and Thought of Patrick Forbes*, 69–70. For subsequent presentations, see Reg. Pres. V, 24–5, 27–8, 33–4.

present at this instant election'. The procedure was similar to that used at the institution of a minister to his benefice,[40] and in both cases served to emphasize the fact that a man was being admitted into a spiritual cure and not merely into a temporal office.

Little is known about the consecration of bishops in Scotland after 1610. No doubt the English Ordinal, that is, the Ordinal of 1552, reissued in the Prayer Books of 1559 and 1604, was used at the consecrations in London. Peter Heylyn wrote that the consecrations were 'according to the Rules of the English Ordination'; although James Melville's addition that the Scots were 'consecrat with annoynting of oyle and uther ceremonies, just according to the Inglish faschioun and Pontificall Papistis' is scarcely credible.[41]

There is less evidence about consecrations in Scotland. Calderwood implied that an adapted version of the English Ordinal was used:

> In the moneth of December [1610] the thrie consecrated bishops returned home to Scotland, and consecrated the Archbishope of St Androes, &c., efter the same maner that they were consecrated themselfs, als neere as they could imitate.

And apparently the same was true for subsequent consecrations:

> Upon the Lord's day, the 23d of Januar, some of the bishops were consecrated by these who were consecrated before. . . . Some, as was alledgit, sturred at the forme and order of the consecration; yit afterward . . . these who were not consecrated before . . . were consecrated in Leith.[42]

It may be more than a coincidence that 'The Form and Maner of Consecrating ane Archbishope, or Bishope' published in Scotland

---

[40] Dalhousie Muniments 13/328.

[41] Peter Heylyn, *Aerius Redivivus*, 387. Melville, *Diary*, 803-4. It is unlikely that Dr Abbot, the Puritan-minded Bishop of London, would have used 'annoynting of oyle and uther ceremonies . . . [of the] Pontificall Papistis'.

[42] Calderwood, VII, 152, 154. According to another seventeenth (?) century manuscript Gladstanes 'was consecrat in the paroche Kirke of St Andrews, the penult of December, and with him the Bischope of Orkney: their war consecrat be the Archbishope of Glasgow, the Bischopis of Galloway and Brichen' (James Maidment, *Analecta Scotica*, II, 10).

in 1620[43] could best be described as the English Ordinal adapted for use in Scotland. There is some evidence that the 1620 form for the ordination of ministers did reflect general Scottish practice between 1610 and 1636,[44] and the same may also have been true for the consecration of bishops. Both the structure and the contents of the 1620 rite of consecration were taken almost entirely from the Book of Common Prayer. However, numerous adaptations were made to conform to Scottish practice. The tradition of the public edict was added, the litany and other responses were eliminated,[45] separate collects were combined into one long prayer in the tradition of prayers in Knox's Liturgy, and the sentence of ordination was made more explicit about the duties and authority of a bishop. I have found no seventeenth-century reference to the use of this Ordinal in a Scottish consecration, but it is quite possible that the Ordinal did describe the usual Scottish tradition of consecrations after 1610. Whatever the rite may have been, consecrations did continue to take place. In May 1611 Archbishop Gladstanes reported to James, 'All the Bischoppis in my Province ar now consecrated'. After consecrating those in the south, he next:

> consecrated the Bischopps of Abyrdein and Cathnes, in the Cathedrall Kirk of Breichine, being assisted with the Bishops of Dunkeld and Breichine, in the sight of such ane multitude of people as I never saw in such a bounds.[46]

Much had been done to restore episcopal income by 1610 and parliament continued to pass occasional acts augmenting the endowments of particular bishoprics.[47] The real income of bishops between 1600 and 1638 still awaits investigation, but testaments left by bishops give some indication of their financial resources. Seven episcopal testaments are extant. Net assets or 'frie geir' range from a low of £3,052 left by David Cunningham, Bishop of Aberdeen from 1577 to 1600, to a high of £22,278 left by Gavin

[43] The Ordinal was reprinted in Wodrow, *Miscellany*, I, 597–615, and in G. W. Sprott (ed.), *Scottish Liturgies of the Reign of James VI* (1901), 111–131.
[44] See below, 145–9.
[45] On the unpopularity of the litany and responses in Scotland, see G. Donaldson, *The Making of the Scottish Prayer Book of 1637*, 73–4.
[46] *O.L.* I, 270.
[47] *A.P.S.* IV, 551–4, 649, 651.

Hamilton, Bishop of Galloway. These figures would be very misleading by themselves, however, for a large part of the assets left by every bishop consisted of 'debts awin to the deid'. Bishop Hamilton's enormous estate consisted of £19,789 in debts due him (much of it in unpaid teinds or rents) and £2,489 in goods and victuals. The following table shows the high proportion in every testament of outstanding debts:

Testaments of Bishops

Date of death	Name and Diocese	Value of movables	Debts owed by the dead	Debts owed to the dead	Net assets
1600	David Cunningham (Aberdeen)	£1,342	£1,038	£2,748	£3,052
1607	James Nicolson (Dunkeld)	£553	—	£2,867	£3,420
1612	Gavin Hamilton (Galloway)	£2,489	—	£19,789	£22,278
1613	David Lindsay (Ross)	£816	—	£3,974	£4,691
1615	George Gladstanes (St Andrews)	£2,000	£1,105	£14,209	£15,104
1632	James Law (Glasgow)	£933	£2,573	£14,737	£13,096
1634	William Forbes[48] (Edinburgh)	£3,133	£333	£5,384	£8,184

Moreover, a high proportion of outstanding debts very probably meant that bishops were often involved in court actions. In 1615 the new Bishop of Galloway, William Cowper, complained to London that 'Neither is my dewtie, nor the dewtie of the Ministers, thankfullie paied, so that I am forced to seeke myne owne be the law'.[49] The records of the court of session have not been indexed or studied for this period. However, even an examination of occasional volumes shows a large number of cases in which ministers were trying to recover their unpaid stipends,[50] and it seems likely that Bishop Lamb's attempt in 1619 to recover rents

[48] Edinburgh Test. 24 November 1600, 35; Edinburgh Test. 4 June, 1608, 44, 8-9; Hamilton & Campsie Test. 16 June, 1612, 2(1), 243-4; Edinburgh Test. 17 December 1613, 47, 352-3; St Andrews Test. 1 February 1616, 6; Glasgow Test. 6 Sept. 1633, 24; Edinburgh Test. 7 March, 1635, 57, 74-6.
[49] O.L. II, 451.
[50] See below, 160-1.

which had been unpaid for three years was typical enough.[51] In spite of outstanding debts, however, the estates left by bishops were substantial for Scotland and could be matched only by the wealthier clergy of such centres as Edinburgh.[52]

In 1610 James sent instructions that 'every archbishop and bishop should make his residence at the cathedral church of his diocese'.[53] Calderwood later charged that bishops 'to this houre have not made residence so muche as within the bounds of the diocie'.[54]

In four dioceses, Caithness, Dunkeld, Galloway and Ross, bishops were clearly not resident for most of the period. John Abernethy, Bishop of Caithness from 1616 to 1638, was minister of Jedburgh and resident there. In 1630 'the provest and bailyies of Jedburgh' reported a rumour that 'the bishop of Caithness thair ordinar pastor was to be removed from thaim'. However, two years later he was still seeking another royal licence allowing him 'to stay frome my residence' in Caithness; and there is no definite evidence that he was living in his diocese until 1638 when he was reported to be 'dwelling there in his own house'.[55]

Alexander Lindsay, Bishop of Dunkeld from 1607 until 1638, was minister of St Madoes throughout the period. He regularly appeared in the presbytery of Perth as the minister of St Madoes, and he was allowed by the general assembly of 1638 to continue as minister there after renouncing episcopacy.[56] William Cowper, Bishop of Galloway from 1612 until 1619, certainly resided in the

---

[51] Register of Acts and Decreets of the Lords of Session, 330, 44–5.

[52] For a comparison of bishops' and ministers' testaments, see below, 167–8.

[53] Spottiswood, *History*, III, 210. Charles repeated the instructions in 1626 (Balfour, *Works*, II, 144).

[54] Calderwood, VI, 626–7. Calderwood's observations were probably written in 1627 (VIII, 4).

[55] Jedburgh Presb. 21 April, 1630; cf. Calderwood, VI, 627, VII, 1–2. Letter from John Abernethy to Sir Robert Ker, Newbattle Portfolio, xiii/72. The bishop had sought a similar licence in 1623 (Newbattle Portfolio, xiii/32). The excuse which Abernethy gave in 1623 that 'the rent of that benefice is so small . . . that it wold not sustaine me and my familie there scarclie half a year . . . beside that I have no resident place there, neither darre I hazard under the feet and tyrnnie of the earle of Cathnes and his sone' was confirmed by letters from the archbishops to James in the same year (*O.L.* II, 708, 710–11). *Chronicle of the Frasers*, 261.

[56] Perth Presb., *passim*; A. Peterkin, *Records of the Kirk of Scotland*, 28.

Canongate as Dean of the Chapel Royal, and it was reported that his successor, 'Mr Andrew Lamb, for the most part maketh his residence in Edinburgh and Leith'.[57] David Lindsay, the veteran minister of Leith and Bishop of Ross from 1600 until 1613, continued to live in Leith. His successor, Patrick Lindsay, was reported to reside 'about Dundie'.[58]

The bishops of Dunblane did not reside in their diocese for part of the period. George Graham, Bishop from 1603 until 1615, probably remained at Scone as minister there for some years.[59] His successor, Adam Bellenden, appeared regularly at meetings of the presbytery of Dunblane between 1616 and 1619. He probably moved to Edinburgh shortly thereafter, for he was described in 1632 as an 'indweller' there.[60]

In the other dioceses bishops appear to have resided at least for much of the time. Peter Blackburn and Patrick Forbes certainly lived in Aberdeen; and both Alexander Douglas and John Guthrie officiated as ministers at Elgin during the time they were bishops of Moray.[61] James Law may have lived in Orkney after the arrest of Earl Patrick, and his successor, George Graham, certainly resided there with his family.[62] Andrew Knox lived in the Isles after 1609, and it seems likely that the bishops of Argyll were also resident.[63] Both archbishops had residence in their dioceses, and William Forbes was resident in Edinburgh during the few months that he was bishop of that new diocese.[64] Little is known about the bishops of Brechin, but none of them were ever accused by their

[57] *O.L.* II, 466; cf. Calderwood, VI, 627; Row, *History*, 258.
[58] He regularly attended meetings of the Privy Council between 1600 and 1613 (*R.P.C.* VI, xxxi, 1037, VII, xxii, 906, VIII, 995, IX, 879–80; Calderwood, VI, 627).
[59] In 1608 Graham was receiving his stipend as minister of Scone (Reg. Assig. Stipends, Scone [Perth], 1607–8).
[60] Dunblane Presb., *passim*; Newbattle Portfolio XIII/72; cf. Calderwood, VI, 627, where he was described as living 'in the Cannongate'.
[61] *Aberdeen K. S.* 30, 32, 42, 66, 82; *Elgin K. S.* 178, 182, 208.
[62] R. S. Barclay, *The Court Book of Orkney and Shetland*, 16–32; *O.L.* II, 638; *Scottish History Society Misc.* II, 237ff.
[63] *R.P.C.* IX, xxxii–xxxiii; *O.L.* II, 372–5; Spottiswood, *History*, III, 82. However, James Fairlie, Bishop of Argyll in 1637, was not (James Gordon, *History of Scots Affairs*, II, 141–2).
[64] He attended council meetings frequently after his admission in February 1634 (*R.P.C.* [Second Series] V, 717). So did his successor (see above, 38).

enemies of being non-resident and Angus would not be a difficult place for a bishop to reside. Although some bishops were non-resident, yet in nine dioceses bishops were resident for the most part. Much would probably depend on whether a bishop had family connections in his diocese and a suitable house in which to live.

One important responsibility of bishops was their work on the controversial court of high commission, first established in 1610. A large number of bishops, barons and ministers were nominated to the court, which was given jurisdiction (later expanded) over 'anie person . . . whom they hold anie way to be scandalous' as well as any minister 'whose speeches in publict have beene impertinent and against the established order of the kirk'.[65] According to contemporary descriptions, bishops probably dominated the court.[66] The court was not popular with the nobility. Archbishop Spottiswood wrote that the court was erected:

> to the great discontent of those that ruled the estate; for that they took it to be a restraint of their authority in matters ecclesiastical, nor did they like to see clergymen invested with such a power.[67]

Nevertheless, both James and Charles continued to support the high commission, to renew its authority, and to expand its jurisdiction. After parliamentary approval of the Perth Articles in 1621, James wrote the bishops:

> The sword is now putt into your hands: goe on therefore to use it; and let it roust noe longer till ye have perfited the service trusted to you, or otherwise we must use it both against you and them.[68]

James probably meant that the high commission was the way they were to use their new sword.

The court of high commission is best known for its activities

---

[65] *R.P.C.* 417–20; Calderwood, VII, 57–62. Actually two courts were established in 1610 to give Archbishop Spottiswood at Glasgow separate jurisdiction, since the Archbishop of St Andrews was in disfavour. A few months after Spottiswood's translation to St Andrews in 1615, the two courts were united into one (*R.P.C.* X, 435–7; Calderwood, VII, 204–10).

[66] Calderwood, VII, 259, 366–7, 370, 388, 414, 442, 519, 534; George I. R. McMahon, 'The Scottish Courts of High Commission', 198.

[67] Spottiswood, *History*, III, 212; McMahon, 'The Scottish Courts of High Commission', 207–8.

[68] Calderwood, VII, 508. For the Perth Articles, see below, 181–92.

against ministers, especially those who opposed episcopacy or who refused to conform to the Perth Articles. No records of the court are known to have survived. However, many prominent cases were cited by Calderwood, and it is possible to form an estimate of the work of the high commission against ministers who opposed the Jacobean settlement. Between 1610 and 1625 forty-eight ministers were tried by the court. Twenty-seven of them were either excused or admonished and dismissed. Two were confined to their own parishes, five were suspended from the ministry and later restored, seven were deprived and later restored, and seven were deprived and not restored. Between 1625 and 1638 at least six cases were tried by the court. The outcome of two is unknown, two were admonished, two were suspended.[69] The majority of ministers tried by the court were from Fife, Lothian and the south-west.

However, the high commission did not limit itself to cases of recalcitrant ministers, and it sometimes served as an effective court of appeal. James sent instructions in 1610:

> that every particular matter should not be brought at first before the high commission ... except the same was appealed unto, or complained by one of the bishops as a thing that could not be rectified in their dioceses.[70]

A wide variety of offences was referred to the high commission after 1610. A visitation by a bishop and presbytery at Newburgh in 1611 ordered an obstinate adulterer 'to compeir befoir the Lords of the High Commissioun to hold in Perth upon Thursday next'. In 1613 the synod of Fife 'dilated David Fotheringham, ... who ... upon the 15 day of August lastbypast, ... being the Saboth day, ... sold his wyff. ... For the foirsaidis filthie crymes he is to be charged to the High Commissioun'. In 1614 the same synod learned that an adulterous couple had been fined fifty merks by the high commission.[71] In 1623 the high commission authorised an excommunication in Elgin during a vacancy in the see of Moray.[72] Disputes over kirk seats were sometimes violent, and serious cases came before the high commission. In 1613 the 'Hie

[69] McMahon, 'The Scottish Courts of High Commission', 200–202.
[70] Spottiswood, *History*, III, 210.
[71] Fife Synod, 56, 135, 174.
[72] *Elgin K. S.* 179. Bishop Douglas died on 11 May, and his successor was not appointed until August.

Commissioun halding at Glasgow' decided that the laird of Dreghorne's kirk seat had been unlawfully removed by the laird of Caprington 'or att lest be the Lady Capringtoun', and ordered the seat to be restored. In 1632 'Mr Patrik Rynd, minister at the Kirk of Drone, [was] apoynted to be summondit befor the High Commission for sum offences', perhaps because he 'wes a verie prophane and dissolute man, given to drunkenness'.[73]

Ministers could also count on support from the high commission in cases of physical assault. In 1632 the presbytery of Perth ordered to the high commission an offender who had quarrelled with his minister and 'threattened to putt a dirke throw his cheekes'. Apparently the action was effective, for a few months later the offender appeared before the presbytery and accepted his censure in sackcloth. In 1618 the presbytery of Jedburgh received a penitent 'reportit from the hie commissioun to satisfie for abuse-ing his minister'.[74]

Moreover, the high commission had a reputation for prompt action. In 1628 a justice of the peace wrote that a 'citation before the hie commissione or befor his majesties secret counsell is upon the first summonds without any forder delay ... and not lyke the summonds befor the commissar or session quhilk is with continuation of dayis'.[75]

The jurisdiction which the high commission exercised was wide and apparently effective. Its powers of enforcement enabled it to deal with cases which could not be satisfactorily handled in ordinary ecclesiastical courts. Parliament in 1639 may well have had in mind the many types of cases heard by the high commission when it ordered the repeal only of sentences passed by the court against ministers who had opposed bishops or the Perth Articles, 'and no farder'.[76]

The high commission was as much a civil court as an ecclesiastical one. However, within the church itself bishops had numerous administrative and pastoral responsibilities. In 1610 James sent instructions 'that all archbishops and bishops be careful in visitation of their dioceses, and every third year at least take

---

[73] Fife Synod, 331; Row, *History*, 457.
[74] Perth Presb. 20 June, 12 September 1632, 15 May 1633; Jedburgh Presb. 18 March 1618. For another case, see Perth Presb. 13 Sept. 1620.
[75] Lord Forbes Papers, I/2.
[76] *A.P.S.* V, 598.

inspection of the ministers, readers, and others serving cure within their bounds'.[77] It is unlikely that this ideal was consistently maintained,[78] but many episcopal visitations did take place. I have found only one extant record of visitation tours, that of Archbishop Gladstanes between 1611 and 1614; but it shows considerable activity on the part of that prelate. During four summers he made fifty-seven visitations, mostly in the northern half of his diocese.[79] If he was equally vigorous south of the Forth, he left a remarkable record indeed. At every visitation the archbishop was assisted by ministers of a presbytery and often by prominent laymen as well. Thus a visitation at St Vigeans was held 'be the Right Reverend Father in God George, Archbishop of St Andrews, assisted be the brethren of the Exercise of Arbroth, and Sir Peter Young of Seatoun, Almoner to the Kings Majestie,' and other laymen.[81] The sederunts on some visitations illustrate the way in which ministers with very different views on ecclesiastical polity worked together. A visitation at Barrie was conducted 'be the Right Reverend Father in God Georg, Archbishop of Saint Androis, assisted by Mrs Arthur Futhie [constant moderator of the Presbytery of Arbroath and a member of the Court of High Commission], Patrik Lyndesy [minister at St Vigeans and Bishop of Ross in 1613], Androw Clayhills [minister of Monifieth], Androw Drummond [a member of High Commission in 1619], Henrie Duncane [one of forty-two ministers who signed a protest against episcopacy in 1606], William Rait [another minister who had signed the same protest], David Williamsone [minister at Methie], Alexander Kinninmouth [minister at Kirriemuir], John Guthrie, clerk [minister at Arbirlot, and bishop of Moray in 1623], My Lord Rector of the University of St Androis and elders and deacons of the parochioners'.[82]

[77] Spottiswood, *History*, III, 210. Charles repeated the instructions in 1626 (Balfour, *Works*, II, 144–5).

[78] Calderwood wrote in 1627, 'See we not that they [i.e. the bishops] use no other visitation of the particular kirks of their dioceis but upon rare occasiouns?' (VII, 109–10).

[79] Fife Synod, folios, 1–8, pp. 19–56, 75–81, 103–5, 127–36, 147–54, 169–70.

[80] The dates of his visitations suggest that he may have been. In 1611 he held ten visitations between 10 April and May 7. No further visitations were held for seven weeks until a tour in Fife began again on 30 June.

[81] Fife Synod, 75.

[82] Fife Synod, 19.

Visitations were also made by other bishops.[83] In 1634:

> the Bishop of Murray, Mr John Guthery, kept on his circular visitations of every church within the diocesse, came up through all Strathspey, Badenoch, Stratharick, to Cilchummen in Abertarfe, through Glenmoriston, in to Kilmore S. Durstan in Urchart, and to Kilarlety, and thence to Kirkhill in Wardlaw parish, ... setling very good order and disciplin.[84]

In 1616 Archbishop Spottiswood made a visitation at Dunfermline; two years later the bishop and presbytery of Dunblane held a thorough visitation at Kincardine-in-Menteith.[85] In 1618 the archbishop of Glasgow reported to James that the bishop of Argyll 'hes all this last sommer travelled throw all the pairts of his diocie, visited and ordoured the churches therof'.[86] Dr Garden declared that Patrick Forbes 'had a custom of visiting all his parish churches, and this without a train of attendants. ... He would arrive in the neighborhood on Saturday without giving notice to anyone and would make his appearance in the parish church on Sunday, carefully noting what he saw and heard'. Bishop Forbes also held more normal visitations with the presbytery of Ellon at parishes with difficult or unusual problems.[87] Most visitations were held by presbyteries themselves,[88] but visitations by a bishop and presbytery were not unknown.

Whether a bishop was present or not, the same procedure was followed. Ministers and elders were examined, as was the fabric of the church and the state of church life. A visitation at Perth by the archbishop and the presbytery of Perth removed an inefficient clerk of the kirk session, ordered elders and deacons to be punished who 'keip thair meitings verie rarelie', settled a quarrel between an assistant minister and the town clerk, and urged that minister (Mr William Cowper, later Bishop of Galloway) not to resign,

---

[83] Records of visitation, however, are more fragmentary. Separate visitation books (now lost) were kept in the Synod of Fife after 1615 and presumably in other synods as well (Fife Synod, 193).
[84] *Chronicles of the Frasers*, 256.
[85] Fife Synod, 192; Dunblane Presb., 6 January 1618.
[86] W. Fraser, *Memoirs of the Maxwells*, II, 73.
[87] Snow, *Patrick Forbes*, 109; Ellon Presb., 5 September 6 September 1620.
[88] See below, 105-6.

seeing 'his people carrie ane constant good affectioun toward him'.[89]

An even more rigorous visitation was held by Bishop Patrick Forbes at Tarves. In 1621 the heritors of Tarves formally promised to pay the stipend of a man who would be their schoolmaster, reader, and session clerk. A year later, however, the presbytery of Ellon learned that the heritors had not fulfilled their promise and reported that fact to Bishop Forbes. Minutes of the presbytery record the events of the morning when the bishop visited Tarves.

Convenit the bischop with sum of the ministrie of uther presbyteris togidder with the presbyterie of Ellon. ... The bischop taucht Psal. 4: vs. 5 etc. The bischope efter lang contestatioun with sum of the gentillmen and elders concerning the execution of the forsaid act and finding na conformitie on thair pairt ordanes the minister to send south *primo quoque tempore*, and rais letters upon the forsaid act and charge the elders and gentillmen heritors of the paroche to put the forsaid act to executioun and in the mein tyme to tak the haill commoun guid of thair kirk and allocat the same for the mantenance of the said clark, reider and scuill maister as he will be comptablie to the nixt assemblie.[90]

In addition to conducting visitations, the Glasgow assembly of 1610 ordered bishops to ordain ministers, 'being assisted be such of the Ministrie of the bounds quher he is to serve, as he will assume to himselfe'.[91] Bishops were accused of violating that act as well as reformed practice by ordaining men 'in anie part of the diocie he pleaseth, and some tyme out of his diocie, and without assistance of the ministers of the bounds'.[92] The accusation is partly justified. I have found no evidence that Archbishop Spottiswood ever ordained a man in his parish church. In 1615 three men were ordained at the opening of a session of the synod of Fife, where the archbishop might well have been assisted by ministers who were present.[93] In 1630 the archbishop of Glasgow ordained the new minister of Kilmacolme 'at Glasgow ... with all due solemnitie', and the same procedure was followed for the

[89] Fife Synod, 24–28.
[90] Ellon Presb., 14 June 1621, 20 April, 25 July 1622.
[91] *B.U.K.* III, 1096 (Calderwood, VII, 100).
[92] Calderwood, VII, 112.
[93] Fife Synod, 186–7.

ordination of ministers for Eastwood and Lesmahagow.[94] Whether the archbishop was assisted by ministers or not is uncertain. However, there are also many records of ordinations conducted by bishops and presbyteries in parish churches where ministers were to serve. At nine of the fifty-seven visitations which Archbishop Gladstanes made between 1611 and 1614, new ministers were ordained by the archbishop and members of a presbytery. In 1633 a minister for Bedrule was ordained 'by the Bishop of Cathnes and Presbiterie of Jedburgh in the kirk of Badreul with consent of the gentlemen, elders and hail congregatioun'. The bishop of Dunkeld and the presbytery of Perth ordained three men in their parish churches between 1622 and 1624.[95] In 1617 the bishop and presbytery of Dunblane met at Logie for the ordination of a new minister. The Bishop preached upon a text from I Thessalonians, 'quhairin the apostill schawis the dew of the peopill to the pastor and the pastoris dewtie to thame', and then ordained the minister 'by laying on of hands by the said reverend father' and ministers of the presbytery. Three subsequent ordinations were also held in parish churches.[96] There are too few surviving records of ordinations to justify any final conclusions, but existing presbytery and synod records suggest that ordination by a bishop and presbytery at the parish church where the new minister was to serve was probably as common as, and perhaps more common than, any other practice.

Administration of discipline involved all of the courts of the church, and bishops had their responsibilities in that work. The Glasgow acts of 1610 which required diocesan bishops to approve excommunications before they were pronounced gave bishops final authority over the highest censure of the church. However, bishops were sometimes involved in disciplinary cases long before a process of excommunication had been completed. The advice of a bishop might be sought in an unusual case. The synod of Aberdeen considered several difficult cases of incest and ordered the cases to be 'given to the bischop and that he acquent my Lord Archbishope thairof requyring his best advyse'. In 1623 the kirk session

[94] Paisley Presb., 8 April, 22 April 1630; Lanark Presb., 17 Nov. 1631.
[95] Fife Synod, f. 7 (20 Sept. 1611), 29, 33, 37, 43-4, 53, 75, 80-1, 103; Jedburgh Presb., 30 Oct. 1633; Perth Presb., 6 March 1622, 29 Oct. 1623, 30 June 1624.
[96] Dunblane Presb., 14 April 1617, 26 March 1619, 31 July, 12 November 1623.

of Belhelvie dealt with a man who 'war delaitit for blaspheming the publict worship of God in our kirk. . . . Quhairpoune the minister resolves to advyse with the bischop anent the censure thairoff giff he be found giltie'.[97]

Occasionally, a process was begun at the direction of a bishop. More frequently episcopal authority was invoked to support or enforce an action initiated by a presbytery. In 1628 the presbytery of Paisley advised their bishop that one of their members, Mr Andrew Hamilton, would not pronounce a sentence of excommunication against a papist. Eventually the presbytery learned that 'it wes the Bishops will that the said Mr Andro shuld be suspended if he did not excommunicate Issobell Mowat'. Under threat of that sentence, the minister obeyed.[98]

Patrick Lindsay, Archbishop of Glasgow, acted promptly to settle a difficult dispute at Carluke. There had been trouble in that parish for some months over the selection of a new minister. The laird of Calderwood had his own candidate and refused to allow temporary ministers sent by the presbytery to preach there. A month after the new archbishop's translation to Glasgow, he sent a letter to the presbytery of Lanark and requested them:

> to send commissioners to Glasgow against the 22 of Maii, first that they may sie the wrong repaired done to the presbiterie by . . . Calderwood and his followers, nixt to gif advyse anent the presentation of the kirk.

The presbytery recommended one of their own expectants, and, with the help of the bishop, he was tried, given a new glebe, and settled at Carluke.[99]

Sometimes episcopal authority sought to mitigate the severity of a sentence imposed by church courts. The presbytery of Kirkcaldy was about to excommunicate a heritor of Auchterderran when Archbishop Spottiswood requested them to confer with the heritor once more.[100] A letter by the same archbishop to an unnamed presbytery in 1628 was in the same tradition. The case concerned the discipline of a justice of the peace who, in the course

---

[97] Ellon Presb., April 1616; Belhelvie K. S., 29 June 1623.
[98] Paisley Presb., 27 March, 17 April, 22 May, 5 June, 10 July 1628.
[99] Lanark Presb., 3 January, 7 March, 16 May, 13 June, 29 August, 21 November 1633, 20 February 1634.
[100] *Kirkcaldy Presb.* 91.

of his duty, accidentally killed a man 'who refused to obey him'. Spottiswood recommended that he be gravely admonished once before the congregation, but without sackcloth, and then received. After referring to the first Book of Discipline and pointing out that the civil courts had discharged the justice, he continued: 'The dejectioun of a sinner in my mynd requyrs at our hands much tendernes in proceding, and when we sie that, we should reverence Gods mercifull work with his creatur, which so far as man can judg I found in him at my conference with him'. And he concluded, 'I would entrait you to tak with him the calmest course that may be'.[101]

This letter suggests that presbyteries were not unduly subservient to bishops, and many other cases confirm this view. Indeed, presbyteries showed a rather surprising freedom and independence in maintaining their own opinion of a disciplinary case when it conflicted with that of a bishop. A typical case was that of Mr William Spittell, assistant minister of Dysart in 1632, whose 'distressed and pitifulle estait' included not only the facts that he was in debt by 'aught hundredth merks' but also that his session had declared their 'unwillingnes thairof to have Mr William Spittell continued with them in his ministrie'. In November the archbishop sent a letter to the presbytery of Kirkcaldy' desyreing them to convene Mr William Spittell befoir them ... and discharge him to preache any more within thair bownds'. Evidently the desire was ignored, for on 7 March 1633 a second letter was received:

> from the Archbishope of St Androis desyreing the brethren to advyse Mr William Spittell not to preache in Dysert, or, if he will not be advysed, to discharge him to preache thair till some cours wer taken betwixt him and the towne for setling of some divisions. ... The brethren considering that the Bishop being informit be one partie onlie [i.e. the enemies of Spittell] hes written so, and thairfoir hes resolved to writt to the Bishope and to informe him further.

A week later a conciliatory letter was sent by the archbishop 'desyreing the brethren to tak the best cours anent the setling of the maters of Dysert betwixt the said Mr William and the towne, and to send one of thair number to Dysert to preache thair ... and to

[101] Dalhousie Muniments 14/792.

exort them to peace and unitie'.[102] The quarrel was eventually settled.

Disagreement over discipline was rare. In general, relations between presbyteries and their bishop seem to have been friendly and co-operative. Presbyteries were much more accustomed to request support from their bishop than to quarrel with him.

Apart from disciplinary cases, bishops had a number of other administrative and pastoral duties. Fasts were announced by bishops. Collections for such diverse purposes as 'the Harborie of Port Patrik', ransom for Scots captured by the Turks, or the distressed church in the Palatinate, were commended by bishops.[103] Bishops supported ministers whose stipend was unpaid or too small. In 1624 Spottiswood ordered a minister to have 'excuse from the taxation by reason of his poverty', and the same year the bishop of Dunkeld settled a dispute over the division of a stipend which had been 'submitted to me and some of our brethren with me'.[104] The presbytery of Jedburgh sought to prevent disadvantageous tacks by requiring its members 'to confer with the Bischop ... [before] the setting of the tacks of the teindscheavis [i.e. tithes of corn]'.[105] Bishops recommended chaplains, private tutors and ministers.[106] In 1623 the minister of Kingussie was having 'many difficulties and oppositionis maid unto him in the building the krik' and the bishop of Moray was requested 'to speak the Marquis of Huntlie ... for giving off his asistance'. Apparently the bishop's intercession was successful, since a few months later a report was received that the marquis 'hes givin directioun to his bailyis for holding hand to the said work conform to the qukilk the roof was alreddie knitt and bound'.[107] In 1633 the bishop of Orkney supported the separation of Hoy and Walls into two parishes and promised one hundred merks annually towards the stipend for a

---

[102] *Kirkcaldy Presb.* 57, 58, 60–1.

[103] Jedburgh Presb., 15 May 1622; *Kirkcaldy Presb.*, 92, 72–3, 62; Perth Presb., 29 March 1620.

[104] Airlie Muniments, 46/23, 47/43; Breadalbane Letters, 638. Cf. Jedburgh Presb., 3 July 1611, when that presbytery threatened to request assistance if a stipend at Harwick was not augmented.

[105] Jedburgh Presb., 24 April 1611, cf. 27 March 1611.

[106] Breadalbane Letters, 656, 690; Morton Papers, 63, 19 May, 1628; O.L. I, 350.

[107] Moray Synod, 1, 5. For a similar case at Urquhart, see Moray Synod, 6.

new minister. In April 1638 the bishop of Caithness, 'with consent of the deane and chapter of the cathedrall kirk' and of the Lord of Reay, made plans to erect a new parish 'in the midst of the cuntrie in Kintaill' because of the 'wyde and spatious bounds' of the former parish, with its 'montanes, rocks ... creiknes and loches'.[108]

James urged the assembly at Aberdeen in 1616 to authorise a modified form of the rite of confirmation, and the assembly did pass an act 'that the Archbischops and Bischops ... [or] the Minister of the paroch, make all young childrein of six yeirs of age be presentit befor them, and to give the Confessioun of Faith'. James was not pleased with the act, declaring it 'a mere hotchpotch, and not so clear as was requisite'.[109] Although the Perth Articles of 1618 avoided the word 'confirmation', this was undoubtedly the intention of the fourth article, which required bishops to:

> cause ... children to be presented before them, and bless them with prayer for increase of their knowledge, and continuance of Gods heavenly graces with every one of them.[110]

However, confirmation was administered very rarely if at all, a fact which was later admitted by the Aberdeen Doctors in their *Duplies*.[111]

Between 1600 and 1638 thirty ministers became bishops in the Church of Scotland. Of the first generation of bishops, one had begun his ministry in the earliest days of the Reformation. David Lindsay, minister of Leith in 1560, was one of the more prominent of the early reformers. Commissioner of Kyle, Carrick, and Cunningham and a visitor for many parts of the country, he was moderator of six general assemblies and a member of numerous committees. In the early years of the Reformation 'no minister's name appears more frequently than that of David Lindsay in the accounts of the General Assembly's proceedings'.[112] He had supported episcopacy throughout the Reformation period, and

[108] Craven Bequest, 9; Reay Papers, 29/3.
[109] *B.U.K.* III, 1127 (Calderwood, VII, 228); Spottiswood, *History*, III, 236.
[110] *B.U.K.* III, 1166.
[111] *Duplies of the Ministers ... of Aberdeen ... concerning the Late Covenant*, 77 (1638).
[112] G. Donaldson, 'David Lindsay', *Fathers of the Kirk*, 30.

his acceptance of the bishopric of Ross in 1600 was a significant link between the Jacobean episcopate and the reformers of the 1560s.

Most of the other early seventeenth century bishops had begun their ministry during the 1580s. Both Alexander Douglas and James Nicolson were ministers in 1580; Andrew Knox became minister of Lochwinnoch in 1581; Peter Blackburn and David Cunningham had been ministers in Aberdeen since 1582. John Spottiswood succeeded his father at Calder in 1585; and James Law became minister of Kirkliston in the same year. George Gladstanes was minister of Ecclesgreig by 1587.[113] Most of these men had begun their ministry during a period when presbyteries were first developing, and they were undoubedly aware of the debate then taking place over the polity of the church.

Moreover, some of the new bishops had close connections with the sixteenth-century episcopal tradition. Archbishop Spottiswood's father had been superintendent of Lothian since 1561, and, along with David Lindsay, had participated in the 'consecration' of John Douglas as archbishop of St Andrews in 1572.[7] John Campbell became bishop of Argyll in 1608. His father, Neil Campbell, was bishop of Argyll in 1580. Some scurrilous verses in 1609 described Neil Campbell as the only pious bishop in Scotland.

> For light in doctrine they may all resign it to Argile, So faith has left the lowland cleane, gone to the hills awhile.[114]

The new bishops were charged by their opponents with hypocrisy and self-seeking because they accepted bishoprics after having served as ministers during the period of presbyterian dominance after 1586. The motives of men are exceedingly difficult to determine. However, some of the new bishops had known some outstanding representatives of the episcopal tradition in Scotland, and their support of episcopacy was probably not due to wholly cynical motives.

John Spottiswood, Archbishop of Glasgow and St Andrews, was the ecclesiastical leader of the church throughout the entire period. Never an exciting or dramatic figure, his administration, like his *History of the Church of Scotland*, was calm, judicious and moderate. His letters, which are found in numerous family

[113] *Fasti*, I, 176; VII, 322, 326, 329, 339, 348, 351.
[114] Calderwood, VII, 2.

collections, testify to his extensive activity in both church and state. Dr Perry, in a Ph. D. study of the archbishop, concluded that 'he was a capable administrator and conscientious servant in the royal government. ... His judgment was sound and his practical experience extensive, but his lack of originality kept him from achieving true greatness'.[115]

George Gladstanes, Archbishop of St Andrews from 1604 to 1615, was much less competent. He was sharply rebuked by James in 1609 and probably lost the confidence of the king thereafter. In 1611 the two archbishops found it necessary to assure James that there was no 'schisme ... amongs us two', but a year later Spottiswood wrote to court that Gladstanes had made a proposal 'in his folly I may say it. which was so absurd 'ye wald not ken qhether to laughe or be angry'.[116] One example of an ill-advised decision by Gladstanes occurred in the presbytery of Ellon in 1613. A couple were being tried for adultery, which they denied. 'Quhairfor, seeing the archbishop of Sant-Androes be his preparative haid taking away all aithis [oaths] in the cace of adulterie, quhilk the said parteis knew verie weill,' the case was postponed indefinitely. One of Spottiswood's first acts after his translation to St Andrews was to restore to presbyteries their right to administer solemn oaths.[117]

Of the bishops appointed by James after 1610, Patrick Forbes of Aberdeen was clearly outstanding. Robert Baron's description of him has been generally accepted. 'There was as great a variety of God's graces in him as in any laick or clergyman of this kingdom'. He was a vigorous and effective administrator of his diocese and the 'second founder' of King's College. Under his leadership, the Aberdeen Doctors developed a sober and learned theology which was to be the only serious theological alternative to the covenants. 'His spirit and his point of view ... inspired the Episcopacy ... of Leighton and the Scougalls and James and George Garden'.[118]

William Cowper, Bishop of Galloway in 1612, was notable for the learning and piety of his sermons and commentaries. Thomas McCrie, the learned and sympathetic biographer of Andrew

---

[115] John Perry, 'John Spottiswood', 239.
[116] W. Fraser, *Memoirs of the Maxwells*, II, 54-5, 57.
[117] Ellon Presb., 8 December 1613, 19 June 1616.
[118] *Funerals*, 73, quoted in G.D. Henderson, *Religious Life in Seventeenth-Century Scotland*, 31, 59.

Melville, wrote that 'the discourses of William Cowper ... are perhaps superior to any sermons of that age'. Not only did Cowper quote freely from Greek and Latin fathers, but he used a number of vivid illustrations, some of them drawn from natural history. 'Prayer is a marvellous kinde of husbandry, it soweth seede in the heaven and reapeth fruit in the earth and heavne also'. Or again: 'Our Prayer to Him is like the flowering of a little strand, but his answere to us is like the flowing of the Ocean'. Yet Bishop Cowper had signed a protestation in 1606 which declared that the 'pre-eminence of bishops is that Dagon which once alreadie fell before the arke of God in this land' and his opponents despised him for accepting a bishopric. Spottiswood declared that Bishop Cowper was 'an excellent and ready preacher ... and a singular good man, but one that affected too much the applause of the popular'. Cowper does appear to have been very sensitive about the charge of hypocrisy, but perhaps the bishop himself should be allowed the last word.

> Say what they will, my workis shalbe witnesses for me: The planting of Preachers, the building of Kirks where never one hes bene, the repairing of others, shall testifie for me, that, after my weaknes, my cair hes bene to do the work of a Bishop there, to the glorie of God, your Highnes honor, and good of the countrey.[119]

Some of the bishops appointed by James had ties with landed and prominent Scottish families. Andrew Boyd, Bishop of Argyll in 1613, was a natural son of Lord Boyd of Kilmarnock. Neil Campbell, Bishop of the Isles in 1633, whose brother and father were also bishops, secured his appointment partly through the influence of his cousin, Lord Lorne, who later became Marquis of Argyll. Adam Bellenden, Bishop of Dunblane in 1613, was the son of Sir John Bellenden of Auchnoull. Archbishop Spottiswood was probably descended from the lairds of Spottiswood in the Merse. Alexander Lindsay, Bishop of Dunkeld, was a kinsman of Sir Robert Ker of Ancrum. David Lindsay, Bishop of Ross, was of the family of Lindsay of Edzell and was a nephew of David, ninth Earl

---

[119] T. McCrie, *Life of Andrew Melville*, 390; W. Cowper, *Works*, 789, 780; G. D. Henderson, *Religious Life in Seventeenth-Century Scotland*, 209; Calderwood, VI, 488, 491; 349–50; Spottiswood, *History*, III, 258; *O.L.* II, 426.

of Crawford. Although Archbishop Gladstanes was the son of a clerk and bailie of Dundee, the marriage of his daughter to the son of John, Lord Glamis, in 1611 indicated his rising position. Patrick Forbes of Aberdeen was the laird of Corse. George Graham was a grandson of William, Lord Graham, first Earl of Montrose.[120]

Henry Guthrie, in his *Memoirs*, charged that Charles's bishops were very different from those appointed by his father. James appointed 'old bishops, who were prudent and humble men' while Charles appointed 'young bishops ... [who] kept a fellowship among themselves apart, [and] ... carried themselves ... loftily'.[121] Some reservations should be made about Guthrie's judgment. Charles did not appoint noticeably young bishops. Twenty-two bishops were appointed by James. Their average age at election was forty-five. Charles appointed eight bishops. Their average age at election was forty-eight.[122] And, unlike the Arminians in England, Charles's Scottish bishops did not hold all the best sees.

However, Guthrie's point does have some validity. Five of the eight bishops appointed by Charles – William Forbes, John Maxwell, James Wedderburn, Thomas Sydserf, and Walter Whitford – do form a separate group, distinguishable from their colleagues both by their theological outlook and their family background. Influenced by the Laudian tradition, they were contemptuously referred to as 'the Canterburians' by their opponents. The most distinguished scholar of the Caroline bishops, and the most extreme in his theological views, was William Forbes, first Bishop of Edinburgh. Usually classified as one of the Aberdeen Doctors, he went far beyond his contemporaries in an attempt to reconcile the theological issues between 'Romans' and 'Protestants'. His major work, *Considerationes Modestae*, found little support in Scotland, but Dr Mathew rightly pointed out the charity and the profoundly irenical temper of his work. Forbes called upon all Christians to 'reverence the judgment of the Ancient Church', and he believed that both 'Romans' and 'Protestants' should re-examine their beliefs, recognise their errors, and

[120] Spottiswood, *History*, V. A 4^r, (1677 edition); Newbattle Portfolio, xiii/72; G. Donaldson, 'David Lindsay', *Fathers of the Kirk*, 28; *Fasti*, VII, 326; *Scots Peerage*, VIII, 287; W. G. S. Snow, *Patrick Forbes*, ch. II; *Scottish History Society Miscellany*, II, 231.
[121] Guthrie, *Memoirs*, 17.
[122] *Fasti*, VII, and articles in the *D.N.B.*

discover the common truth which underlay their dispute. Thus, after a long discussion on purgatory, he concluded, 'To remove or at least to diminish this controversy, let the Romanists neither hold themselves as an article of faith, nor obtrude as such upon others, their opinion about a punitive purgatory'. Protestants, on the other hand, should approve 'the custom of praying and offering for the dead, which is most ancient, and thoroughly received in the universal Church of Christ almost from the very times of the Apostles'.[123]

John Maxwell, Bishop of Ross in 1633, was one of the most competent of Charles' appointments. He was the leading figure in the preparation of the Prayer Book of 1637. Spottiswood wished to see him as his successor at St Andrews, and even Henry Guthrie, who thoroughly disliked the 'young bishops', made an exception in the case of Bishop Maxwell.[124]

James Wedderburn spent much of his early ministry in England. According to Laud, Wedderburn was appointed to Dunblane so that he might enforce the full English liturgy in the chapel royal. And Wedderburn appears to have been the main author of the final, radical changes introduced into the Prayer Book of 1637 – changes which looked to the English Prayer Book of 1549 for their inspiration.[125]

Moreover, Maxwell and Whitford were the only 'Canterburians' who had any ties with prominent or ancient families. Bishop Maxwell was probably the son of William Maxwell, laird of Cavens, and Bishop Whitford was the grandson of Sir James Somerville of Cambusnethan in Lanarkshire. However, William Forbes was the son of a burgess of Aberdeen, Thomas Sydserf was the son of a merchant in Edinburgh, and James Wedderburn was the son of a mariner and shipowner.[126] Both by theological outlook and by family ties, the 'Canterburians' were ill-equipped to support the radical liturgical policy which Charles wished to introduce.

Episcopacy between 1600 and 1638 was in many ways similar to episcopacy as restored in 1661. The authority and jurisdiction of

[123] David Mathew, *Scotland under Charles I*, 89; *Considerationes Modestae*, II, 139.
[124] Spottiswood, *History*, I, cxxxii–cxxxiii; Guthrie, *Memoirs*, 16–17.
[125] Robert Baillie, *Letters and Journals*, I, 437; Gordon Donaldson, *The Making of the Prayer Book of 1637*, 49–53, 81–2.
[126] *Scots Peerage*, III, 127; *Dictionary of National Biography*, XXI, 127 (cf. *Scots Peerage*, IV, 581); *Fasti*, VII, 338, 341, 353.

the two episcopates within the church were fundamentally the same. However, episcopacy in the early part of the century was somewhat more moderate. The bishops appointed by James VI did not licence schoolmasters or readers, nor did they have a technical veto over decisions of their synods. Presbyteries and kirk sessions were not required to procure a licence from a bishop before meeting.

More significant than these minor formal differences was the more moderate attitude of the Jacobean bishops toward nonconformity. Or, to put the point more strongly, Archbishop Spottiswood and his colleagues were more interested in preserving the unity of the church than in imposing unpopular liturgical practices. The chief point at issue was conformity to the Perth Articles. These articles will be discussed more fully later,[127] but they required certain liturgical practices – chiefly kneeling to receive communion – which James forced through a general assembly at Perth in 1618 and which were resented and ignored by an important minority. The bishops were almost openly unenthusiastic about the unpleasant job of enforcing these articles. This fact was recognised by the editor of Samuel Rutherford's letters in 1664:

> Our late furious Prelates [i.e. the Restoration bishops] ... are a little more hot then their predecessors: It's true, these went so high in their persecution & drave so hard, that it was thought scarce possible, for any to out-doe them in persecuting. ... But Alas! The Church finds this day, that in respect of their successors, they were mere novices & had scarce served their Aprentiship in the *blake Art*.[128]

A more sober estimate was made by another presbyterian historian in 1676. Although the Perth Articles were urged, he wrote:

> yet the persecution then was nothing so hot and violent as now; for then the bishops (especially Spottiswood) were more moderate, and dealt with the King for moderation, and did strive to keep off innovations, such as surplice, liturgy, &c, and did depose very few of the nonconformists; for in the province of Fife there were only two deposed; and then they never challenged

[127] See below, 181–92.
[128] Samuel Rutherford, *Letters*, f. C6^r, (1664).

deposed ministers for public preaching and assisting at the celebration of the communion. And that was the cause why in these times there were no meetings in the fields.[129]

This estimate was confirmed by the bishops' own actions, and there is no reason to doubt the sincerity or candour of Spottiswood's opening sermon to the Perth assembly:

> The convencie of them [i.e. the proposed articles] for our Church is doubted of by many, but not without cause. They are new and uncouth; such things as we have not been accustomed with. ... Had it beene in our power to have disswaded or declined them, mostly certainly wee would; and if any of you thinke otherwise, yee are greatly mistaken.[130]

Bishops often did insist upon conformity, but, unlike Restoration prelates, there is no suggestion that they would have continued to do so had an indulgence been granted by the crown. In fact, the very moderate accommodation offered to some ministers in 1626 may have been due to Spottiswood's influence.[131]

The development of episcopacy in Scotland between 1600 and 1638 was not merely a revival of medieval prelacy, nor a copy of English episcopacy. The whole programme of confirmation tours well known in England had no parallel in Scotland. Indeed, as already mentioned, confirmation by bishops in any form was conspicuously absent, in spite of attempts to introduce that practice. Scottish bishops did hold visitations in local parishes, although bishops were invariably assisted by members of a local presbytery, and sometimes by representatives from other presbyteries as well. However, both before and after 1610 most visitations were held by presbyteries alone.

In the ordination of clergy and consecration of bishops, the Scottish experiment followed somewhat more traditional lines. Presentations were directed to bishops after 1610. Presbyteries continued after 1610 to examine candidates before ordination, usually upon warrant from a bishop. Between the Glasgow assembly

---

[129] William Row, *The Life of Robert Blair*, 137.
[130] *Spottiswood Miscellany*, I, 65-6.
[131] *R.P.C.* I, 344n. For the attitude of Restoration bishops, see my *Bishop and Presbytery*, 26-7. Nonconformity was, of course, much more serious during the Restoration.

of 1610 and 1637 presbyteries also often assisted at ordinations, but the evidence for ordinations by presbyteries alone during these years is very slight.[132] A bishop was invariably present at an ordination, and he presided. Yet bishops did not ordain men to the diaconate[133] and priesthood, but simply to the ministry. Bishops were consecrated by bishops and the ancient practice of at least three consecrators was retained.

The extensive administrative and pastoral work of Scottish bishops was in the usual western tradition. Less common was a sharing of authority with the courts of the church in the administration of discipline. Kirk sessions, presbyteries and synods were well-established by 1610. Bishops worked with those courts and often supported them in difficult disciplinary cases. An Englishman who visited Scotland during the Restoration wrote a description of Scottish episcopacy which could apply to bishops throughout the century:

> Their Kirk-Sessions and Presbyteries savour of the Presbyterian Classes, and are, as one might conceive, derived from 'em, and follow 'em so close in the Methods of Governing the People, yet because they allow and respect the Name of Bishop, and give him an Account at their Six Months Synods of what they did in their Presbyteries and Parishes, because as Perpetual Moderator he influenced their Consultation, and had the Power of Mission and Ordination as with us; therefore this Government of their Church was called Episcopal, tho' hardly to be discern'd for such; by Travellers who have seen what Episcopacy is in other places.[134]

Clearly Scottish episcopacy was not exactly 'what Episcopacy is in other places'. Episcopacy in early seventeenth century Scotland was an interesting and in some ways a unique development of the ancient office of bishop.

[132] See below, 151–2.
[133] For the introduction of 'preaching deacons', see below, 150–1.
[134] Thomas Morer, *A Short Account of Scotland* (1702), 49.

CHAPTER FOUR

Kirk Sessions

I

Kirk sessions existed in the reformed Church of Scotland from the earliest years of the Reformation, and by 1600 many parishes had established kirk sessions. There is little information in early presbytery records about the way kirk sessions were established, probably because this matter was handled during visitations and entered in special visitation registers which are no longer extant.[1]

Fortunately, full records exist for the establishment of the kirk session of Udny in Aberdeenshire; and the struggles to establish discipline there must have been repeated with variations in many rural parishes.

The parish of Udny was created by an act of Parliament in December 1597 and was formed from sections of four neighbouring parishes: Foveran, Ellon, Tarves and Logie-Buchan.[2] It was part of the presbytery of Ellon. In May 1598, that presbytery appointed a reader, 'Robert Murray, ... to reid the word at the Kirk off Udny till forder ordour be taken'. Four months later the presbytery met at Udny and appointed nineteen 'eldairs and givers up of public offendaris,' including the most prominent parishioner of the parish, 'the Laird Udny'. The chief problem was the lack of a resident minister at Udny, and it was immediately clear that the new session would be allowed to handle no cases of discipline unless a minister presided and moderated their meetings. Several temporary expedients were tried by the presbytery. Neighbouring ministers were asked to visit Udny, 'teache thair', and meet with the elders for 'the grand wark off disciplein'. However, neither that nor other schemes worked well and in June 1599 the presbytery itself took over the disciplinary cases at Udny. The session of Udny continued to meet 'every secund sabboth at the kirk befoir the

[1] See below, 105–6.
[2] *A.P.S.* IV, 157.

prayers at aucht houris'. They issued baptismal and marriage testimonials and received fines collected by the presbytery of Ellon, but they did not try disciplinary cases. It was not until 1604, when a regular minister, Mr Thomas Mitchell, was at last instituted at Udny, that discipline became a regular part of the work of the session.[3]

Several aspects of this account are striking. There was, of course, no suggestion here (or elsewhere) that members of the session were to be elected by the congregation. Even more striking was the unspoken assumption that a session could not handle cases of discipline unless a recognised minister moderated the session meetings. Nor was the Udny arrangement unique. In 1614 the synod of Fife considered:

> the kirk or chapell of St Michael [?Tarvit] ... in respect the parochinars will gif no moyen for intertainement of ane minister, it is thairfoir ordained that ... the Exercise of Coupar salbe to thame in place of sessioune befoir whome immediatlie sall thair slanderis come.

And the church at Abbotrule did not even have elders until a minister was settled there in 1610.[4] It seems likely that the settlement of ministers in parishes, which continued steadily throughout the early seventeenth century,[5] was a major factor in the establishment of fully functioning kirk sessions which could carry out 'the grand wark off disciplein'.

Where kirk sessions were established, both presbyteries and bishops used their authority to require sessions to fulfil their duties. A presbytery regularly examined the registers and work of a kirk session at a parish visitation, often requiring elders to leave the meeting and the minister to give a full account of their work. In 1621 the presbytery of Ellon rebuked negligent elders in the parish of Ellon and ordered all elders 'newlie admitted and suorne and causit solemnelie promeis concurrance to discipline'. Two years earlier the session of Methlick was reformed by a presbytery and commissioners sent by the synod of Aberdeen.[6] Archbishop

[3] Ellon Presb., 3 May, 28 August 1598; 24 January 1598–99; 6 June 1599; 29 May 1600; 8 July 1601; 26 January 1603; 11 January, 25 April 1604; 28 March 1605.
[4] Fife Synod, 174; Jedburgh Presb., 16 May, 29 August 1610.
[5] See below, 153–4.
[6] Ellon Presb., 4 November 1619, 6 September 1621.

Gladstanes reorganised many kirk sessions during his visitation tours of 1611–14, adding some new members, charging sessions to meet weekly, and requiring them to secure a session book. At the first court which Bishop Law held in Orkney in 1612 he 'ordanit that the saidis magistrattis and counsell [of Kirkwall] sall assist and fortifie the minister and sessioun of kirk for putting to executioun of all actis and statutis maid be thame for mentenance of Godis glorie'. In 1630 the court of high commission reorganised the kirk session of Leith in an attempt to settle quarrels there. Precise rules about membership, election of elders and deacons, and conduct of meetings were set down.[7]

Although James VI wrote in 1610 that 'laic elders have neither warrant in the word, nor example of the primitive Church', he agreed that it was 'expedient that some be appointed to assist the minister' and to try 'all public and notorious offenders, and enjoin the satisfaction according to the canons of the Church'.[8] And, in spite of James's reservations, all the evidence indicates that both civil and church authorities used their influence to establish kirk sessions or improve their efficiency wherever possible.

Kirk sessions normally met once a week, usually on Sunday. Few matched the industry of the session of Elgin, which met 'ilk Wedinsdaye, Frydaye and Sondaye'.[9] In 1641 Alexander Henderson wrote that 'the Minister of the parish is always moderator of' the session. Not only was he moderator, but apparently some ministers were also exercising a right of veto over session actions.[10] Strong and well-established sessions occasionally met even if their minister was temporarily absent, but the typical pattern was the action of the kirk session of Culross, which held no meetings in 1634 between 19 October and 9 December because 'the Minister, Mr John Duncan, wes sick'.[11]

---

[7] *Fife Synod*, 47–50; R. S. Barclay, *The Court Book of Orkney and Shetland*, 17; *Extracts from the Records of the Burgh of Edinburgh, 1626–41*, 68–70.

[8] Spottiswood, *History*, III, 211.

[9] E.g. *K. S. Dundonald, passim*; Ellon Presb., 12 August 1601; *St Andrews K. S.* II, 936; *Elgin K. S.*, 60.

[10] *Government and Order of the Church of Scotland*, 36. The general assembly of 1638 ordered 'that no Minister moderating his Session, shall usurp a negative voice over the members of his Session', implying that this had, in fact, been done (A. Peterkin, *Records of the Kirk*, 37).

[11] *Elgin K. S.*, 60; Culross K. S., note after 19 October 1634 meeting.

Annual elections of elders and deacons were the custom in some prominent parishes, the session normally electing its own successors. The kirk session of St Andrews elected a new session every October between 1583 and 1600, although many elders and deacons were re-elected year after year. However, few parishes maintained that ideal in the early seventeenth century.[12] The kirk session of Dundonald held only one election between 1602 and 1612. In Belhelvie three elections were held between 1623 and 1632. In the royal burgh of Culross no election took place between 1632 and 1637. Eight elections were held in Stow between 1626 and 1652. There were fourteen elections in Canongate between 1630 and 1652.[13]

The general assembly of 1597 ordered 'that all Sessiouns be electit with consent of thair awin congregatiouns', and congregations sometimes had a formal right to object to any person nominated as an elder. However, there is no evidence that congregations themselves elected members of a session.[14]

Who were elected as elders? Dr W. H. Makey has carefully investigated the elders of Stow, Liberton, Canongate and St Cuthbert's.[15] Broadly the pattern which emerged was that elders on these sessions were prominent citizens but often were not the leading or most powerful persons in the parish. In Stow about a tenth of the elders were village craftsmen and a further tenth were millers; but most of the rest were working farmers, some of them

---

[12] *St. Andrews K. S.* II, 511, 542, 560, 574, 607, 624, 650, etc.. Edinburgh maintained an annual election into the seventeenth century (W. H. Makey, 'The elders of Stow, Liberton, Canongate and St Cuthbert's', 157).

[13] *Dundonald K. S.*, 92, 100, 108; Belhelvie K. S., 6 January 1623, 19 July 1629, 22 February, 8 July 1632; Culross K. S., 30 September 1632, 16 April 1637; W. H. Makey, 'The Elders of Stow, Liberton, Canongate and St Cuthbert's', 156.

[14] *B.U.K.* III, 926 (Calderwood, V, 643). Cf. *St Andrews K. S.* II, 822; Culross K. S. 7, 18 October 1632; *Dundonald K. S.* 105; Trinity College K. S. 20 December 1627; Belhelvie K. S. 19 July 1629. In 1641 Alexander Henderson wrote, 'Where particular Elderships are already constitute, the Pastor and the Elders who are now in office, do choose such as are to succeed those who are removed by death, or any other way' (*Government and Order of the Church of Scotland*, 14).

[15] W. H. Makey, 'The elders of Stow, Liberton, Canongate and St Cuthberts in the Mid-Seventeenth Century'. I am endebted to Mr Makey for most of this paragraph.

tenants and some small proprietors. In the barony of Craigmillar, which formed part of the parish of Liberton, the elders were the tenants of the Laird of Craigmillar. But neither Craigmillar nor any of the other lairds of the parish were themselves elders. 'For the most part, the Lairds held aloof, they had power to spare'. In the urban parish of Canongate, on the other hand, the elders were often drawn from the wealthier elements of the congregation. They tended to be wealthy middlemen or master craftsmen and they often held office either as councillors or as the deacons of their incorporations. If these three sessions are at all typical, the kirk session system successfully enlisted the second-rank leadership of the nation to carry out the important though routine work of local discipline and church administration.

After election, elders and deacons were admitted at a public service of the church. On the Sunday following the annual election in St Andrews, the elders and deacons were 'solemnly convenit in the kirk ... [and] war all admonished and informit of the burding of thair offices, quha all, being resavit, maid promeis be uphalding of thair handis to discharge the samin'. Similar services took place elsewhere.[16] No distinction was made between those who had previously been elders and those who had not, and there is no evidence in practice of any idea of an 'indelible ordination'. All alike were 'solemnly received with lifted up hands, giving their promises to be faithfull'.[17]

The position of deacons on kirk sessions varied considerably in different parts of the country, probably reflecting some uncertainty about deacons' status and duties.[18] None of the kirk sessions in the presbytery of Ellon had deacons; there were two to four deacons on the session of Elgin; Trinity College kirk session in Edinburgh was usually composed of six elders and six deacons; and the kirk session of Dundonald in 1606 had eight elders and nineteen deacons.[19]

It was often difficult to draw any clear line between the ecclesiastical jurisdiction exercised by sessions and civil jurisdiction

---

[16] *St Andrews K. S.* II, 905. For other examples, see Fife Synod, 52; *Maitland Misc.* I, 467.
[17] *Government and Order of the Church of Scotland*, 14–15.
[18] Deacons are discussed below.
[19] Ellon Presb. *passim*; *Elgin K. S.*, 5, 9, 32–3; Trinity College, K. S., 27 December 1627; *Dundonald K. S.*, 108.

exercised by government officials. This overlapping of jurisdictions was especially obvious in burghs, where burgh officials usually not only shared in the election of elders and deacons but also attended and participated in meetings of a session. For example, the elders and deacons of Trinity College kirk session were elected every December by 'the provost [of Edinburgh], baillies, deyne of gild, treasurer, and remanent counsell' as well as the present minister, elders, and deacons. The kirk session at Leith was elected 'be the ministers, baillies and sessioun for the tyme'. Usually a provost or bailie in a burgh was also elected an elder of a session, although occasionally, as in South Leith, the bailie was entitled to sit on the session whether he was elected as an elder or not.[20]

There appears to have been uniformity in the way kirk sessions were constituted in different parts of the country. By the early seventeenth century a common order and pattern was widely established, and the institution of kirk session did a remarkable job of enlisting the lay leadership of the church in an active and vital organisation.

II

The Scots Confession of 1560 declared that the notes of 'the true Kirk of God' were:

> First, The true preaching of the word of God; . . . Secondly, The Right administration of the sacraments of Christ Jesus; . . . Last, Ecclesiastical discipline uprightly ministered, as God's word prescribes whereby vice is repressed and virtue nourished.[21]

Whatever may have been the theological status of 'ecclesiastical discipline', its importance in the life and practice of the reformed Church of Scotland would be difficult to overestimate. No parish would have been regarded as 'reformed' which had not accepted the discipline of the church and which did not bring offenders against that discipline to at least formal repentance. Indeed, any parish without a kirk session to enforce discipline was usually described as 'desolate'. Discipline was one of the most enduring features of the Scottish Reformation, and its administration was retained by the church throughout the seventeenth century.

[20] Trinity College K. S., 20 December, 27 December 1627; *Extracts from the Records of the Burgh of Edinburgh, 1626–41*, 69.
[21] John Knox, *History of the Reformation* (Dickinson), II, 266.

Administration of discipline was first of all a responsibility of local kirk sessions. Practically all cases began in a kirk session court, and the vast majority of cases were settled by that court. The work of discipline began in the duties assigned to individual elders. Many sessions divided their parishes into districts and assigned one or more elders to each portion. Although their primary responsibility was a disciplinary one – 'the better tryell of vice and punishing thairof', elders were also often charged – as at St Andrews – to inform the minister if 'ony persoine be seik within ony familie ... that the ministeris may ... cum and comfort thame with holy admonitioun'. But the basic responsibility was to carry out the work of discipline, and instructions issued to the elders at Stirling in 1600 were typical. They were:

> to tak attendence to the maneris of the pepill thairin ... [to] attend quhat straingearis resortis to the toun, and to quhat effect; ... [and to search for] any Jesuistis or seminarie Preistis ... within this toun.[22]

Most cases tried by a session were probably initially begun by the activity of an elder.

The weekly kirk session meeting was an important occasion when elders were expected to be present. If late or absent, they were fined.[23] Sessions began with the 'invocatioun of God his holie name' and then turned to the work of discipline. By 1600 the competence of kirk sessions was clearly recognised in most areas, and sessions throughout the church tried the same types of cases.

The Sabbath was especially the church's own day; offences such as drunkenness or fighting, which might be tried in a civil court if they occurred during the week, came before the session if they violated the sanctity of the Sabbath. In 1632 the kirk session of Culross summoned seven men and women for 'scolding and flyting [quarrelling] on the Lords Day', and the kirk session of Perth tried a man who on the Sabbath had become 'so beastly drunk that he knew not what he did'.[24]

The church had a clear idea of the behaviour it expected of its

---

[22] *St Andrews K. S.* II, 871, 817–8; *Maitland Misc.* I, 136. See also Culross K. S., 13 November 1632.
[23] E.g. Trinity college K. S., 3 January 1628; Fife Synod, 154; *St Andrews K. S.* II, 805, 872, 913; Belhelvie K. S. 13 January, 1623.
[24] Culross K. S., 26 August 1632; *Spottiswood Misc.* I, 279.

members on the Sabbath. That ideal was set forth in 1604 by the session of Aberdeen in a notice sent to all heads of families.

> The haill famelie sall keip halie the Saboth day, and that by abstinence from play and corporall labour thairon; sall resort to thair awin paroche kirk, heir all the sermones thairin, and quha can reid sall learne to sing and prais God publictlie.[25]

It was a popular ideal, supported by magistrate and churchman alike. Those who were 'absentis frome sermon', those who profaned the Sabbath by 'playand', 'gatherin kaill', 'fisching both of whyt fisch and salmond fisching', and similar offences could expect a summons before the session.[26]

The right of parishioners to be married on Sunday was a controversial topic. That right has been affirmed by a general assembly in 1602 and reaffirmed in 1610. 'The holy band of matrimonie [was to] be refused to no Christians . . . upon Sunday'.[27] Yet sessions and presbyteries were reluctant to permit Sabbath marriages because marriages were frequently accompanied by parties with 'publict dansing at the croce . . . [and] on the publict streitis'. In 1614 the presbytery of Jedburgh roundly ordered 'that na marriage be geven one the sabboth day inder the pane conteinit in the act of the synodole assembly',[28] which suggests that Jedburgh's actions was not unique. That implication is further borne out by extant parish registers, where marriages on Sunday steadily declined. In 1604 sixty-three per cent of the marriages in Aberdeen took place on Sunday. By 1612 the percentage had dropped to forty-three. And similar declines took place at Dunfermline, the Canongate, and Inverness.[29]

If the medieval practice of Sunday marriages was opposed, one medieval custom which did continue was the observance of Lent as a time when marriages were not solemnised. Only rarely did a

---

[25] *Aberdeen K. S.*, 34-5.

[26] Belhelvie K. S., 13 April 1623; *Elgin K. S.*, 103; *B.U.K.* III, 996 (Calderwood, VI, 184).

[27] *B.U.K.* III, 1002, 1101 (Calderwood, VI, 183, VIII, 83).

[28] *Maitland Misc.* I, 136, Cf. Ellon Presb., 10 June 1601; Jedburgh Presb., 24 August 1614.

[29] Aberdeen Parish Register, 168a (12), 1604, 1612; Dunfermline Parish Register, 424 (1), 1600, 1605, 424 (2), 1612, 1620; Canongate Parish Register, 685³ (12), 1601, 1611, 1625; Inverness Parish Register, 98 (1), 1604, 1610.

marriage take place during Lent, although there appears to have been no reformed legislation forbidding the practice.

Regulations about marriage services were only a small part of the jurisdiction which sessions exercised over the obligations of marriage or violations against its sanctity. Cases of incest and adultery often came before sessions in the earlier part of the century, although jurisdiction over these offences gradually passed to presbyteries.[30] However, kirk sessions continued to try many cases of fornication. Fornication 'under promise of mariage' was especially common.[31] Kirk sessions usually tried to get the guilty couple to marry after their penalty had been paid. A variety of other marriage and family problems were handled as well. A quarrelling couple were summoned before an Edinburgh session and ordered to:

> leive in peice and love and in the feir of God as Godis word allowed . . . and that nane of tham shall ingriyit uthers [i.e. harm each other] be word or deid . . . under the paine of sevir punischementis of thair persouns and estaite.

And considering the ample authority of an Edinburgh session, the threat was no empty one. A son who failed to support his aged father was ordered 'to do his dewtie to his father anent his interteinement of meit and claith'. A man was required to guarantee support for his illegitimate child before his marriage was permitted.[31]

Although cases of slander belonged to the jurisdiction of commissary courts, many trials for slander were also held in kirk session courts, especially if the slander implied superstitious practices. In 1627 Trinity College kirk session tried Isabel Monteith, who had some money and clothes stolen from her. At the trial Isabel admitted that she had wronged William Mactear by calling him a thief. She explained:

> that scho haud writtin the said William his name and certane uther boyis names on paper and putt thame in watter to try qhus name did sink to the grund and the said William his name

[30] See below, 96.
[31] E.g. Trinity College K. S., 16 October 1633, 26 November 1629; Culross K. S., 27 May, 5 August, 7 October 1632, 9 December, 14 December 1634.
[32] Trinity College K. S., 14 July 1636, 14 March 1633; *Dundonald K. S.*, 203–5.

did onlie sink to the ground and thairfore scho judged him to be onlie theiff.[33]

She was punished for both slander and superstition.[33]

Committing superstitious acts often brought an offender before his session. The session of Dundonald tried a woman who healed a sore breast with 'hir husbandis left foot scho'. 'S. Geregynes [St Gerardine's] cave' regularly troubled the session at Elgin, and the elders at Dundonald used much effort to obtain a stone used by Katherine Macteir to make butter when others 'could get no buttir'.[34]

Cases of blasphemy were occasionally tried by kirk sessions, although usually offenders were more guilty of ignorance or foolishness than of blasphemy. Thus Margaret Underwood, a beggar, was accused 'of hir blasphemous speich in saying Christ wald not being so daft as to haif died for hir', but she granted that it was 'said of witlesnes'.[35]

The number and variety of cases tried by kirk sessions can be seen in the following tables. The number beside each offence indicates the number of persons who were tried. Each person might come before a session for several meetings.

Dundonald Kirk Session – 1605

Profanation of the Sabbath	31
Violation of the Sabbath fast	13
'Awayabiding' from the kirk	5
Assault on the Sabbath	3
Observance of Yule	3
Absence from precommunion examination	3
Failure to communicate	3
Misbehaviour on the stool of penitence	2
Alteration of a testimonial	1
Fornication	20
Adultery	5
Slander	10
Witchcraft	2
Attempted murder	1

[33] Trinity College K. S., 13 December 1627.
[34] *Dundonald K. S.,* 170, 9; *Elgin K. S.,* 87. For other cases, see *Elgin K. S.,* 96, *Dundonald K. S.,* 37, 51.
[35] *Dundonald K. S.,* 49.

Belhelvie Kirk Session – 1624

Profanation of the Sabbath	9
Absence from sermon	12
Failure to communicate	3
Fornication	20
Adultery	2
Breach of promise	3
Irregular marriage	1
Blasphemy	1
Reception of strangers without testimonial	3
Slander	3
Assault	2

Culross Kirk Session – 1632

Profanation of the Sabbath by drinking	31
Profanation of the Sabbath by working at the salt pans	23
Profanation of the Sabbath	10
Absence from sermon	3
Absence from communion	1
Assault on the Sabbath	10
Fornication	27
Slander	1
Trespassing (allowing cattle in kirk yard)	1

Occasionally kirk sessions did refer cases to their presbytery or their bishop. Those charged with adultery were usually sent to a presbytery, especially after 1625. And the advice of a presbytery might be sought on an unusual matter. However, most kirk sessions seldom found it necessary to mention presbyteries, synods, or bishops. Although the kirk session of Belhelvie decided in 1623 to charge two suspected papists 'befor the presbytery', this case was the only one in 1623 which the session did not conclude by itself.[36] Again, the kirk session of Dundonald sent only one matter to its presbytery in 1605.[37] Most cases of discipline which came before the courts of the church were tried and concluded in kirk sessions.

Trials held in kirk sessions were usually short and simple.

[36] Belhelvie K. S., 23 March 1623.
[37] *Dundonald K. S.*, 73.

Occasionally witnesses were summoned and an extended trial held. But in most cases the facts appear to have been well-known, and the majority of those accused pleaded guilty and were assigned a sentence.

Primarily, the church was interested in that inner repentance of the heart which alone is worthy to be called Christian penitence. And the church recognised that external systems of discipline could easily mask a proud and impenitent heart. In 1599 the kirk session of St Andrews complained that many 'in making repentance befoir the pulpeit ... uteris proud and querelling speiches, testifying thairby the pryid of thair hartis and the litill regaird of God and disciplene'. And a preacher in 1590 put the point more fully. He condemned:

> all the penitentis of our age, all the feined repentances that are drawin out of yow by force of argument and reasoun, and ar not wroucht be the Holie Spirit. That repentance may weill satisfie a visible kirk ... bot it will nevir satisfie the pearceing eye of a living God .... The thing that ye do, do in sinceritie, that as ye are humbled outwardlie in your bodie, so your saull may be humbled inwardlie befoir the living God. Ye may weill beguyll us, bot ye will not begyll the living God.[38]

But God alone could judge the heart, and the church had to be content with more external signs of penitence. The stool of penitence – often called simply the 'stool' – was the chief means by which the church 'humbled outwardlie' its penitents. Sir William Brereton described the use of the stool in 1635.

> The stool is a public and eminent seat, erected towards the lower end of the church about two yards from the ground, either about some pillar, or in some such conspicuous place, where the whole congregation may take notice of them; this seat is capable of about six or eight persons. Here this day, 28 *Junii*, I was at sermon in the Gray Friors, where there stood three women upon the stool of repentance, who are admitted [i.e. allowed] to sit during the sermon.[39]

A woman who was guilty of a serious offence might be required to

---

[38] *St Andrews K. S.* II, 910, lxxxi.
[39] Sir William Brereton, *Travels*, 107.

appear 'in sackcloth' or even 'with her half heid schavein', while a man was often required 'to satisfie . . . in . . . sackcloth, bair fuittit and bair leggit'.[40] Penitents were expected to appear for several Sundays – three Sundays being the usual penalty for fornication and six Sundays for adultery. The church even attempted – with some success – to require the wealthy and powerful to undergo public humiliation. In 1636 'My Lord Bishop and the Synod [of Moray] ordenes that non of the brethren sall ovasee [i.e. overlook or disregard] the repentance of anie man for the payment [of] his penalties how great soever it be', and similar edicts were made by other courts.[41]

But any offence against the church was also an offence against the state, and civil penalties were often demanded of offenders before they were admitted to the stool. The purpose of a civil penalty was expressed by the elders of Stirling, who sent an offender to the bailies to be punished, 'quhairby she may be movit to abstein fra the lyk in tymes cuming, and that utheris may tak exampill'.[42]

This practice meant, of course, cooperation from civil authorities; and that co-operation was usually readily given. Burgh kirk sessions normally had bailies and sometimes a provost among their members who were expected to exact civil penalties. A town council might pass an ordinance supporting kirk discipline.[43] A really serious offence might be tried at a joint meeting of council and session. In 1620 a man in Perth:

> upon a Sabbath-day at night . . . pressed to misuse Giles Lowry in her returning . . . [and] having entered the kirk, he rang the common bells, thereby setting the haill town under fear either of fire or sword. His offence being so great

he was tried by both the council and session of Perth and punished severely.[44]

Rural sessions could not appeal to a burgh council, but they had other methods of securing assistance from the magistrate.

[40] Ellon Presb., 20 March 1605.
[41] Moray Synod, 85.
[42] *Maitland Misc.* I, 131.
[43] E.g. *Extracts from the Council Register of the Burgh of Aberdeen. 1625–42*, 1, 2; Culross K. S., 28 June, 1635.
[44] *Spottiswood Misc.* I, 296–7. For a similar case in Aberdeen, see Aberdeen K. S., 66–7.

A direct appeal to a powerful nobleman might be made. Occasionally a session might even appeal to the privy council.[45] But the most common method used by rural parishes was to request a commission from the privy council authorising the session to impose civil penalties directly. The need for such a commission was recognised at many of the visitations made by Archbishop Gladstanes after 1610. At Rescobie it was:

> regraited be thame [the elders] that thei gett no payment of the penalties quhairin offenderis ar convict, they are ordained with diligens to purchas ane commissioun quhairin salbe the minister, the Lairds of Cars, Strickmartine [and other members of the session].

Similar injunctions were issued at Forgan, Kilmany, Uphall, Slamannan, Abdie, Kinfauns, Rait, Liff, Murroes and Errol.[46]

Once a session possessed a commission, they were able to impose both civil and ecclesiastical penalties. The kirk session of Belhelvie secured a commission in 1630. Thereafter the session fined almost all offenders, and the fines were promptly paid. When Thomas Robertson was found 'grinding upoun the sabbathe daye' he was ordered 'to pay tene schillinges and mak publick repentance' which was done 'boith in penaltie and repentance' two weeks later.[47]

The most common civil penalty imposed by sessions was a fine. Sometimes presbyteries set up tables of fines for sessions to use. The presbytery of Ellon ordered 'that four marks be the penaltie of ilk fornicator in tyme cumming for the first time and aught marks the secund tyme'.[48] However, a more popular ideal than a fixed table of fines was reflected in the injunction of the kirk session of Belhelvie 'that pecunniall penalties of publict offenders be imposit proportionallie to thair estait', and their practice followed that principle.[49]

[45] E.g. Morton Papers, Box 63, Letter from Mr John Wemyes to the Earl of Morton, 1597–1616; *R.P.C.* (First Series), VIII, 330–1.
[46] Fife Synod, 31, 35, 38, 40, 50, 54, 127, 129, 131, 134, 154.
[47] Belhelvie K. S., 21 March 1630, 2, 16 January 1631. Cf. *Dundonald K. S.*, 268.
[48] Ellon Presb., 6 August 1617.
[49] Belhelvie K. S., 9 February 1623. For examples of proportional fines, see Belhelvie K. S., 14 March, 24 October, 26 November, 3, 10, 31 December 1625.

Persons who could not (or would not) pay their fines were either put in prison or in the jougs. In Dundonald the partly ruined castle of Dundonald served as a prison. At Aberdeen and St Andrews, confinement was in the kirk steeple.[50] However, the jougs were more common in rural parishes. The jougs consisted of a short chain, one end of which was attached to the door or wall of the church and the other to a collar fastened around the offender's neck. Those who did not pay their fine were often ordered to 'stand in tym of sermon in the jogges'.[51]

The records of kirk sessions indicate that these courts were much more efficient than either presbyteries or synods. Those summoned to a kirk session appeared promptly, usually after the first summons. Trials were short, sentences were imposed at once, and the sentences were usually obeyed within a few weeks. Presbyteries often had to issue numerous summonses before an offender would appear. A difficult case might last for months or even years. And presbyteries frequently found difficulty in enforcing their sentences.

There were a number of reasons for this difference. Kirk sessions dealt with less serious crimes; their meetings did not require a journey to a neighbouring parish on a working day; and their sentences were not as severe as those given by presbyteries. Furthermore, a session consisting of leading laymen of a parish may well have seemed even more formidable to the average parishioner than a presbytery of ministers. Also, the fact that those who came before a session had to satisfy 'boith in penaltie and repentance' undoubtedly contributed to the effectiveness of kirk sessions. Archbishop Spottiswood wrote, 'To be punished by the purse is a thing that ever hath bene most grievous to Scottishmen, and keepeth them most in aw'.[52] Fines have kept many men in awe, including the Scots, and they were one of the reasons why 'the grand wark off disciplein' was so effective in many of the parishes of Scotland.

III

Apart from discipline, the major responsibility of kirk sessions was the care of the poor within their parishes. The first Book of

[50] *Dundonald K. S.*, viii, x, 127–8; *Aberdeen K. S.*, 24–5, 44–5, 78; *St Andrews K. S.* II, 893.
[51] Belhelvie K. S., 10 August 1623; cf. Ellon Presb., 10 May, 1620'.
[52] *O.L.* II, 756.

Discipline declared, 'Every several kirk must provide for the poor within the self; for fearful and horrible it is, that the poor ... are universally so contemned and despised'.[53] This ideal remained in force throughout the seventeenth century and was repeated in many kirk session records. In 1597 the kirk session of Stirling 'ordains everie eldar and diacun to tak up the namis of all the nateive puir within this toun ... that they ... may tak sum gude ordur for thair sustenatione'.[54]

A visitation at Ellon in 1617 reported that 'thair is a collectioun for the puir ilk saboth day and the puir of the paroche helpit'.[55] The same report could have been made in most of the parishes in Scotland where a minister was settled and a kirk session in operation. Alms were usually collected at the door of the church by elders or deacons. Alms were also collected at a week-day sermon, at a service held on a special fast day, at marriages, or at burials.[56] Alms given on communion days were much higher than those given on ordinary Sundays. At Aberdeen two magistrates were appointed to 'stand at the end of ewerie tabill in ... the tyme of the ministratioun of the holie communioun, and demand of ewerie communicant, at thair ryising from the tabill, sume almes to the poore, according to the forme obserwit ... in the south pairtis of this realme'.[57]

During the period there appears to have been a general rise in the amount collected for the poor. There was some rise and fall from year to year, but the trend was clearly upwards, as the following table of amounts collected for the poor shows.[58]

	Belhelvie
1624	£31 6s. 11d.
1630	£62 7s. 3d.
1633	£83 15s. 7d.
1637	£80 7s. 0d.

[53] Knox, *History of the Reformation* (Dickinson), II, 290–1.
[54] *Maitland Misc.* I, 130.
[55] Ellon Presb., 27 November 1617.
[56] *Elgin K. S.*, 180, Belhelvie K. S., 27 May 1636; Trinity College K. S., 17 May 1627, 29 August, 5 September 1633; *St Andrews K. S.* II, 845, 883, 884, 906.
[57] *Aberdeen K. S.*, 86.
[58] These figures were compiled from the weekly reports of alms collected for the poor in the Kirk Session Records of Belhelvie, Elgin, and Trinity College.

Elgin

1614	£93	9s. 11d.
1616	£71	1s. 2d.
1625	£190	14s. 5d.
1634	£184	5s. 8d.

Trinity College, Edinburgh

1626	£1034	12s. 10d.
1631	£1926	15s. 4d.
1633	£2514	3s. 1d.
1636	£2423	8s. 2d.

In these three parishes alms for the poor had more than doubled. The rise was one of many signs of the increasing prosperity of church and nation.

Each parish was expected to have a list of its own poor and to give them seals or 'cognisances' as evidence of their status. In all of the parishes of the presbytery of Dunfermline 'seales of lead wer ordanned to be maid and given to our own poir and non to receave almis but such as have these markis'. A more elaborate system was introduced into Belhelvie in 1636. 'Some were given two tokens, one of leade and another of brasse, to shew that they were most indigent and could no wayes helpe to mainetaine themselves'. Others were given 'one onelie brasen token' because they 'myt make some reliefe for themselves'.[59] Alms were distributed to the poor at regular intervals, often five or six times a year. In addition, small sums were given for special needs throughout the year. In Belhelvie there was given 'Henrie Davidsoun pauper – 6s.', 'ane pour woman bedfast – 6s.', 'and woman namit Urquhard distrest in mynd – 18s.', 'ane pour man with his wyff and fyve barnes – 15s. 8d.'[60]

But if kirk sessions were willing to assist their own poor, they were equally determined not to help strangers, those 'sturdy and idle beggars' condemned by many church courts. A general assembly in 1596 described them as 'ane great number of idle persons without lawfull calling, as pypers, fidlers, sangsters, sorners,[61] pleasants, strang beggars, living in harlotrie and having thair children unbaptizit'.[61] Several acts of parliament were passed against 'sturdy and idle beggars'; kirk sessions and presbyteries

---

[59] Culross K. S., 20 November 1631; Belhelvie K. S., 15 August 1636.
[60] Belhelvie K. S., 10 January, 9 May 1630, 25 September 1631, 8 June 1633.
[61] Sorner: one who takes free quarters.

were charged to enforce the acts.[62] Some sessions did appoint an officer to 'hald away all uncouthe and strange beggeris', but little was done other than attempt to keep them out of a local parish. Society was expected to be stable with little movement of people, and there was no place in that structure for 'ane great number of idle persons without lawful calling'.

Although kirk sessions would not assist wandering strangers, they did raise special sums for authorised projects outside their own bounds. In 1634 the bishops of Orkney and Caithness sent appeals to many presbyteries 'conserning the deplorable famine of Orknay and Zetland'. Within a month collections had been taken for the 'distressed peopll of Orknay and Catnes'. Collections included fifty-three merks from Belhelvie, £26 from Culross, and £40 from Elgin.[64] Many similar projects were supported by parish collections.

It is not possible to form an accurate estimate of the extent of poor relief from kirk session registers. There are too many breaks, and too little information is to be found. However, the church's care for the poor was clearly widespread and continuous. The most frequent entry found in typical kirk session minutes was the amount collected for the poor. On the other hand, the attitude of both church and state toward wandering beggars was almost wholly repressive. Both kirk sessions and justices of the peace sought, probably without much success, to compel sturdy beggars to take up permanent employment and residence.

IV

The kirk session was *the* fundamental unit of ecclesiastical administration in Scotland during the Reformation period. A generation older than presbyteries, kirk sessions continued to function whether

---

[62] *A.P.S.* III, 86–9, 139–42, IV, 140, 232–3; *R.P.C.* VI, 98–9, XI, 33–4. Much of the text of the 1617 proclamation is illegible in the *R.P.C.* For the full text, see Ellon Presb., 22 April, 1617

[63] *Elgin K. S.*, 185; Ellon Presb., 17 August 1620; Belhelvie K. S., 20, 28 February 1631, cf. 17 January, 31 July 1636, 26 February, 19 March 1638.

[64] *Maitland Misc.* I, 473. See Jedburgh Presb., 16 July 1634 for a letter from the Bishop of Caithness. Belhelvie K. S., 17 August 1634; Culross K. S., 143; *Elgin K. S.*, 228.

bishops were active or not. A revived seventeenth-century episcopate did help to increase the number of effective kirk sessions, either directly by visitations and acts of synod, or indirectly by the 'planting' of ministers. Otherwise, however, episcopacy had no significant effect upon the work of kirk sessions. Their membership remained the same, and they exercised the same kind of authority in 1600 as they did in 1620. Most disciplinary cases were heard by kirk sessions, and neither bishops nor presbyteries were very successful in establishing discipline in a parish which had no effective kirk session. A kirk session might correspond with a bishop about the selection of a new minister, but otherwise session records seldom have any occasion to mention episcopacy. Local collections for the poor, support of bursars in theology, general collections for a distressed area, or even collections to support such public projects as 'reparatioun of the brig of Don'[65] depended ultimately upon the work of vigorous kirk sessions.

The overlapping of civil and ecclesiastical authority within a kirk session itself was a distinctive feature of efficient sessions. All church courts relied to some extent upon civil authority, but the support of the magistrate was especially prominent at kirk session meetings. Although the second Book of Discipline might draw a theoretical distinction between 'the Power of the Sword' and 'the Power of the Keyes',[66] offenders who were summoned to a kirk session soon learned that the sword was not absent.

Kirk sessions were the oldest, most enduring and efficient institution developed by the reformed Kirk. Sessions successfully enlisted much of the leadership of the church and nation. Week by week the minister, the elders, and sometimes the deacons met together to see to it that 'true preaching, ... right administration of the sacraments ... [and] ecclesiastical discipline uprightly ministered' were a reality for the people of God in that place.

[65] Ellon Presb., 24 May 1609.
[66] Calderwood, III, 531.

CHAPTER FIVE

The Brethren of the Presbytery

I

The presbytery was the last major ecclesiastical court to develop in Scotland after the Reformation. It was not until 1581 that a general assembly proposed the erection of some fifty presbyteries and ordered the establishment of thirteen at once 'that ane beginning be had'.[1] Formal erection of presbyteries went ahead fairly rapidly, and by 1593 Calderwood could list forty-seven presbyteries then in existence.[2]

Even where presbyteries were formally established, their existence in 1600 was sometimes insecure and their ability to maintain effective discipline limited. In March 1595–6 the presbytery of Glasgow reported that although seven ministers composed that presbytery, only four attended meetings. Two were too poor to come and one kept 'nather exercise nor discipline'. In May 1597 the presbytery of Dumbarton, 'in respect of the fewnes of thair number, [requested] that certaine of the Presbytrie of Paislay might be adjoynit to them'.[3]

A vivid example of the difficulties which outlying presbyteries had to face was recorded in the minutes of the newly established presbytery of Ellon. In 1602 that presbytery summoned George Gordon and Lady Haddo on suspicion of adultery. The charge was not proved, but the couple were publicly admonished to avoid suspicious behaviour in the future.

[1] *B.U.K.* II, 481–7 (Calderwood, III, 523).
[2] *B.U.K.* III, 799–800. Calderwood's list has some inaccuracies. He included Shetland, which probably existed in name only (G. Donaldson, *Shetland Life under Earl Patrick*, 128–9). Surprisingly, he omitted Stirling, which almost certainly was in existence by 1593 (*Records of the Scottish Church History Society*, IV, 184).
[3] *Maitland Misc.* I, 79; *B.U.K.* III, 917. For a similar situation in the presbytery of Inverness, see *B.U.K.* III, 847.

And quhil as the moderator was delyvering to tham the ordinance [he] was stayed be a tumult rasit in the kirk through the persuit and minaceing off Mr John Mercer [minister of the couple] and remanent presbiterie be the said George... and thair complices.[4]

At the beginning of the seventeenth century, the presbytery was the newest and probably the weakest unit of church government. One major need facing the church was to increase the number and extent of presbyteries and to strengthen and establish their authority. The Kirk needed to become in fact a church of presbyteries. And one of the major accomplishments of the next forty years was the achievement of that goal.

New presbyteries continued to be established after 1600. At least four new ones, Cullen (Fordyce), Ellon, Alford and Kelso, had been erected by 1606.[5] Revival of episcopal authority during the early seventeenth century meant no change in this policy, for the presbytery of Forfar was established by the synod of Fife and the archbishop of St Andrews in 1611, while the same archbishop erected that of Earlston in 1613.[6] Dunblane appears to have been separated from Auchterarder before 1616.[7] The presbytery of Stranraer may have begun in 1622 and was certainly in existence by 1635.[8] Inveraven was listed as a presbytery of the synod of Moray in 1623, and in 1632 that presbytery had been divided into two, creating Aberlour and Abernethie.[9] The presbytery of Penpont was established by 1627; and in 1629 the privy council had business with presbyteries in Argyll and Bute. Lochmaben was in existence in the same year. Middlebie (Annan) had been established by 1632, and Dingwall was probably in existence by the following

[4] Ellon Presb., 28 July, 1602.
[5] Ellon Presb., 30 November 1597; *B.U.K.* III, 1035–8 (Calderwood, VI, 622–4); *R.P.C.* VII, 301–2. Alford was in existence by 1598 (Ellon Presb., 19 April 1598).
[6] Fife Synod, 18, 22–3; *Fasti*, II, 146.
[7] The extant register of Dunblane begins in 1616 and does not include the parishes of Auchterarder.
[8] 'Its records begin 13 November 1622' (*Fasti*, II, 330). These records cannot now be found. On 14 July 1635 a testimonial was signed 'by the moderator and brethren of the presbytery of Stranrawer' (*R.P.C.* [Second Series], VI, 51).
[9] Moray Synod, 1, 39.

year.[10] In all, sixteen (and possibly eighteen[11]) new presbyteries came into existence between 1594 and 1637. Such progress was a remarkable achievement and was one of many signs of the growing stability and expansion of the church during this period.

The recent origin of presbyteries was reflected in their boundaries, which exhibited a logical and systematic pattern long lost by both parishes and dioceses with their detached portions and erratic borders. The jurisdiction of presbyteries ignored diocesan limits where necessary and often included parishes from several dioceses. This was true even when a presbytery was established by a bishop. The presbytery of Perth, for example, contained eleven parishes from the diocese of St Andrews, three from Dunblane, and five from detached sections of the diocese of Dunkeld; and the new presbytery of Forfar, erected by the archbishop of St Andrews in 1611, included nine parishes from the archbishop's diocese and four from the diocese of Brechin.[12]

The Register of the Presbytery of Ellon contains a rare example of the establishment of a presbytery. On 14 October 1597 eight parishes presented a supplication to the synod of Aberdeen to establish them as a separate presbytery, the parishes being 'farre distant frome the seatis off thair presbiterie' of Aberdeen. The synod agreed, and 'ordained the erection off an presbyterie at the kirk of Ellon ... and earnestly desyred the commissioneris off the Generall Assemblye be thair power and authoritie to authorize and establishe this necessarie erection!' The action was approved by

[10] *R.P.C.* I, 602; III, 54, 87, 341; IV, 425; VI, 191. *Records of the Presbytery of Inverness and Dingwall*, 252. On 21 April, 1653 the old and retired minister of Dingwall 'did exhibit and delyver the old presbytrie booke being at the beginning thairoff of the daite 12 Novemb[er] 1633 zeires'. Since this (now lost) book contained matters concerning the glebe of Dingwall, and since none of the ministers in Dingwall were members of the presbytery of Inverness in 1632 (*Ibid.* 24–5), it seems likely that this book was not the Presbytery Register of Inverness but was that of another presbytery, probably Dingwall. In any case, the presbytery of Dingwall had been established by 1638 (Peterkin, *Records of the Kirk*, 38).

[11] According to a (probably contemporary) report on the 1638 assembly, sixty-six presbyteries were represented at its first session (Peterkin, *Records of the Kirk*, 129). If accurate, eighteen presbyteries had been established since 1593.

[12] For the diocesan affiliation of parishes, see Robert Keith, *An Historical Catalogue of the Scottish Bishops*, and the 'Ordnance Survey Map of Monastic Britain (North Sheet)'.

the two commissioners, Mr James Nicolson, later Bishop of Dunkeld, and Mr James Melville, nephew of Andrew Melville. And on 30 November the new presbytery held its first meeting.[13]

The establishment of Forfar in 1611 followed a similar pattern, being authorised by the archbishop and synod in April and erected at a visitation of Archbishop Gladstanes two weeks later.[14] Instructions given to the presbytery of Forfar were typical. The brethren were to meet weekly on Wednesday at ten, fortnightly meetings being permitted in winter. Presbytery records show clearly the conscientious way in which this duty was fulfilled. Although no presbytery had a perfect record, the usual pattern for an established presbytery was a weekly meeting in summer and a meeting every fortnight during the rest of the year except when there was 'no . . . meitting because of the tempestuous weather be winds and raine'.[15]

II

Meetings of presbytery were attended by ministers, expectants,[16] a presbytery officer, and a clerk. Almost every presbytery passed a general act (enforced with only moderate success) imposing fines on ministers who were tardy or absent.[17]

One of the more distinctive features of presbyteries prior to 1638 was the absence of elders as regular members of this court. The second Book of Discipline apparently expected elders (but not deacons) to be members of every ecclesiatical court, although that document did not, at least in its original form,[18] distinguish the presbytery as a separate ecclesiastical court.[19] Opinion was

[13] Ellon Presb. 14 October, f. 3 (?12 November), 1597.
[14] Fife Synod, 18, 22–3.
[15] Perth Presby., 20 December 1626.
[16] Expectants were candidates for the ministry. See below, 135–8.
[17] E.g. Perth Presb., 11 November 1618.
[18] There were apparently later revisions of the second Book of Discipline (1577). On 15 June 1592 the presbytery of Dalkeith appointed 'William Carbrayth to spek Mr James Richie willing him to recognoss [i.e. revise] and correct of new againe our copy by collationing it with the last editioun of the buik of discipline' (Dalkeith Presb.).
[19] There is some uncertainty about the point. The second Book of Discipline did not provide for a separate court called a presbytery, but it has been suggested that the word 'eldership' as used in that book sometimes meant a presbytery (J. H. S. Burleigh, *A Church History of Scotland*, 200).

divided on the right of elders to attend presbyteries in 1597. In response to some questions by James VI, the synod of Fife affirmed that presbyteries should be composed of pastors, elders and deacons; while Patrick Galloway, the respected minister of Stirling who was later to decline an appointment to the episcopate, roundly affirmed that presbyteries should be composed of 'Pastors onlie,' and a third set of anonymous answers agreed with him.[20]

Whatever the theory, there is remarkably little evidence that in fact elders were ever regular members of presbyteries for any length of time or over any wide area between 1600 and 1638. The presence or absence of ministers at presbytery meetings was recorded in practically every presbytery register. Some (as in Dunblane) even record the names of expectants. Nowhere does one find the names of elders listed as either present or absent until their appearance in 1638. Injunctions requiring ministers to attend presbyteries (and fining them when they were absent) were commonplace, but acts requiring elders to attend presbyteries were apparently nonexistent. Decisions were universally rendered by 'the brethren' or, when a diocesan bishop was present, by 'the Bischope and ministers present'.[21] On the rare occasions when elders or prominent laymen were present, their presence and usually their names were recorded. Much of the evidence is negative, of course; but it is hard to believe that elders could have been in regular attendance at presbyteries and have left no trace of that fact in the registers of those presbyteries.

The relationship which did exist between prominent laymen (whether elders or not) and presbytery courts was shown clearly at the formal establishment of the presbytery of Ellon on St Andrew's Day, 1597.

> The said day after prayeris and doctrine the conclusion [of the] provinciall assemblie ratified be the commissioners off the Generall was [read in] presence and audience off the baronis and gentlemen quha wer c[ome] out off all quarters within the precincts off the presbyterie. The [all] be ane [voice] approved the erection concludit, and beand requ[ired] be the brethren promised at all necessarie occasions upon ane c[itation?] thair

[20] Calderwood, V, 589, 598, 601.
[21] Dunblane Presb., 26 December 1616.

presence at our meitings and sicklyke assistance, and co]ncurrence on] everie occurance that concerned the glorie off God. . . .[22]

The 'baronis and gentlemen' of the presbytery of Ellon agreed to be present for special meetings, although only on very rare occasions were they ever asked to come. More important was their willingness to give their support, backing and authority to decisions of a presbytery. Presbyteries often had difficulty establishing their authority in the early decades of the seventeenth century, and they could only succeed in doing so if they had the 'assistance and concurrence' of the leading laymen of the presbytery. That support, rather than weekly attendance, was the real need.

It is not difficult to understand the absence of elders. Presbyteries met frequently – in summer a weekly meeting was normal. The court met for most of a working day and for many members involved a ride of some miles as well. It was difficult enough to get ministers to attend with any regularity, but to expect prominent elders to attend frequent presbytery meetings as well as weekly kirk sessions was not very practicable. Even after 1638, when elders were inducted as members of presbyteries, it was apparently not common for them to attend regularly. In 1641 Alexander Henderson wrote that ministers who were absent from presbytery were:

> censured as guiltie of the contempt or neglect of the order of the Church. But the Elders are not so strictlie tied to ordinarie attendance; but if there be any matter of great weight to be handled, they are all warned to be present.[23]

In September 1638 the brethren of the presbytery of Lanark thought 'it most expedient . . . *to renew the old practise of our kirk,* in useing the concurrence of Laicke Elders to keep the Presbyterie, with their ministers'. However, the evidence certainly suggests that the historical precedents quoted by the brethren of Lanark were based more upon pious imagination than actual practice: and when in 1662 the Restoration synod of St Andrews ordered the establishment of presbyteries as 'meetings of the ministers', they

---

[22] Ellon Presb., 30 November 1597 (f.4). The manuscript is torn in several places, and the words in brackets have been added by conjecture.
[23] *Government and Order of the Church of Scotland*, 47.

were restoring a practice which had been normal for most of the century.[24]

One change which did take place in the organisation of presbyteries early in the century was the introduction of 'constant moderators'. Prior to 1607 the normal practice, at least in the south, was a semi-annual or annual election of a moderator by his own presbytery.[25] However, a different practice was followed, at least in sections of the more conservative north, where moderators of presbyteries were sometimes chosen by the synod, not by the presbytery. In 1599 the presbytery of Aberdeen reported that 'Mr David Coningaime being moderator [was] chosin be the last provincial assemblie haldin at Aberdeen', and similar entries are found for subsequent years.[26] If the moderator of the presbytery of Aberdeen, the leading presbytery of the synod, was elected by the synod, it seems likely that moderators of the other five presbyteries in that province would be elected in the same way; and the minutes of the presbytery of Ellon, which simply record the names of new moderators,[27] suggest that this was so. The right of presbyteries to elect their own moderators was not universal in Scotland at the beginning of the century.

However, the practice of all presbyteries was altered by the decisions of the assembly or convention at Linlithgow in December, 1606. That assembly, under pressure from James, gave approval to constant moderators – that is, moderators chosen by a general assembly. Where a bishop was resident in a presbytery, he was always to be moderator. The assembly action was reinforced by an act of council.[28] Calderwood wrote, 'Some obeyed willinglie, others yeelded for feare. Some refused. . . .'[29] Opposition was not

[24] Lanark Presb., 13 September 1638. Italics added. *The Diocese and Presbytery of Dunkeld, 1660–1689*, edited by John Hunter, I, 314.
[25] See, for example, Paisley Presb., 12 April 1604, 13 Sept. 1604, 21 March 1605, 5 September 1605, 13 March 1606, 21 August 1606; or Edinburgh Presb., 12 May 1602, 13 April 1603.
[26] Aberdeen Presb., 20 April 1599. David Cunningham was also Bishop of Aberdeen, but he was not always moderator of this presbytery. See 28 September 1599, 26 September 1600, 23 October 1601, 23 April 1602, 29 October 1602, 28 October 1603.
[27] Ellon Presb., 2 November 1603, 28 March 1604, 14 August 1605.
[28] *B.U.K.* III, 1032–4 (Calderwood, VI, 617–21). Cf. below, 122–3. *R.P.C.* VII, 301–2.
[29] Calderwood, VI, 644.

always to be found in expected areas. Of the six presbyteries in the synod of Lothian, 'Edinburgh, Dunbar and Linlithquo had satisfied the king's Majestie's commissioners, . . . but Peebles, Hadintoun and Dalkeith had not'.[30] There was even opposition in the north. The presbytery of Ellon told two lairds that:

> they thocht it necessar to sie the said act authentiklie extractit befoir thai culd give thair answar to the same, and that efter the sicht thairof, they suld give ane ressonable and discreit answer in reverence and humilie as becom them.[31]

Three months later the presbytery of Aberdeen had still not accepted its assigned moderator, Peter Blackburn, Bishop of Aberdeen, Significantly, both northern presbyteries did so only after their constant moderators were approved by the synod of Aberdeen, thus preserving at least the external form of their former practice.[32]

The Register of the Presbytery of Jedburgh shows vividly the internal debate which took place within that body as well as their long and ultimately futile resistance to the Linlithgow decision. In April 1607 the presbytery was charged by two noblemen 'to ressave ane constant moderator'. The presbytery successfully postponed action until July when, threatened with horning, the brethren 'be maisest votis consentit to admit ane constant moderator . . . as brethren off utheris presbiteries hes done', but after a protest by two members, David Calderwood and James Johnston, the brethren changed their minds and 'gaiff negative votis.' Jedburgh continued its opposition throughout the year, although by February 1608 they found 'it expedient that ilk exerciser sould for that day be moderator'. A visitation at the end of March by the bishop of Orkney was inconclusive, and in June three leading oppositionists, including David Calderwood, were summoned before the privy council, threatened with imprisonment, and eventually warded (or confined) in their own parishes. A week later 'Mr Johne Abernathy was admittit constant moderator be the

---

[30] *Ibid.*, 645.
[31] Ellon Presb., 7 April 1607, The folio is out of place. It follows that of 11 April 1627.
[32] Aberdeen Presb., 3 July, 17 July, 1607; Ellon Presb., July, 1607 (Aberdeen Synod).

votes off the brethren'.³³ Jedburgh was an extreme example and one of the last presbyteries to submit.³⁴ Yet its ultimate defeat must have made it clear to all that there was little chance of successful opposition to the dominant ecclesiastical tendencies of the time. Throughout the remainder of the period moderators continued to be appointed by a bishop and synod, and probably the actual choice was made by the bishop. In the synod of Fife, whose extant records began in 1611, one regularly finds at the end of synod meetings such entries as 'My Lord Archbishop nominate moderators of the exercises', or (less frequently) 'My Lord Archbishop nominate be advyse of the brethren moderateris of the particular exercises'.³⁵

Rather surprisingly, presbyterial elections were revived in a few places after 1620. In 1623 a minister in the presbytery of Ellon 'wes chosin moderator be voit of the brethren of the presbyterie', and two years earlier the presbytery of Dunblane 'for electioun of ane moderator' put 'thrie on leit' and one was 'electit moderator to the nixt Synod'.³⁶ Yet these elections appear to be isolated exceptions to the general pattern, perhaps allowed in places where episcopal authority was already sufficiently established by other means.

III

Regular meetings of presbyteries usually began in the morning with an opening exercise and addition. The exercise had been recommended by the first Book of Discipline, which urged ministers and laymen to meet together to study a portion of Scripture.³⁷

---

[33] Jedburgh Presb., 22 April, 15 July, 28 October 1607; 24 February 30 March, 13 July 1608. *R.P.C.* VIII, 126, 509–10, 103.

[34] On May 31 James appears to have believed that the only presbyteries which had not conformed were Jedburgh and Chirnside (*O.L.* I, 397*–8*). The presbytery of Melrose (Selkirk) might be added to this list. Their constant moderator was accepted on 5 July 1608 (Melrose Presb. 5 July 1608).

[35] Fife Synod, 14, 74, 100, 115.

[36] Ellon Presb., 2 April 1623. For subsequent elections in this presbytery, see 15 October 1623, 14 April 1624, 12 October 1626, 10 October 1627. Dunblane Presb., 30 November 1621. For subsequent elections, see 14 November 1622, and 12 November 1623.

[37] Knox, *History of the Reformation* (Dickinson), II, 315. Cf. G. D. Henderson, 'The Exercise', *Records of the Scottish Church History Society*, VII, 13–29.

That recommendation commended itself, and exercises were established during the early years of the Reformation. In fact, some early presbyteries may have developed from these exercises.[38] Although exercises may have originally included addresses by both laymen and ministers, by the seventeenth century the exercise and addition were in effect two public sermons by ministers or expectants upon an assigned text.

Most contemporarly legislation about the exercise consisted of efforts to limit the volubility of ministers. In 1587 the presbytery of Edinburgh 'be reasoun of the greit prolixitie and langsumnes of sum of the brethren' ordained a fine of 18d. for any preacher 'quho pass the hoir glass in making the exerceiss' and a similar fine for any addition which passed 'the half hoir glass'.[39]

The two sermons were always censured, that is examined, in the privacy of a presbytery meeting. Alexander Henderson's description, written in 1641, is a good summary of ordinary seventeenth-century practice.

> The exercise ... ended in publick, the people depart, and the Ministers and Elders, with others who are permitted to bee present, goe to the private place of their meeting, where, ... the Moderator having begun with prayer, the doctrine delivered in publick is examined.[40]

Usually the sermons were 'approvit', but the injunctions which one minister received 'to avoyde divisions off interpretationes (quhilk is more weirsome then edifying)' were common enough; and sometimes more important matters than homiletical style were involved. In 1634 the presbytery of Paisley severely rebuked the minister of Paisley for teaching 'that a man once justified, might possiblie fall away from justifiing faith'.[41]

The exercise and addition may be of more significance than is apparent at first. Probably no single duty of presbyteries was as widely and faithfully performed as that of making a public exercise

---

[38] G. Donaldson, *Scottish Reformation*, 204–5. Some presbyteries continued to be called exercises throughout the century.

[39] Edinburgh Presb., 24 October 1587. For a similar act in the seventeenth century, see Ellon Presb., 22 February 1604.

[40] *Government and Order of the Church of Scotland*, 50–1. Elders, of course, did not meet with ministers and expectants prior to 1638.

[41] Ellon Presb., 28 December 1597; Paisley Presb., 15 May, 1634.

and addition. This was the one invariable part of a presbytery meeting, even when no other business was at hand, and rare indeed was the meeting when there was 'na exercise'. The wide and enduring character of an orthodox Calvinist theology throughout the parishes of the kirk has often been noted. Surely one of the reasons for the persistence of this tradition was the regular exercise. Those who have had to preach before their fellow clergy know what a disciplining experience this can be. Regularly the brethren of the ministry heard the gospel proclaimed as the reformers understood the same, and they were quickly made aware of any serious departure from the accepted norm.

IV

With the censure over, and assignments made for the next exercise, the presbytery became an ecclesiastical court prepared to summon offenders, hear accusations, sift evidence, swear in and receive the testimony of witnesses, issue judgments, and impose sentences. The majority of entries in presbytery books were cases of discipline, for presbyterial discipline was of great significance in determining the life of both kirk and nation.

Presbyteries had been authorised by parliament in 1592 to 'enquyre diligentlie of nauchtie and ungodly personis and to travell to bring thame in the way agane be admonitioun or threatning of goddis Jugementis or be correctioun'.[42] The Glasgow assembly of 1610 did not mention presbyterial discipline, and the parliament of 1612 actually repealed the earlier 1592 acts.[43] There were even threats in 1610 to discharge presbyteries.[44] However, as Calderwood wrote, the presbyteries 'needed not feare; for presbyteries could not be altogether abolished'.[45] Indeed, the abolition of presbyteries does not seem to have been seriously contemplated, and the government was more interested in controlling than suppressing them. James instructed Archbishop Spottiswood in 1610 to authorise meetings of ministers:

> and over them a moderator placed by the ordinary of the diocese ... with power to call before tham all scandalous

[42] *A.P.S.* III, 541–2.
[43] *A.P.S.* IV, 470.
[44] Calderwood, VII, 97; *O.L.* I, 235.
[45] Calderwood, VII, 97.

persons within that precinct, and censure and correct offenders according to the canons of the church.[46]

This was simply a continuation of earlier practice. As will be seen later, some important modifications of presbyterial authority were made, but these changes had little effect on the ordinary work of discipline. Habit and tradition are strong forces – the procedure and disciplinary jurisdiction of presbyteries were well established by 1610 and little sense of discontinuity is revealed by the records of those courts.

Most disciplinary cases were handled by kirk sessions and the majority of offenders never came before a presbytery. In general, presbyteries dealt with more serious offences, cases where the offender was contumacious, or cases which involved the long process of excommunication.

In most years the largest class of cases which came before a presbytery were those involving sexual offences or violations of marriage vows. Simple fornication was regularly handled by kirk sessions; but relapses in fornication, adultery and incest came to be regarded as matters for presbytery action. In the early part of the century kirk sessions often did handle cases of adultery, but by about 1625 presbyteries appear to have established their exclusive jurisdiction over this offence.[47]

References to the treatment of adulterers were often cursory, but occasionally one gets a vivid glimpse of all that was involved for a penitent adulterer. It must have been a sobering experience. In 1618 Andrew Dyk confessed to the presbytery of Perth that he had committed adultery and was still living with the woman. The presbytery:

> ordane him to put away the said woman out of his company this same nigt and mak his repentance for the slandellis done be him on Soinday nixt and humblie confes his syne befoir the congregatioun and promois obedience to the disciplyn of the kirk and to mend his life in tyme coming and humilie on his kneis hes begun

[46] Spottiswood, *History*, III, 210.
[47] *Dundonald K. S.*, 84–94, 97, Belhelvie K. S., 8, 15, 22 February 1624 and Trinity College K. S., 8 August 1627 are examples of kirk sessions handling cases of adultery. However, even Trinity College referred cases of adultery to its presbytery after 1627. Trinity College K. S., 4 June 1629, 21 July 1631, 3 January 1633.

his repentance this day befoir the presbyterie and to pay his penaltie as salbe appointit.[48]

Although offences against chastity were an important part of presbyterial discipline, the court's jurisdiction covered many matters other than violations of the seventh commandment. Cases of slander were technically part of the jurisdiction of commissary courts, but presbyteries often tried such cases if the slander was against a minister. In January 1594–95 the presbytery of Glasgow 'findis thame juges competent to the cognitioun of ony sclandir . . . aganis the persone of ony minister within thair presbyterie',[48] and many other presbyteries shared this view of their jurisdiction. In 1632 the presbytery of Perth heard evidence in an especially violent case of slander and assault. The action began with a complaint 'upon George Fillan in the paroch of Tibbermore, who, beeing reproved be his minister for some misdemenors and unorderly carriage the day off his marriage, first abused him with evell words and . . . thereafter threattened to putt a durke throw his cheekes'.[49]

At least in a case like this it was easy to tell who the offender was. However, the same presbytery also acted vigorously and wisely in the much more difficult case of general parish gossip and slander. The brethren of the presbytery received a report that the minister of Kilspindie 'was calumniat and traduced be some of his parochiners, alleadgeing that the penalties of his kirke war not keepit . . . for the easing of the parochiners in the reparation of their kirk but wer otherways bestowed'. The brethren noted that in a recent visitation it was found 'that these penalties war faithfully imployed' but ordered the minister to 'produce before them an particular compt since his entrie how the said penalties has been imployd'. At the next meeting the minister produced:

ane particular compt of the imployment of his penalties . . . as also compeired certan of his elders . . . who faithfully declarit that the saids penalties war faithfully and lawfully bestowed to gud and charitable uses and that the Bischop of Dunkeld (heritor of the bounds) his owne man did keep the key of the box. The brethren haveing considerit the same ordeins that such as speake the contrar be reput as calumniators.[50]

[48] Perth Presb., 9 December 1618.
[49] Ibid., 20 June 1632.
[50] Ibid. 2 December, 12 December 1632.

When a disciplinary decision was unpopular, the minister was an obvious target for local resentment, and the authority of a presbytery court was one important way by which ministers were protected from local attacks.

Presbyteries handled a wide variety of other cases. In 1605 the presbytery of Ellon learned that 'Thomas Smyth ... wes presentlie at feud with James Mill and his freinds' and appointed two ministers 'to travell for a full reconsiliatioun betuix the saidis parteis'. In 1622 a man was summoned by the presbytery of Jedburgh 'for desarting off his wyff'. Two weeks later he appeared and 'promesit obediens in all poyntis'. Persons delated by kirk sessions as contumacious, or disobedient to session injunctions, were summoned to the presbytery. In 1613 the presbytery of Glasgow censured a painter who 'painted the crucifix in mony houses ... quhilk is liklie ... to turne the heartes of the ignorant to idolatrie'.[51]

Those suspected of loyalty to the Roman Catholic Church were summoned before presbytery. Even in the north, cases of 'papistrie' were only a small percentage of the total number of cases handled; but those who were tried were sometimes persons of power and influence, and their trials were long and arduous.[52]

Some idea of the scope of presbyterial discipline can be seen in a few sample years. The number beside each offence indicates the number of persons tried. Usually each person appeared before a presbytery for several meetings.

                Presbytery of Paisley 1606
    Adultery   22
    Fornication and contumacy   17
    Incest   1
    Nonadherence   1
    Failure to communicate   5
    Profanation of the Sabbath and contumacy   2
    Nightwalking   4
    Slander   1
    Assault on the Sabbath   4

[51] Ellon Presb., 3 April 1605; Jedburgh Presb., 5, 19 October 1622, 29 October 1606; *Maitland Misc.* I, 420.

[52] The presbytery of Ellon had a number of such trials, some of which are summarized in Thomas Mair, *Narratives and Extracts from the Records of the Presbytery of Ellon*, 7–13, 42–4, 64–9, 130–4.

Presbytery of Jedburgh 1622

Adultery	11
Fornication and contumacy	9
Irregular marriage (married in England)	2
Desertion	1
Profanation of the Sabbath and contumacy	15
Violation of Sabbath fast	3
Neglect of duty by an elder	1
Murder	1

Presbytery of Perth 1632

Adultery	12
Irregular marriage	2
Irregular baptism	1
Contemptuous behaviour to a minister	2
Profanation of the Sabbath and contumacy	1
Irreverent behaviour at communion	1

Although the scope of presbyterial jurisdiction was certainly a wide one, much would depend on the effectiveness with which trials were conducted and sentences enforced. There was much variety of practice, but in general presbytery courts seem to have been reasonably effective, although not as efficient as kirk sessions.

Offenders summoned to a presbytery who were prepared to confess their faults (and many were) often appeared in the garb of penitents, admitted their guilt, and were either sentenced, or more usually remitted to their session for sentencing. Andrew Ruthven, accused of adultery by the presbytery of Perth, 'compeired in sackecloath and barefutted, confessed his adultrie' and, 'after humiliation, promised to obey his minister.[53] Similar cases occur in all presbyteries. Those who denied the accusation were usually put to trial, witnesses were summoned, and the accused were given a chance to object to them. Once admitted, witnesses were sworn, their testimony taken, and often entered in the presbytery record.

Those found guilty were either remitted to the session for sentencing, or the sentence was determined by the presbytery itself. The public place of repentance, sackcloth, jougs, and fines were the usual penalties, although immediate enforcement of a sentence was, with rare exceptions, the work of local kirk sessions.

[53] Perth Presb., 27 February 1628.

Ideally, the discipline of the kirk applied to all without regard to rank or power; and in the case of the lairds and lesser nobility this ideal was often realised. Sometimes a presbytery was quite literally able to put down the mighty from their seat. The presbytery of Lanark, after considerable effort, succeeded in requiring the laird of Loy to appear before them. He was ordered 'the nixt Sabbothe day to come out of his awen seat within the paroch kirk of Lanark befoir his awin minister, Mr William Livingstoun, and thair to humble himself upone his knees, crave God and the congregatioun forgiveness for misregaird of God and his sabboth in drawing ane quinger within his house'.[54] Attempts to discipline the nobility were more difficult. The presbytery of Paisley in 1627 learned that the Earl of Abercorn 'had made apostasie and defectioune from the true religioun ... and that he openly doth avowe himselfe to be a papist and verie contemptuouslie despiseth the word of God preached publictlie'.[55] He was summoned for trial; and by December of that year an episcopal warrant for his excommunication had been signed, although apparently the excommunication itself was never pronounced.[56]

Presbyteries had an important place in the total disciplinary work of the church. They were a superior court to kirk sessions; and, unlike the session, they were given jurisdiction over 'the terrible sentence of excommunication'. They met far more frequently than synods and did not hesitate to discipline at once a prominent elder who might have overawed his kirk session. Certainly, one of the reasons why presbyteries continued to flourish after 1610 was the important disciplinary work which they were doing – work which probably could not have been done as efficiently by any other church court then in existence.

V

One of the reasons for the effectiveness of presbyteries was their right to supervise the process of excommunication. Excommunication would indeed be a terrible sentence. If a person was 'strucken with the terrible sentence of excommunication' the minister from the pulpit called 'upon the Name of God to ratifie the sentence

[54] Lanark Presb., 25 January 1627.
[55] Paisley Presb., 19 April 1627.
[56] *Ibid.* 20 December 1627, 10 January, 30 January, 1628.

in Heaven, and the people warned to hold him as a Heathen ... and to shun all communion with him'. The name of the one excommunicated was published in all kirks of the presbytery and persons warned not to 'haunt, frequent nor intercommoun' with the outcast, a warning which, after 1610, might be reinforced with an episcopal injunction.[57]

Moreover, those who had been excommunicated were liable to civil penalties as well. An act of parliament in 1609 reinforced several earlier acts by ordering that no excommunicated person:

> salbe sufferit ... [to] injoy the possessioun of thair landis, rentis and revenewis, bot that the same salbe mellit with, intrometit with [i.e. managed] and upliftit to his maiesteis vse.

Although excommunicated persons were 'permitted to come to the preaching of the Word' yet it must 'appear that he commeth as one not having communion with the Church'.[59]

Clearly excommunication was a serious and formidable sentence, and the right of presbyteries to initiate and supervise the process which led up to excommunication was one of the more distinctive features of presbyterial jurisdiction. Kirk sessions usually did not handle cases of excommunication but referred that matter to presbyteries.[60] If a kirk session tried to do so, it might be rebuked. In 1609 the presbytery of Jedburgh warned one of its ministers who had tried to act without presbyterial sanction 'that in no case he excommunicate any off his people untill that the process intendid on ... be him be sein and examinat be the presbitery', and an excommunication he had pronounced was actually annulled.[61]

The normal process of excommunication followed a pattern of

---

[57] *Government and Order of the Church of Scotland*, 42. Cf. W. McMillan, *Worship of the Scottish Reformed Church*, Chapter XXVI: 'The Order of Excommunication' in The Book of Common Order. *Elgin K. S.*, 133, 145. The necessity to repeat these orders from time to time suggests that the prohibition was not too easy to enforce. See e.g. *ibid.* 144.
[58] *A.P.S.* IV, 407. For earlier acts, see III, 71–2, 421, IV, 63.
[59] *Government and Order of the Church of Scotland*, 43. Cf. Paisley Presb., 25 October 1626. This was a concession from earlier practice. Cf. *A.P.S.* III, 431.
[60] E.g. *Spottiswood Misc.* II, 276; *St Andrews K. S.* II, 891n; Ellon Presb., 29 May 1600; Jedburgh Presb., 13 November 1606, 3 June, 24 June, 30 December 1607.
[61] Jedburgh Presb., 3 October, 26 April 1609.

three weekly summonses, three public admonitions, three public prayers, and the sentence itself, thus taking a minimum of ten weeks. Most cases took longer than this, since the process was suspended whenever there was any hope of conformity from the impenitent. An example shows how long the process was; formal actions were often accompanied by numerous pastoral attempts to reach the sinner. In May 1605 the presbytery of Paisley reviewed the process of the minister and elders of Erskine against a contumacious trilapse in fornication. The presbytery found that the kirk session:

> hes lawfullie proceidid aganes the said William be thrie severall admonitiouns, upoun thrie severall sabbathes, and efter travell privatlie takin with the said William baith be the said Mr William [Brisbane, his minister] and his eldership, without ony proffeit or hope of obedience, hes nixt, conforme to the buke of discipline, used publict prayer thrie severall sabboths lykwayes for the better induceing of the said William to obedience. . . . And now seing the said William persevering in his contumacie, . . . The brethren haveing caused travell with his friends . . . and finding no hope of obedience: thairfoir . . . give expres warrand and . . . ordens the said Mr William to proceid to the pronounceing of the sentence of excommunicatioun . . . upoun the nixt sabboth except the said William come and offer his obedience in humility.[62]

One important change in this process was introduced by the Glasgow assembly of 1610, which ordered that 'no sentence of excommunicatioun, or absolution therfra, be pronouncit against or in favours of any person, without the knowledge and approbation of the Bischop of the Dyocie, quho must be ansuerable to his Majestie'.[63] And the practice of the church after 1610 appears to have conformed to this new regulation with occasional exceptions. Presbyteries continued to institute and supervise the process of excommunication; but at the end of that process one regularly

[62] Paisley Presb., 23 May 1605; cf. *Government and Order of the Church of Scotland*, 40–2; Knox, *History of the Reformation* (Dickinson), II, 306–8.

[63] *B.U.K.* III, 1096 (Calderwood, VII, 100). Parliament ratified this act in 1612 but without the provision that bishops should be subject to general assemblies in their exercise of jurisdiction over excommunications (*A.P.S.* IV., 469).

finds an order that a process 'be extractit and ane warrant to be gottin from the Bischop for excommunicatioun'.[64]

What effect did this new requirement have upon excommunications? The number of excommunications steadily declined after 1610, and it seems likely that the requirements of the Glasgow assembly were an important reason for this decline. In 1602 the presbytery of Ellon excommunicated thirty-five persons in one year – an astounding figure. On one day the names of eleven persons were presented for excommunication, the 'saids personis being for the maist part vagabund harlotts'. All were excommunicated. In 1608 seven persons were excommunicated by that presbytery, and eight were sentenced the following year. However, between 1611 and 1617 there was only one excommunication by the presbytery of Ellon, and only rarely after that was the sentence pronounced.[65]

In the presbytery of Paisley the decline was not quite as dramatic, but it was clear enough. Between 1603 and 1606 excommunications averaged one a year. When the extant records begin again in 1627 four were ordered, and three more in 1628. However, excommunications disappeared completely between 1629 and 1638.[66] The presbytery of Kirkcaldy between 1630 (when its extant records begin) and 1638 excommunicated one person, and that one probably without episcopal authority.[67]

Sir William Brereton's description in 1635 seems accurate enough. 'Very rarely, not once in many years, do they [i.e. the ecclesiastical courts] denounce any excommunicate'.[68] It seems clear that the 'terrible sentence of excommunication' had altered during the course of the period from a fairly frequent and not unusual decree to that of a rare and extraordinary sentence.

The requirement that a presbytery must complete all formal

[64] Lanark Presb., 24 Jeb. 1625.
[65] Ellon Presb., 13 January, 10 February, 24 March, 25 June, 8 September, 5 October 1602; 30 March, 25 August, 6 October, 21 December 1608; 25 January, 14 June 1609; 3 April 1611, 27 December 1620.
[66] The figures for the presbytery of Paisley are: 1603, 0; 1604, 2; 1605, 1; 1627, 4; 1628, 3; 1629–38, 0.
[67] *Kirkcaldy Presb.*, 70, 74.
[68] Brereton, *Travels*, 108. Cf. Alexander Henderson's description in 1641. 'They proceed to excommunication ... with great meeknesse, longsuffering, and by many degrees, the censure being so weighty' (*Government and Order of the Church of Scotland*, 40).

details of a long, involved process before requesting episcopal approval would itself have a limiting effect on the number of excommunications; no presbytery whose process was shortened or irregular could expect episcopal sanction.[69] Moreover, episcopal approval, although customarily granted, was not automatic. In 1627 the presbytery of Paisley requested approval for eight excommunications, six of which were granted.[70] In 1628 the presbytery of Lanark found itself in sharp disagreement with its bishop over its request for the approval of the excommunication of Patrick Dickson, servitor to the Earl of Angus. No approval was forthcoming, and a month later the presbytery ordered the excommunication to be pronounced anyway. Soon, however, there was 'produced the Bischops letter for staying the sentence of excommunication' because Dickson had promised to conform. Whereupon the presbytery sent two ministers:

> to go downe to Glasgow and in the name of the brethren of the presbyterie to regrat unto the bishop how by reason of letters purchasit from him by ... obstinat papists the discipline is continued [i.e. postponed] ... and stayit to thair great gref.

Dickson did not conform; Archbishop Lindsay eventually gave his approval, and the excommunication was pronounced.[71]

Bishops were also used by James to express royal displeasure at presbyterial actions. In 1628 the presbytery of Lanark received a letter:

> from thair ordinar the Bischop of Glasgow, desyring thame to desist frome any farther proceiding against the erle of Anguse for his papistrie, in respect his Maiestie hes writtin to the two archbischopes to this effect.[72]

[69] Shortcuts had evidently been taken on earlier occasions. In March 1596/7 James insisted that summary excommunications, which even omitted three citations, be forbidden. (*B.U.K.* III, 896 [Calderwood, V, 615]). James had first raised the issue in 1595 (*B.U.K.* III, 852–3 [Calderwood, V, 367–8], cf. *A.P.S.* IV, 111). For subsequent actions, see *B.U.K.* III, 926, 247 (Calderwood, V, 643, 708).

[70] Paisley Presb., 24 June, 16 August, 27 August, 15 November, 29 November, 20 December 1627; 10 January, 30 January, 7 August 1628; 19 March 1629.

[71] Lanark Presb., 21 August, 25 September, 16 October, 23 October, 7 November 1628.

[72] *Ibid.* 17 January 1628. Before 1610 James used the Privy Council for the same purpose. E.g. *R.P.C.* V, 509–10; VI, 272, 586–9; VIII, 328–9, 381.

Excommunication of a nobleman had serious civil consequences, and James had insisted as early as 1605 that no nobleman was to be excommunicated without approval by the privy council.[73] Disagreement or conflict between bishops and presbyteries about excommunication is rarely found in the records. Bishops served as a check upon irregular presbyterial actions; they were probably an informal court of appeal; and their supervision probably helped to make excommunication a rare and solemn matter. But a presbytery that had carried out a full and regular process could usually count on support from its bishop, and the 'terrible sentence of excommunication' was imposed by presbytery and bishop alike.

VI

Visitations of local parishes were another major responsibility of presbyteries. Throughout the period visitations were conducted by a variety of officers: sometimes by two or more visitors appointed by a presbytery, frequently by an entire presbytery, sometimes by a presbytery with commissioners sent by the synod, sometimes – after 1610 – by a bishop with members of a presbytery.[74] The Glasgow act of 1610 ordered 'the visitation of ilk dyocie . . . done be the Bischop himselfe', and, as was seen earlier, episcopal visitation was not uncommon. Nevertheless, the Glasgow act also allowed a bishop 'to mak speciall choise, and to appoint some worthie man to be visitour in his place', and in practice visitations by an entire presbytery continued to be the normal procedure.[75] Synod records contain many injunctions urging and requiring 'everie presbyterie to visit the kirks thairof within thair bounds'.[76] The main problem was to persuade presbyteries to fulfill their their duty, and their record was only fair in this respect. The presbytery of Ellon conducted no visitations between 1611 and 1617. In that year Bishop Alexander Forbes held an extremely

---

[73] *O.L.* I, 354*–355*.
[74] Paisley Presb., 12 July 1604; Lanark Presb., 24 July 1623; Jedburgh Presb., 25 April 1609, 22 July 1612; Ellon Presb., 6 June 1599; Fife Synod, folios 1–8, pp. 19–56, 75–81, 103–5, 127–36, 147–54, 169–70.
[75] *B.U.K.* III, 1097 (Calderwood, VII, 101).
[76] Ellon Presb., 22 April 1617 (Aberdeen Synod). See also Fife Synod, 182, 243; Moray Synod, 22; Jedburgh Presb., 19 October 1608.

thorough and searching visitation of the presbytery itself; among other orders, he instructed 'the moderator and everie minister yeirlie [to] visit his paroche . . . anis [once] in the yeir at the lest and gif possiblie thai mai twyse in the yeir'.[77] Ellon continued to hold visitations irregularly until 1621, when its record improved. The presbytery of Dunblane made only isolated visitations between 1616 and 1628. Between 1623 and 1638 the kirk of Belhelvie was visited once, presumably by the presbytery of Aberdeen. Although occasional visitations were held earlier, the first systematic visitations held by the presbytery of Jedburgh were in 1628.[78]

The record may not be quite as mediocre as these figures suggest. Visitations by a bishop and presbytery were not usually recorded in presbytery minutes; and some presbyteries probably kept separate books of visitations, none of which appear to have survived.[79] Yet when allowance is made for these exceptions it still seems that visitations were conducted by many presbyteries rather infrequently.

Most visitations followed a similar pattern. A day was announced and a preacher was appointed. The brethren assembled at the kirk to be visited, a collection for the poor was taken and a sermon preached. Thereafter the presbytery met with the kirk session, the minister was removed and his life was examined. The elders in their turn were examined. The records of the parish, the state of the kirk building, manse and glebe, the behaviour of the reader, the support of the school (if any) and difficult disciplinary cases were all considered. Frequently much of the regular disciplinary work of the presbytery was carried on as well. For many parishioners the chief visible sign of ecclesiastical authority beyond that of a local kirk session must have been presbyterial visitations, when all the brethren of the presbytery met in a local kirk, solemnly examined the minister, the elders, and the state of that parish. Especially where a bishop was inactive or non-resident, presbyteries must have seemed to many to be the real overseers of the kirk.

[77] Ellon Presb., 6 September 1617.
[78] Dunblane Presb., 6 January 1618; Belhelvie K. S., 10 June, 1624; Jedburgh Presb., July-September 1628.
[79] Perth Presb., 11 June 1628; Lanark Presb., 21 August 1628; Linlithgow Presb., 24 July 1616. In 1616 the synod of Fife ordered all 'Moderatours, having power of Visitatione from my Lord Archbishop, to have registers of visitations (Fife Synod, 193).

VII

Presbyteries also had a number of other responsibilities. (Their work in the examination, ordination, and admission of ministers will be considered later.)[80] Many of them were involved in public projects of various kinds, occasionally initiating a project, but more usually helping to implement a plan recommended by the government or a bishop. In 1624 the presbytery of Lanark received 'ane letter direct from the Bischop for ane support to be collectit . . . for the support of the towne of Dumfermling, brunt with fyre', and by September £597 had been collected by that presbytery.[81] In 1622 there was a general collection for the distressed Church of France, for which, according to Calderwood, the sum of 30,000–35,000 merks was raised. The minutes of the presbytery of Jedburgh show the careful way that the presbytery planned for the collection, accounted for the total, and saw to its safe delivery to Edinburgh.[82]

Presbyteries were also responsible for the trial and admission of both readers and schoolmasters. The synod of Moray in 1626 ordered that 'no man be allowit to read in publict with [out] the speciall allowance of the brethren of the presbytery',[83] and this seems to have been the practice throughout the period.

A similar procedure was followed for the admission of schoolmasters, and presbyteries successfully defended their right to licence schoolmasters against the encroachments of both bishops and burgh councils. Before 1616 there are many examples of schoolmasters receiving their licences from presbyteries.[84] However, the general assembly of 1616 required schoolmasters both to have 'the approbation of the Bishop of the Diocie' and to be 'tryit be the Ministers of the Presbytrie'.[85] If episcopal licences were issued, no evidence of them appears to have survived; and after 1616 examinations and licences continued to be granted by

[80] See below, Chapter Seven.
[81] Lanark Presb., 17 June, 23 September 1624.
[82] Calderwood, VII, 543; cf. *Scottish History Society Misc.* III, 181–202. Jedburgh Presb., 28 February, 3 April, 24 April 1622.
[83] Moray Synod, 25; Ellon Presb., 11 April 1635.
[84] E.g. Jedburgh Presb., 20 July 1611.
[85] *B.U.K.* III, 1120 (Calderwood, VIII, 99–100).

presbyteries. In 1622 the presbytery of Jedburgh examined a candidate. 'His testimoniallis sein and considered and he examined and fund qualified. The brethren . . . did admit him schoolmaster'. 'His testimoniallis' may possibly have included an episcopal licence; but the presbytery of Perth, in considering a similar case, examined only a candidate's testimonials from the Universitie of St Andrewse' and thereafter accepted him as 'reader at Kilspindie kirke and teacher off the schoole there'.[86]

Presbyteries also successfully resisted attempts by burgh councils to install schoolmasters without approval by the brethren. At least this was the case in 1632, when the presbytery of Perth learned that 'the towne of Perth hade made nomination and aggreament with a schoolmaister, not acknowledgeing them nor seikeing their consent contrair to the custome. . . .' Three months later the offending schoolmaster appeared and 'acknowledged his oversight in entering to the said schoole without beeing tryed by them'. He was 'admonished . . . off his dewtie in . . . instructing off the bairnes in literature and manners' and the brethren, 'in toakine off their acceptation, taks him be the hand'.[87]

The authority which presbyteries exercised over the admission (and deposition) of schoolmasters and readers during this period was in marked contrast to Restoration practice where bishops regularly licensed men for both these offices,[88] and serves to underline the rather more moderate character of episcopacy during the early part of the century as compared with that after 1661.

VIII

A pamphlet in 1606 asserted 'as all men know, that the discipline and governement of the kirk, exercised by presbytereis and by bishops, are so opposed one to another, that when the one is sett up, the other must doun of force'.[89] However, presbyteries did not 'doun of force' after the revival of episcopacy; on the contrary, records from the early seventeenth century show that presbyteries increased in number, strength, and stability. By 1638 presbyterial discipline was more effective over a wider area in Scotland than

[86] Jedburgh Presb., 8 May 1622; Perth Presb., 28 September 1636.
[87] Perth Presb., 23 May, 15 August 1632.
[88] W. R. Foster, *Bishop and Presbytery*, 43-4.
[89] Calderwood, VI, 513.

in any previous generation. In the records of such presbyteries as Ellon (one of the few presbyteries whose extant records are almost unbroken) one can see signs of the growing stability and authority of that presbytery over the people within its bounds. During the early years of the century, advice and support were often sought from other presbyteries.[90] After about 1607, however, requests for assistance from other presbyteries were rare, and thereafter the presbytery of Ellon seems to have been more stable and better established.

Presbyteries between 1600 and 1638 continued to be important and effective agents of the church. They helped to maintain the authority of reformed theology on a practical and parochial level; they brought clergy into close and frequent contact with one another at a time when travel was not easy, and they protected ministers from the ire of angry parishioners. They were disciplinary courts for more serious offences, as well as courts of appeal and sources of advice for kirk sessions. They supervised the process of excommunication, examined candidates for ordination, conducted institutions, and held most visitations of local parishes. They were responsible for a wide variety of administrative activities and exercised effective control over most of the officers of the kirk: elders and deacons, kirk officers, schoolmasters, and readers. Their work was of immense importance in establishing law and order within the bounds of their jurisdiction.

Nevertheless, the first decade of the century saw some important modifications of presbyterial authority, of which perhaps the most important was the introduction of constant moderators. The Linlithgow act of 1606, reinforced by the Glasgow act of 1610, placed the immediate appointment of moderators in the hands of bishops and ultimately in those of the crown. It is not surprising that the rebellion of 1638 should have begun in many presbyteries with an election of their own moderator.[91]

Final authority to pronounce excommunications was transferred from presbyteries to diocesan bishops in 1610, and presbyteries were likewise no longer responsible for presentations, collations, or (by themselves at least) ordinations. It is less obvious that the 1610 act meant any real change in the rights of presbyteries to conduct

[90] E.g. Ellon Presb., 19 April 1598, 17 December 1600, 4 August 1602.
[91] *Kirkcaldy Presb.*, 125 (15 March 1638); Paisley Presb., 27 June, 5 July 1638; Perth Presb., 16 May 1638; Haddington Presb., 16 May 1638.

visitations. Visitations by superintendents, commissioners and bishops were common enough before 1610, and after that date episcopal authority seems to have been used to urge presbyteries to hold visitations, rather than to restrain them.

The reformed Kirk of the sixteenth century knew little or nothing of presbyteries for a generation. Yet by 1600 'the brethren of the presbyterie' had become an important part of the ordinary administration and life of the Church. The revival of episcopacy meant some reduction in the autonomy of presbyteries, but those bodies continued to function, to increase in number and effectiveness, and to be vigorous and vital agents in the pastoral and disciplinary work of the Church.

CHAPTER SIX

The Senior Courts of the Church

I

SYNODS

The Scottish reformed synod was a descendant of the medieval diocesan synod of bishop and clergy.[1] After the Reformation, synods continued to be organised along diocesan lines for the most part, although the inclusion of the presbytery of Peebles (diocese of Glasgow) in the synod of Lothian (Diocese of St Andrews) in 1590 suggests that some revision of synod boundaries was taking place where medieval diocesan lines were impractical.[2]

The reformed synod also showed its medieval heritage in its organisation. Superintendents were permanent moderators and all ministers of the area were expected to attend. The reformed Church added representation by elders or deacons. An act of the general assembly of 1562 revealed the character of the early synod when it ordered superintendents to:

> appoint there Synodall Assemblies twyce in the yeir ... that the minister with ane elder or deacon may repair toward the place appointed be the superintendents.

And a general assembly act in 1567 suggests that synods did not meet where there were no superintendents.[3]

The oldest extant synod record is that of the synod of Lothian and Tweeddale, which begins in April 1589. By that date changes had taken place in the synod, probably in part because of the rise of presbyteries and the Melvillian party, and probably in part because of practical difficulties in the earlier pattern. By 1589 the

[1] Duncan Shaw, *General Assemblies of the Church of Scotland, 1560-1600*, 174-5.
[2] *B.U.K.* II, 649; Synod of Lothian and Tweeddale, I, 14-15, 17, 24-5, 34.
[3] *B.U.K.* I, 29, 111 (Calderwood, II, 208). Cf. G. Donaldson, *Scottish Reformation*, 124.

superintendent had disappeared and the moderator of each synod was elected at the first session. Even in Aberdeen, where bishops were never suppressed, Mr David Rait (and not Bishop David Cunningham) was 'principall and moderator of the last provinciall assemblie' in 1589.[4] That change was in accordance with the second Book of Discipline. However, the disappearance of elders and deacons from synod meetings violated the ideals of that book.[5] By 1589 elders and deacons had disappeared from synod records, and the synod was composed entirely of ministers. The difficulty of persuading laymen to attend church courts regularly has been noted before, and attempts to revive lay participation in synods of the early seventeenth century were not very successful.[6]

The rise of presbyteries and changes in synodical organisation did not mean that synods declined in importance. The synod of Lothian and Tweeddale met regularly twice a year, examined each presbytery within its jurisdiction with great care, and conducted considerable general business as well. Presbyteries were rebuked for negligence of duty, ministers were rebuked or deposed, a suspended minister was restored.[7] If the synod of Lothian and Tweeddale was at all typical, synods continued to be active and vigorous courts of the church during the latter part of the sixteenth century.[8]

As part of his programme to revive episcopacy, James urged a general assembly at Linlithgow in 1606 to commit 'the moderation of the Provinciall Assemblie ... unto the Bishop'. Probably the assembly did not approve that proposal, and James rewrote the minutes to indicate approval after the Assembly had disbanded.[9] This action was reinforced by privy council injunctions charging synods to accept their constant moderators, and probably royal commissioners were sent to all synods.[10]

James' proposal looked very much like diocesan episcopacy, and

[4] Synod of Lothian and Tweeddale, I, 1, 11; Aberdeen Presb., 20 October 1589.
[5] Calderwood, III, 539 (4) (18).
[6] See above, 88–91.
[7] Synod of Lothian and Tweeddale, I, 1, 2, 4, 13, 14.
[8] The extant records of this synod cover the years 1589–96.
[9] *B.U.K.* III, 1030, 1032–4 (Calderwood, VI, 615, 618–20); Calderwood, VI, 624; *O.L.* I, 105. Cf. the suspicion of the Presbytery of Ellon about the minutes (above, 92).
[10] *R.P.C.* VII, 380, 416–7.

there was widespread opposition at first. Mr James Melville learned in June 1607 that 'there is not a province in Scotland that has accepted as yitt the provinciall moderator except Angus, and that not without oppositioun'. According to Spottiswood, opposition was especially strong in Perth, Fife and the Merse;[11] but it seems to have been widespread throughout the south. In August 1607 the Earl of Abercorn reported on his commission to the synod of Clydesdale. He ordered that synod to 'admit the Archbishope of Glasgw thair Moderator; quhairunto, in the beginning, thay maid greit oppositioun'. However, 'in end, fynding thame selffis straittit with a present aunsuer, and haveing signifeit to thame quhat command I haid for denunceing thame rebellis, ... the haill Synode (two onlie exceptit), voittit to his acceptatioun'.[12]

Although intense at first, opposition did not last long. All 'opposition proved vain, and they in end forced to obey', wrote Archbishop Spottiswood. At the synod of Lothian in November 1610 three ministers protested against their episcopal moderator:

> the thrie brethren forsaid thought that others sould have assisted them; but they found noe assistance as was promised them.[13]

The Glasgow assembly of 1610 repeated the Linlithgow injunction by ordering 'that the Bischops salbe Moderatours in every Diocesian Synod',[14] and this practice was apparently followed between 1610 and 1637. During those years the moderator of the synod of Fife was always either the Archbishop of St Andrews or a commissioner assigned by him, and the same was true in the synod of Moray.[15]

Attempts were also made around 1610 to revive the early Reformation practice of lay delegates to a synod. In October 1610 Archbishop Gladstanes summoned a meeting of the synod of

---

[11] Calderwood, VI, 666; Spottiswood, *History*, III. 189. Cf. Calderwood, VI, 653, 658, 672–7, 679–81; *O.L.* I, 119–20; *R.P.C.* VII, 521–3, 540.
[12] *O.L.* I, 104–5. For opposition in Lothian and Teviotdale, see n. 11 above. Even in the north it was necessary to send royal commissioners to synods (William Fraser, *The Chiefs of Grant*, II, 4–5).
[13] Spottiswood, *History*, III, 189; Calderwood, VII, 128.
[14] *B.U.K.* III, 1096 (Calderwood, VII, 100). The act did allow two or three synods to be organized in a diocese 'quher the Dyocies are large'.
[15] Fife Synod, 190, 207, 259, *passim*; Moray Synod, passim.

Lothian, and required ministers to be present 'accompanied with two or three commissioners from everie paroche'.[16] The minutes of the synod of Fife record the presence of lay commissioners between 1611 and 1617. In September 1611 thirteen were present, and twenty-one attended in April 1612. Thereafter, the number of lay commissioners slowly declined, until by April 1617 only one was present.[17] The extant records of the synod of Moray begin in 1623. There is no evidence of laymen in that synod by 1623.[18] As in presbyteries, it was difficult to get laymen to attend meetings two or three days in length, especially since much of the business of the synod concerned the trial of presbyteries and the disciplining of ministers.

Meetings of synods were held twice a year, normally in April and October. The synod began with a public sermon, usually by the bishop. The people of the parish where the synod met were urged to 'frequent the preitching that day', and alms from the opening session were turned over to the local kirk session.[19] Thereafter, absentees were recorded, and 'visitors' were appointed to examine minutes of each presbytery in the synod.

As in the late sixteenth century, synods continued to be courts of appeal from presbyteries and dealt with unusual cases or those involving powerful persons. In 1628 the presbytery of Jedburgh learned that 'certaine of my Lord of Jedburgh his folkes cam to the Kirk of Oxnam', broke into the church, and admitted 'ane Inglish curate, quho against all order . . . did marie Lilias Ker upon ane Inglish gentlemen'. The case was referred 'to the Synode'.[20] A typical example of matters brought by one presbytery were those presented to the synod of Fife by the presbytery of Kirkcaldy in April 1632. The presbytery asked the synod to settle a quarrel between two parishes over a burial bell, to raise a ransom for two Scots who had been captives of the Turks and the Spaniards for eleven years, and to issue a judgment in a difficult case of adultery. Judgments were issued on all three matters.[21]

[16] Calderwood, VII, 124-5.
[17] Fife Synod, 57, 82, 106, 116, 137, 155, 171, 179, 191, 199, 207.
[18] Moray Synod, 1623-38. The synod was known as 'the assembly of the ministeris'. Cf. Elgin K. S., 7 April 1629, 29 April 1634.
[19] *Elgin K. S.*, 149, 152; Elgin K. S., 17 May 1625, 7 April 1629, 29 April 1634.
[20] Jedburgh Presb., 5, 19 March 1628.
[21] *Kirkcaldy Presb.*, 37; Fife Synod, 329-30,

In addition to hearing specific cases, synods often issued general instructions designed to improve discipline and order within their boundaries. The synod of Aberdeen was especially active after the consecration of Patrick Forbes. In October 1620 that synod issued twenty-eight general disciplinary acts. Ministers were not to travel on the Sabbath, destitute widows of ministers were to be supported, as were students in theology, servants were to be in the kirk on Sunday 'except ane to keip the hous', and wandering beggars were to be returned to their own parishes.[22]

A large part of each meeting was devoted to an examination of presbyteries and disciplining of ministers. Presbyteries who allowed Scottish winters to prevent regular meetings were sharply rebuked. Ministers who lacked either manse or glebe were ordered to secure the same, and sometimes a bishop agreed to intercede with a powerful parishioner to provide a glebe. A minister who solemnised a marriage without proclamation of banns was 'suspendit . . . for the space of ane moneth'. The congregation of Forfar asked the synod of Fife to require their minister to 'preache . . . upon Sonday efternoon', and the minister was so ordered by 'my Lord Archbishop and this present Synod'. The synod of Moray warned the brethren of the presbytery of Inverness 'that non of them be found heirafter on Saturday in Inverness or ony where from thair studies'.[23]

Controversial presentations were sometimes tried by synods. In 1627 the synod of Moray considered the presentation of Mr Thomas Ross to Calder. The synod decided that:

> he had obtained the forsaid presentatioun by ane sinonicall pactioun quherupon he was rejected from the said place, yit becaus he was found to haif the Irishe language the synod thocht guid to offer unto him some uther charge in Highlands.[24]

Translation of ministers from one parish to another[25] as well as trials for deposition of ministers were handled by the synod. The most common offence for which ministers were deposed was fornication. Usually an accused minister was suspended by his

---

[22] Ellon Presb., 19 October 1620.
[23] Fife Synod, 8, 146, 157, 183, 276; Moray Synod, 3, 63.
[24] Moray Synod, 30.
[25] E.g. Moray Synod, 35; Ellon Presb., 3 April 1616 (Aberdeen Synod); Fife Synod, 7, 139, 162, 163.

presbytery and tried at the next synod. Thus in 1630 Mr John Wood, assistant minister at Rhynd and son of the minister there, was accused of fornication. A month later he confessed his guilt and 'humblit himself upon his knees with tears craveing mercie of the Lord'. The presbytery 'suspends him from his ministrie unto the nixt Synod of Saint Andrews', and at the April synod he was deposed.[26]

The archbishop or bishop of a diocese was clearly the dominant member of any synod. He appointed the clerk of the synod and was either moderator or appointed a substitute. He issued warrants to offenders to appear before the synod.[27] Calderwood added that he also 'suffereth nothing to come in voting but what he pleaseth' and that 'the diocesan assemblie has not power to conclude anie thing without the bishop's consent'.[28] That judgment seems likely enough, although I have found no evidence in extant records to verify it.

Whether ministers privately approved of this arrangement or not is probably impossible to determine. However, lists of absentees make it clear that most ministers were at least willing to participate in a court which might well be described as a 'bishop and synod'. There were about one hundred ministers in the synod of Fife. Between 1617 and 1620, an average of twenty-one ministers were absent. The synod of Moray had about fifty ministers in its jurisdiction. Usually absentees were limited to three or four ministers who were sick.[29] Although the number of absentees in Fife was not insignificant, yet most ministers did not agree with Calderwood that it was unlawful to attend a synod, or that the moderator of a synod after 1610 was an 'anti-christian bishop'.[30]

Unlike general assemblies, the frequency or regularity with which synods met was not interrupted by the revival of episcopacy. Although only a few synod records have survived, there are references in every presbytery to semi-annual meetings of synods. Indeed, after the virtual suspension of general assemblies in 1618, the synod was the highest regular court of the church. As in the

[26] Perth Presb., 6 January, 10 February, 14 April 1630; Fife Synod, 230. For other cases, see Moray Synod, 9; Fife Synod, 213.
[27] Barclay Allardice Papers, 347; cf. Fife Synod, 139, 141.
[28] Calderwood, VII, 110, 133.
[29] Fife Synod, 207, 212, 216, 220, 226, 231, 235; Moray Synod, 16, 21, 27, 33.
[30] Calderwood, VII, 132

1560s, the synod had a permanent moderator; but, unlike the early years of the Reformation, bishops were not subject to the discipline of either synod or general assembly. Not only were many important disciplinary cases tried by synods, but the synod was also the main agent of the church responsible for discipline and order among the ministry. The seventeenth century church had a high conception of the life, the duties, and the privileges of a minister; and synods were effective courts in maintaining that ideal among the ministers of the kirk.

II

PROVINCIAL ASSEMBLIES

Little is known about either the composition or the work of provincial assemblies. No minutes of their meetings are known to be extant. Even the term 'provincial assembly' can be misleading, since it was sometimes used to describe synods.[31] Apparently, at irregular intervals bishops and sometimes ministers of each archiepiscopal province (St Andrews and Glasgow) met together to consider major disciplinary or administrative matters. As early as 1607 the bishops made plans to hold regular meetings 'everie sex weikis, anis at the leist, . . . quhair we intend to communicat our intelligence mutuallie'.[32]

By 1612 the provincial ideal had appeared, when there was a meeting of 'the provinciall synode of the prelatis of the province of St Androis'. By 1614 'dyvers of . . . the ministrie' met with the archbishop of St Andrews and four other bishops.[33] An act in 1614 implied that members of chapters were to attend 'provinciall meetings from yeir to yeir' with their bishop.[34]

Several assemblies were called to discuss issues raised by Charles's Act of Revocation. Apparently these were not limited to provinces but were meetings with representatives from the whole church. In October 1626, 'in respect of the weightie maters of the kirk to be handled in the nixt meiting of the Bishopes, the synod

[31] E.g. *B.U.K.* III, 1030 (Calderwood, VI, 615).
[32] *O.L.* I, 90.
[33] Fife Synod, 101, 166.
[34] *Ibid.* 168.

[of Moray] eftir advyss thinks expedient to direct three commissionars of the ministrie from this diocie with the bishop'. And at the end of the year 'there was a convention of Bishops and other ministers ... in Edinburgh' to consult about the revocation.[35]

Another meeting was held in July 1627 and presbyteries were requested to send commissioners. The presbytery of Lanark received 'ane letter frome the Bischop of Glasgow schawing of ane meitting of some brother out of everie presbiterie in Edinburgh to advyse anent the kirk effaires', and two ministers were chosen. This meeting was not limited to the province of Glasgow, since the archbishop of St Andrews sent similar requests to presbyteries in his diocese. Indeed at the meeting 'some feared that it should stand for a Generall Assemblie; but the Bishop of St Androes came not to it, but wrote his excuse, and desyred the Bishop of Rosse to moderat that meeting'.[36]

Apart from topical issues such as the consequences of the act of revocation, provincial assemblies dealt with disciplinary cases involving powerful and important persons, and they passed minor regulations as well. Prominent papists were summoned and sometimes referred to the court of high commission. A case involving a suspected adulterer who was a servitor of the Earl of Orkney was referred to a provincial assembly by the bishop and synod of Aberdeen. Bishops were ordered to discipline ministers who 'hes not celebrate the communioun upon the day appoynted be his majestie becaus it was Easter Day'. Plans were made to remove unqualified commissary judges who 'have not obtained ane testimoniall of the Lords of the Sessioun'.[37]

Not enough is known about provincial assemblies to form any definite conclusions. Tentatively, provincial assemblies were meetings of bishops and ministers summoned at irregular intervals to consider those more routine matters which had often come before general assemblies when they met. The early Scottish reformers taught that certain matters must be considered by an assembly of the whole church, and provincial assemblies may well have been an attempt to maintain that tradition during the years when no general assemblies were held.

[35] Moray Synod, 26; Row, *History*, 342; *R.P.C.* I, 456.
[36] Lanark Presb., 7 June, 1627; Perth Presb., 11 July, 1627; Row, *History*, 344.
[37] Fife synod, 101, 102, 166, 168.

III

GENERAL ASSEMBLIES

In March 1573-74 a general assembly declared that:

for preservatioun of the holie Ministrie and Kirk in puritie, the Lord hes appointit Assemblies and Conventiouns, not only of the persons of the Ministrie, but also of *the haill members of the Kirk* professing Chryst.

And the assembly went on to rejoice that 'the most noble ther of the hiest Estate, hes joynit themselves, be their awin presence in the Assemblies, as members of ane body, concurreant, voteand, and authorizand in all things their proceiding with their brether'.[38] From its beginnings, the general assembly appears to have been composed of the same three estates as were represented in parliament: clergy (ministers, superintendents and bishops), barons (nobles and lairds), and burgh commissioners. Because all were represented, it was a 'generall assemblie of this haill Realme'.[39]

The second Book of Discipline proposed a very different arrangement. 'Nane ar subject to repair to this Assemblie to voitt, bot ecclesiasticall personis', that is ministers and elders. Indeed the assembly was to be called 'the generall eldership of the haill kirk'. Those who had attended earlier, namely the king or his commissioners, the lords, and the commissioners of burghs, shires and universities, were still allowed to come 'to propone, heir, and reason' but not to vote.[40] These proposals were too radical to be implemented; no immediate reorganisation of the general assembly took place, and throughout the sixteenth century members of the nobility continued to attend occasional assemblies, not as elders but 'in their own right'.[41] The persistence of the old tradition was clear when commissioners of the general assembly, meeting in Edinburgh in October 1596, appointed 'a Generall Assemblie to be

[38] *B.U.K.* I, 292 (Calderwood, III, 305); italics added.
[39] *A.P.S.* III, 23; Duncan Shaw, *General Assemblies of the Church of Scotland, 1560–1600*, 18–20; Gordon Donaldson, 'The Church Courts', *Introduction to Scottish Legal History* (Stair Society), 372–3.
[40] *B.U.K.* II, 500 (Calderwood, III, 542).
[41] Duncan Shaw, *General Assemblies of the Church of Scotland, 1560–1600*, 74; *B.U.K.* II, 762–7.

conveened of the ministrie from all the parts of the countrie; with a good number of the best affected noblemen, barons and commissioners of burghes'.[42]

Between 1597 and 1618 twelve general assemblies were held in Scotland.[43] None were held between 1618 and 1638. Seventeenth-century assemblies continued to be composed of representatives from several estates. A contemporary commented on the noblemen present at the Dundee assembly of May 1597. At the assembly of March 1597–98 'were conveinit the Kings majestie and Commissioners from all Shyres and Townes of the countrey'. At Burntisland in 1601 'the Kings Majestie, with his Commissioners of the Nobilitie and Burrowes, were present'. The assembly at Edinburgh in 1602 was composed of five noblemen, seven representatives from burghs, and one hundred and two bishops and ministers.[44]

By now (and probably earlier) James was encouraging non-ministerial representatives to attend since they could usually be counted on to support his ecclesiastical plans. At Linlithgow in 1606 'of ministers there were reckoned one hundred thirty-six; of noblemen, barons, and others, thirty and three'; and in 1608 'the number of noblemen and gentlemen present at that Assemblie by his Majestie's directioun was above fourtie'. In 1610 seventeen noblemen, thirteen barons, seven burgh representatives, twelve bishops and one hundred and twenty-six ministers attended the Glasgow assembly.[45]

After 1610 James and his advisors considered altering assemblies 'to the form of the Convocatioun House heir in England';[46] but nothing came of the plan, and the next assembly – at Aberdeen in

[42] Calderwood, V, 447.
[43] Perth (1 March 1596–97), Dundee (10 May 1597), Dundee (7 March 1597–98), Montrose (18 March 1600), Burntisland (12 May 1601), Edinburgh (18 November 1602), Linlithgow (10 December 1606), Linlithgow (26 July 1608), Glasgow (8 June 1610), Aberdeen (13 August 1616), St Andrews (25 November 1617), Perth (25 August 1618). This list does not include the 'illegal' assembly held at Aberdeen on 2 July 1605.
[44] *Calendar of Scottish Papers*, XIII (I), 543–4; *B.U.K.* III, 934, 963, 974–9.
[45] 1606: Spottiswood, *History*, III, 183; *B.U.K.* III 1022 (Calderwood, VI, 604). 1608: Calderwood, V2, 751; Spottiswood, *History*, III, 197). 1610: *B.U.K.* III, 1085–91 (Calderwood, VII, 104–7).
[46] Spottiswood, *History*, III, 211; *O.L.* II, 446.

1616 – followed the usual custom. The kirk session of Aberdeen purchased supplies for the 'nobilitie, bishoppis, ministris, barones and commissionaris of burrowes' who were to meet in Aberdeen.[47] And at the Perth assembly of 1618 all three estates were again present in force.[48] The tradition that general assemblies consisted of the 'haill members of the kirk' remained a strong one in the early seventeenth century.

The resurgence of royal authority which began in 1597 resulted in a renewed and successful claim by the king to his prerogatives over general assemblies. James began by altering the time and place of meetings. This was not a completely new procedure. In 1586 and again in 1587 assemblies met after being summoned by royal proclamation, and in 1588 James moved the date of an assembly forward from July to February.[49] After the Edinburgh riot in 1596, James began by moving assemblies forward again. An assembly scheduled to meet at St Andrews on 27 April 1597, was summoned to Perth on 1 March. Next, an assembly which was to be held at Aberdeen was moved to Montrose and postponed by a year.[50] The assembly of 1601 was moved forward by some months, while that of 1602 was postponed from July to November.[51] An assembly planned for 1604 was postponed by the king.[52] When twenty-nine ministers attempted to hold an assembly in 1605, the arrest of many of them, the banishment of six, and the submission of the rest made it clear that henceforth assemblies, like parliaments, would meet only upon licence from the king.

However, the royal prerogative included more than the right to summon an assembly. James himself attended the assemblies held between 1597 and 1602. Two days before an assembly convened at Dundee in March 1597–98, George Nicolson wrote that the question of 'the bishops will receive end now at this Assembly . . . whitherward the King took journey yesterday. If the King had not gone the ministers would sure have prevailed, but now it will go doubtful what will be the end of these things'. And at the assembly

[47] *Aberdeen K. S.* 84; cf. Calderwood, VII, 223. Two commissioners from the burgh of Edinburgh received £692 for their expenses (*Extracts from the Records of the Burgh of Edinburgh, 1604–26,* 144).
[48] *B.U.K.* III, 1143.
[49] *R.P.C,* IV, 60–1, 174; *B.U.K.* II, 702–3, 713.
[50] *B.U.K.* III, 889, 912, 948 (Calderwood, VI, 606, 626).
[51] *R.P.C.* VI, 231; *B.U.K.* III, 962, 973 (Calderwood, VI, 105, 160).
[52] Calderwood, VI, 264.

'the first two dayes nothing was done, but from morne till late at night the ministers sent for to the king, and their votes procured'.[53] James did not of course attend any assemblies after his departure for England; but royal messages, read and re-read to the crucial assemblies of 1610 and 1618 from a distant and powerful king, were probably even more effective.[54]

The right to summon assemblies and to participate actively in their meetings was at least a defensible royal prerogative. Far less defensible was a third practice, namely James's attempts to pack assemblies or to choose and appoint compliant ministerial commissioners.

The method of choosing ministerial representatives to general assemblies had varied in the sixteenth century. Prior to 1568 superintendents 'attended every Assembly in their own right without any election or commission from the lower courts'. Moreover, superintendents selected the other ministers who would attend.[55] In 1568 an assembly ordered ministers 'chosen at the synodall conventioun of the dioces' to attend;[56] and thus probably introduced an elective element, although the influence of a superintendent would be weighty at any 'synodall conventioun'. Presbyteries began to send delegates soon after their formation in the 1580s, although they were not formally authorised to do so until the Dundee assembly of March 1597–98.[57]

There is no evidence that James tried to pack the six assemblies held between March 1596–97 and 1602. However, the Linlithgow assembly of 1606 (where James intended to introduce constant moderators) was a different matter. Calderwood charged: 'About the beginning of December [1606] letters were sent from his Majestie to everie presbyterie, commanding them to send suche men as were nominated in the missive to Linlithquo'. Presbytery records sustain Calderwood's charge in part. The presbytery of Jedburgh received their notice on 4 December:

Quhilk day his Majesties letters came to the presbiterie de-

---

[53] *Calendar of Scottish Papers*, XIII (I), 171; Calderwood, V. 682.
[54] Calderwood, VII, 95, 308–11; *B.U.K.* III, 1093–5.
[55] Duncan Shaw, *General Assemblies of the Church of Scotland, 1560–1600*, 81, 89.
[56] *B.U.K.* I, 124 (Calderwood, II, 421).
[57] *B.U.K.* III, 947 (Calderwood, V, 709).

clairing that it wes his will that thei direct Mr John Abernethye ... and Mr Richart Thomsone ... of thair presbitery to be present ... that be thaim the presbitery micht know his Majesties godlie and just desyris.

A similar letter was sent to the presbytery of Dunfermline.[58] However, it seems likely that letters were not sent to every presbytery; perhaps only those where opposition was expected received letters from James. There is no record of a royal message in the Records of the Presbytery of Ellon. In addition to appointing some ministers to the Linlithgow assembly, the Earl of Dunbar was reported to have spent 40,000 merks among 'the most neiddey and clamorous of the ministrey, to obteine ther woyces,[59] at the assembly.

Less drastic measures were used for the assembly of 1608. The presbytery of Melrose received a visit from:

> Mr James Law, Commissioner off the General Assemblie [and Bishop of Orkney], ... having commissioun off his Majesty ... that we suld nominat to the nixt general assemblie the moist wise, discret, peacable brethren to be commissioners.

The presbytery proceeded to elect, as one of their commissioners, Mr John Knox, who that year had refused to be a constant moderator.[60]

In 1610 James returned to his practice of appointing ministers. Before the Glasgow assembly, the presbytery of Jedburgh received 'ane letter direct from the kingis majestie, ... the tenor quhairoff wes that the presbitery sould send thair commissionares to the generall assemblie ... and to mak choiss off theis his Majestie had nominat'. The presbytery obeyed but protested 'that in all frie generall assemblies the presbitryes had power to nominat thair awin commissioners'. The presbytery of Turriff received similar instructions. And the Earl of Dunbar was ordered by James to have 10,000 merks ready to use at the assembly to be 'dealt amonge

---

[58] Calderwood, VI, 601; Jedburgh Presb., 4 December 1606; *O.L.* I, 67–8.

[59] Balfour, *Works*, II, 18; cf. *O.L.* I, 429*.

[60] Melrose Presb., 27 April 1608. A similar election took place in the Presbytery of Jedburgh (Jedburgh Presb. 13 July 1608). However, some presbyteries were subject to episcopal pressure in their choice. Cf. *O.L.* I, 131.

suche personis as you sall holde fitting by the advyise of the Archbishoppis of St Androis and Glasgowe'.[61]

Selection of commissioners to the assembly at Aberdeen in 1616 was based on a compromise. In July 1616 the moderator of the presbytery of Linlithgow 'did present ane letter sent from the Bishoppe off Sanct Androwis requyring [them] to send ther Moderator and ane uther Brother with him off ther choosing to the Generall Assemblye', and the presbytery elected one. Similar elections took place in the presbyteries of Haddington and Melrose.[62]

Elections to the 1617 assembly were officially free. In November, the moderator of the presbytery of Jedburgh 'presented the Bishop off Glasgow his letter deyreing the brethren ... to dirett two or thrie off the presbiterie as commissioners to the generall assembley. ... The brethren efter advisement maid choise of Mr Thomas Abernethy', a staunch opponent of episcopacy, and two other ministers. The presbyteries of Peebles and Melrose held similar elections. Commissioners from the diocese of Aberdeen were elected at a meeting of the synod on 22 October. Two ministers from each of eight presbyteries were chosen.[63]

The 1617 assembly refused to pass the Five Articles demanded by James;[64] and it is somewhat surprising, therefore, to discover that elections were not suppressed for the next assembly, at Perth in 1618. The synod of Fife did take the precaution of ordering 'that such men salbe nominat furthe of evrie presbyterie as ar wyse and discreit, and wil give his Majestie satisfaction anent their articles'.[65] But formal, and apparently free, elections were held in many presbyteries. The presbytery of Melrose 'nominatit thair brother Mr Jhon Knox and Mr Patrik Shaw as commissioners to the generall assemblie'; the presbytery of Haddington 'chose' three ministers: the presbytery of Jedburgh 'did appoynt and ordaine' three commissioners; and the presbytery of Perth 'with

---

[61] Jedburgh Presb., 30 May 1610; *O.L.* I, 236–7, 425*.

[62] Linlithgow Presb., 24 July 1616; Haddington Presb. 24, 31 July 1616; Melrose Presb. 6 August 1616. Cf. Calderwood, VII, 223.

[63] Jedburgh Presb., 19 November 1617; Peebles Presb., 20 November 1617; Melrose Presb., 18 November 1617; Ellon Presb., 22 October 1617. (Aberdeen Synod).

[64] Spottiswood, *History*, III, 248–9. For the Five Articles, see below, 181–92.

[65] Fife Synod, 219.

ane uniforme consent nominates, maks and constitutis' four ministers as their commissioners.[66] And the convictions of some who arrived at Perth also suggests that free elections were held. Lord Binning wrote to James:

> At oure cumming to this towne, finding that the most precise and wilfull Puritanes wer chosin commissionars by manie of the presbiteries, speciallie of Lowthain and Fyfe, I wes extreamlie doubtfull of the succes of your Majesties religious and just desires.[67]

Regardless of the way in which commissioners might be selected, the dominant voice at most seventeenth-century assemblies was clearly that of the king. During the sixteenth century there was much uncertainty in the church about the relationship between assemblies and royal authority. The assembly may not have 'made up its mind about the place and status of the godly prince',[68] but there was no uncertainty in James's mind. He made his own position clear when he summoned the general assembly at Perth in 1596–97:

> Wee, therefor, . . . have thought, comely following the loveable exemple of Christian Emperours of the primitive Kirk, to conveen and assemble a National Council, as well of the Ministry, as of our Estates.[69]

And after 1603 James increasingly emphasised his royal prerogative over all courts of the church.

The revival of episcopacy was not in itself fatal to the existence of general assemblies, as the full agenda passed by the assembly of 1616 made clear. However, James's emphasis upon his own prerogative, which, he declared, 'is a power innated, and a special prerogative which we that are Christian kings have, to order and dispose of external things in the policy of the Church',[70] did make assemblies almost superfluous.

James never relied solely upon his prerogative to introduce important changes into the church, but Charles I was less cautious.

[66] Melrose Presb., 4 August 1618; Haddington Presb., 22 July, 1618; Jedburgh Presb., 29 July, 1618; Perth Presb., 12 August 1618.
[67] *O.L.* II, 573.
[68] Duncan Shaw, *General Assemblies of the Church of Scotland, 1560–1600*, 65.
[69] *B.U.K.* III, 903.
[70] Spottiswood, *History*, III, 246.

A proposal to call an assembly in 1627 received the support of at least one bishop, and the Canons of 1636 did allow 'NATIONALL SYNODES, called by His Majesties Authoritie'.[71] However, the Canons themselves were introduced solely by royal prerogative as were an Ordinal and a Book of Common Prayer. Indeed, no assembly met during the reign of Charles I until he was forced to call one at Glasgow in 1638.

The manipulation and eventual suspension of general assemblies in the early seventeenth century was a new feature of Scottish reformation history and probably marks the greatest break with past reformation tradition. Between 1560 and 1596 sixty-four assemblies were held by the church. Between 1597 and 1638 – a slightly longer period – twelve official assemblies met.[72]

IV

THE GENERAL ASSEMBLY AT ABERDEEN: 1616

The best known assemblies of the period were those of 1606, 1610 and 1618, at which important changes in government or worship were made.[73] However, the general assembly of 1616 also has considerable interest as one which passed a number of important acts designed to improve the efficiency and discipline of the church. The Aberdeen assembly was certainly composed of the 'haill members of the Kirk'. The nobility were present, as were burgh representatives, commissioners from the king (with royal instructions), bishops and ministers. As has been seen, about half of the ministers were appointed by bishops (the constant moderators of presbyteries), and the other half elected by presbyteries. It was an assembly which derived much of its authority from both bishop and presbytery and was a notable example of the achievements which such an assembly could make in improving the ordinary administration of the church. Not all of its projects were successful, but on balance its accomplishments were considerable.

In its fifth session the assembly turned to an old project, the establishment of a common set of laws or canons for the whole

[71] *R.P.C.* (Second Series), I, 639n; *Canons and Constitutions Ecclesiastical . . . for the Government of the CHURCH OF SCOTLAND* VIII, 3 (1636).
[72] Calderwood, VIII, 306–11.
[73] For the activities of these assemblies, see, 26, 91, 181–8.

church. The need for 'ane uniformitie of discipline' had long been recognised in the church. An assembly in March 1574–75 ordered the production of a compilation of former acts of assembly, but the project was not completed until 1595 and was never published.[74] In 1611 the synod of Fife returned to the same theme and appointed a commission to draw up 'ane uniformitie of discipline'. Six months later the synod urged its committee to meet with representatives from the southern half of the diocese to prepare a common code of discipline which would then be 'presented to ane Provinciall or Generall Assemblie' and to the king. By 1612 a committee of the whole diocese had been appointed, but it apparently produced little. After Spottiswood's translation to St Andrews in 1615, the synod of Fife again 'earnistlie desyris the archbishop with advyse of the bishops and uther learned brethren to tak ordour for setting doune ane uniformitie of discipline', and the archbishop himself observed in the same year that 'Canonis and Constitutiounis must be concludit and set forthe, for keping bothe the Clergie and Kirkis in ordoure'.[75]

The need for uniformity of discipline was obvious. Not only did the same offence receive different sentences in different church courts, but trials of candidates for the ministry also varied from presbytery to presbytery.[76]

In its fifth session the Aberdeen assembly tried to deal with this problem when it ordered that 'a Booke of Canons be made, published in wryte, drawin foorth of the bookis of former Assemblies; and quher the same is defective, that it be supplied be the Canons of Counsells and Ecclesiasticall Conventiouns, in former tyme', and a committee was appointed to prepare the book.[77]

Once again, however, no progress was made. The work of the committee was mentioned at the Perth assembly of 1618, but there is no evidence that canons were ever issued, and complaints about lack of uniformity continued to be made.[78]

[74] *B.U.K.* I, 325, II. 566, 628, III, 815, 856 (Calderwood, III, 343, 618, 732–3, V, 371); cf. Duncan Shaw *General Assemblies of the Church of Scotland, 1560–1600*, 4–6.
[75] Fife Synod, 7, 66, 180; *O.L.* II, 446.
[76] See below, 139.
[77] *B.U.K.* III, 1128, 1157 (Calderwood, VIII, 106). James had sent instructions to pass this act (*B.U.K.* III, 1124 [Calderwood, VII, 229]).
[78] *B.U.K.* III, 1128, 1157 (Calderwood, VIII, 106); Dalhousie Muniments, 14 792.

The attempt by the Aberdeen assembly to establish a Book of Canons was not very successful. More successful was the injunction of the assembly 'that the simple Confessioun of Faith underwrytin be universallie receivit throughout this whole kingdome'.[79] Production of a new confession of faith was not an idle theological exercise but was directly related to the administration of discipline. A confession of faith was regularly used by kirk sessions, presbyteries, and synods in dealing with non-communicants and suspected Roman Catholics. A parishioner who was doubtful about the reformed faith might be given a copy of a confession of faith to study, or a suspected papist might be ordered to read and sign a confession. For these purposes the two confessions of the sixteenth century had certain limitations. The Confession of 1560 was not as precise on certain theological issues as was desired in seventeenth-century Scotland. Nowhere in the 1560 Confession can one find the clear statement that:

> God, before the foundation of the world was laid, according to the good pleasure of his will, for the praise of the glory of his grace, did predestinat and elect in Christ some men and angels unto eternal felicity; and others he did appoint for eternal condemnation.[80]

Moreover, the 1560 Confession might seem needlessly offensive to persons whom the Church was trying to win to the reformed faith. Roman Catholics were described as 'impudent blasphemers, who boldly condemn that which they have neither heard nor yet understand', and the Roman Church was described as a 'pestilent Synagogue', a 'filthy synagogue', 'that horrible harlot the Kirk malignant'.[81]

The Negative Confession of 1581 was even harsher. Not only did it contain little positive teaching, but it required a signer to 'detest and refuse the usurped authoritie of that Romane Antichrist', 'his fyve bastard Sacramentis ... his divilishe Mes; his blasphemous priesthood'.[82]

The need for a new confession of faith had apparently been proposed to James by the Scots bishops in 1611. At least this is suggested by James's reply 'anent that newe Confession of Fayth,

---

[79] *B.U.K.* III, 1127 (Calderwood, VIII, 105).

[80] Confession of 1616, *B.U.K.* III, 1132–3 (Calderwood, VII 233–4).

[81] Confession of Faith of 1560, printed in Knox, *History of the Reformation* (Dickinson), II, 257, 266.

[82] *B.U.K.* II, 516.

... [which] is so agreeable unto us, as it shall have no farder hinderance then so muche time as you shall spend for setting suche frame upon it as in your judgements shalbe founde most expedient'. Work was probably done on a new confession during the next year. On 21 April 1612 the synod of Fife appointed a small committee to prepare 'ane short and cleir Confessioun of Fayth' and two days later a confession was ready. It was 'publicklie red and ... wes found ... orthodox and thairfor ordainit to be sent to the kings majesty' for his licence. And the Fife Confession was used the next year, when 'Andro, Lord Gray, ... subscryved and solemnlie swore the Confessioune of Fayth'.[83]

The Aberdeen Confession of 1616 was probably a revised and extended version of the earlier Fife Confession.[84] And, like the

---

[83] William Fraser, *Memoirs of the Maxwells*, II, 13; Fife Synod, 84, 95–8, 118–20.

[84] The Aberdeen Confession follows a different order and is longer than the Confession of Fife. However, a number of sections in the Aberdeen Confession are found in the earlier work.

Fife 1612	Aberdeen 1616
I *believe* and confes *that thair* ar *two sacraments only* apperteining to all Christians in *The New Testament* viz. *Baptisme & the Lordis Supper*	We *believe that there* be *only two sacraments* appointed by Christ under *the New Testament* *Baptisme, and the Lords Supper*.
I *believe* and confess that the sacrament of the *Supper* of the *Lord* aucht *to be* celebrate and *giffen to all* the faythfull *communicants under* both *the elements of bread & wyne according to Chrystis institutioun*.	We *believe* that the *Lords Supper* is *to be* given to all *communicants, under* *the elements of bread and wine, according to Christs institution*.
I *believe* and confess that the *soules of* the godlie *quhilk departe in the* trew *fayth of Chryst after* thair *separatione from thair bodies* directly and *immediatelie pas* to *heavine and rest thair frome thair labouris.* (Fife Synod, 96–7)	*We believe,* that *souls of* Gods children *which depart* out of this life *in the faith of* Jesus *Christ, after* the *separating from their bodies immediately pass* into *heaven, and there rest from their labours.* (*B.U.K.* III, 1137–8 [Calderwood, VII, 239–40].)

Fife Confession, it was admirably suited for disciplinary purposes. Although less than half as long as the Confession of 1560, the Aberdeen Confession set forth as thoroughgoing, though not as detailed, a Calvinism as did the Westminster Confession. And it described the errors of Rome with moderation and restraint. Dr McCrie concluded:

> There is nothing [in the Aberdeen Confession] of the vehement vituperation, the heaping of terms of opprobrium, which disfigure the two earlier products of Scottish compilers.... In point of calmness and fairness of judgment, historical balance, and moderation of language, the northern Confession of 1616 is entitled to rank alongside of the Thirty-nine Articles of the Church of England and the thirty-three chapters of the Westminster symbol.[85]

The Aberdeen Confession was used by church courts after 1616. The Marquis of Huntly signed it in 1616. In 1620 a suspected papist appeared before the bishop and session of Aberdeen and 'solemplie sworne to the haill articles of the Confessioun of Fayth ... as the samen wer severallie and distinctlie red to him be the bishop', and a few months later an undecided parishioner was given 'the Confessioun of Faith' and told 'whairin he sall have ony dout ... to cum to the bishop or ony of the ministrie, and gett resolutioun'.[86]

The Aberdeen assembly also ordered 'that a Catechisme be made, easie, short, and compendious, for instructing the commoun sort' and appointed three ministers to prepare one.[87] Both authorised and unauthorised catechisms had been used in Scotland since the Reformation. One of the more popular was that of John Calvin, included with most editions of the Book of Common Order until 1611. It was a long catechism, covering fifty-five Sundays, which may have accounted for the injunction of the kirk session of St Andrews that the minister was 'to teache upon Maister Calvins *Catechise*, and the bairnis to ansuer him conform to the *Common Cathechise*'.[88] The Assembly of 1592 authorised the use of John

[85] C. G. M'Crie, *The Confessions of the Church of Scotland*, 33–4.
[86] *B.U.K.* III, 1130 (Calderwood, VIII, 108); *Aberdeen K. S.*, 90, 92.
[87] *B.U.K.* III, 1127 (Calderwood, VIII, 105).
[88] *St Andrews K. S.* II, 848. The 'Commoun Cathechise' is uncertain. It may have been the *Little Catechism* used since 1564, John Craig's *Shorte Summe of the Whole Catechisme*, or a private catechism.

Craig's *Forme of Examination before the Communion*, and the Heldelberg Catechism was translated into English and published in Edinburgh in 1615.[89] The Catechism authorised by the Aberdeen assembly was soon prepared. A royal licence was issued in February 1618 authorising its publication, and the Perth assembly ratified the 'Catechism allowed at Aberdeen, and printed since with Priviledge'. However, the Aberdeen Catechism was no more successful than previous attempts to secure uniformity of instruction in the catechism. Within two years the synod of Fife appointed a committee to revise the Aberdeen Catechism 'in so intelligable and edificative terms as possibly they can'.[90]

More successful than the Catechism was the injunction by the Aberdeen assembly 'that every minister have a perfyte and formall Register' of baptisms, marriages, and burials. Bishops and presbyteries had ordered individual parishes to keep full parish registers, but no general assembly prior to 1616 had ordered all ministers to keep complete parish registers. The Aberdeen act was reinforced by an order from the privy council in the same year;[91] and it was probably due to those acts, as well as to the general stability of the church, that so many of the extant parish registers begin about this time.[92]

[89] *B.U.K.* II, 788; the Catechism is reprinted in H. Bonar, *Catechisms of the Scottish Reformation*, 273–85; H. B. Aldis, *Books Printed in Scotland*, No. 476.

[90] R.S.S. LXXXVII, 67; *B.U.K.* III, 1167; Fife Synod, 238.

[91] *B.U.K.* III, 1129 (Calderwood, VIII, 107); Fife Synod, 130; Ellon Presb., 5 June 1605; *R.P.C.* X, 669–70.

[92] For example, Mid-Calder, 1604 (694), Dumfries 1605 (821), Elgin, 1609 (135), Alloa, 1609 (465), Inverurie, 1611 (204), Pittenweem, 1611 (452), Tranent, 1611 (722), Brechin, 1612 (275), Monikie, 1612 (311). (311), Kirkcaldy, 1614 (442), Montrose, 1615 (312), Kinneff and Catterline, 1616 (262), Lasswade, 1617 (691), Newbattle, 1618 (695), Inchture, 1619 (359), Fetteresso, 1620 (258), Scone, 1620 (349a), Abdie 1620, (400), Longside, 1621 (218) Baldernock, 1622 (471), Peebles, 1622, (768), Alyth, 1623 (328), Kinfauns, 1624 (366), Liberton, 1624 (693), Kinglassie, 1627 (440), Newburn, 1628 (451). There are a few registers from the sixteenth century, e.g. Perth, 1561 (387), Aberdeen, 1563 (168a), Dysart, 1582 (426), Clackmannan, 1595 (466). (*Detailed List of the Old Parochial Registers of Scotland*, annotated copy. Scottish Record Office). The Synod of Aberdeen ordered each presbytery within the diocese to enter a copy of the 1616 act requiring registers in its minutes (Ellon Presb., 22 April 1617).

The assembly's injunction that 'every Dyocie sall intertaine two ... students in Divinitie' and the further requirement 'that the halfe at leist be the sonnes of pure [i.e. poor] Ministers' soon resulted in contributions taken up by many kirk sessions to assist the growing number of candidates for the ministry.[93] And the act 'that ane uniforme ordour of Liturgie or Divyne Service be sett down to be red in all kirks' led to the production of a liturgy which might have been accepted in Scotland if the Five Articles had not soon dominated all liturgical discussion.[94]

The acts of the Aberdeen assembly were neither spectacular nor uniformly successful. However, they were an attempt to improve the efficiency and well-being of the church. The Aberdeen assembly was an interesting example of what assemblies might have achieved under 'bishop and presbytery' had assemblies met more regularly and their meetings been less dominated by major changes in polity or worship.

[93] *B.U.K.* III, 1129 (Calderwood, VIII, 107); see below, 137.
[94] *B.U.K.* III, 1127–8 (Calderwood, VIII, 105); G. Donaldson, *The Making of the Prayer Book of 1637*, 32–4.

CHAPTER SEVEN

Admission to the Ministry

The first book of Discipline demanded that only 'godly and learned men' be admitted ministers of the reformed church. Even if learned ministers were scarce, standards were not to be lowered. Indeed 'no Minister at all' was better than 'an idol in the place of a true minister'. And the authors urged 'fervent prayer unto God that it will please his mercy to thrust out [i.e. thrust forward] faithful workmen into this his harvest.'[1]

By 1600 the reformed kirk had made remarkable progress towards achieving this goal. A sample from scattered presbyteries in 1600 makes this clear.[2]

	Ministers with degrees	Ministers without degrees
Kincardine O'Neill	15	2
Paisley	12	1
Melrose	11	4
Auchterarder	10	2
Orkney	6	8

Only in Orkney and similar remote areas could a substantial number of ministers without degrees be found. By 1638 even these exceptions had disappeared, and rare indeed was the minister in 1638 who was not addressed as 'Mr' – a title reserved in the seventeenth century for university graduates.

In addition to completing an arts course, a learned minister was expected to have spent some years in the study of theology as well. Usually theological study meant even more years at a university. The financial problems of spending years in university study were about as great for seventeenth century students as they are today, and the church had made some effort to assist men in their theological years. An assembly in 1596 recommended the support of a

[1] Knox, *History of the Reformation* (Dickinson), II, 286–7.
[2] Compiled from the Reg. Assig. Stipends, 1601.

bursar to the synods of the church, and in 1602 the synod of Lothian and Tweeddale agreed that one bursar 'suld [be] entertenit in this province for the studie of theologie'. Fifteen merks was contributed to his support by the presbytery of Edinburgh.[3] However, references to bursars occur only rarely in church records prior to 1616.

The first systematic programme of support was established by the Aberdeen assembly of 1616 which decided not only that the 'Divinitie Colledge foundit at Sanct Androes ... sould be the seminarie of the Kirk', but also ordered 'that for the provisioun of some students in Divinitie, every Dyocie sall intertaine two, or according to the quantitie of the Dyocie so many as the number may arise to twentie sixe in haill'.[4] The act was remarkably effective; the church had both the resources and the desire to support a bursary system, and thereafter references to bursars in divinity are found in many church records. Synods usually supervised the system; the actual funds for bursars were raised by kirk sessions.

Almost at once the synod of Fife set up a plan to support five bursars, each of whom was to have 'for thrie quarters buird fourscoir punds'. Each bursar was to be supported for four years. By 1623 six men were being supported by this one synod alone.[5] The synod of Moray had several bursars. The diocese of Aberdeen supported three bursars in 1617; by 1620 the number had increased to four. Each parish in the diocese was expected to contribute 'of ilk hundreth communicants, nyne s.'.[6] In 1619 the presbytery of Dunblane ordered its sessions to take up their first collection for a 'Burser of St Androis'. In Belhelvie almost nothing was given for bursars until 1630, when 'ane dolor' was contributed. Thereafter the kirk session annually gave four pounds or more. In 1633 Trinity College kirk session, Edinburgh, appropriated fifty pounds for a bursar's 'fie and pensioune payit to him yeirlie'.[7]

[3] *B.U.K.* III, 871-2 (Calderwood, V, 414); Edinburgh Presb., 31 March 1602.
[4] *B.U.K.* III, 1128-9 (Calderwood, VIII, 106-7).
[5] Fife Synod, 205, 229, 248, 256, 259, 261.
[6] Moray Synod, 9, 14, 59, 63-5; Ellon Presb., 22 October 1617, 19 October 1620 (Aberdeen Synod).
[7] Dunblane Presb., 21 January 1619; Belhelvie K. S., 4 April 1630, 27 March 1631, 8 July 1632, 12 May 1633, 7 May 1634; Trinity College K. S., 10 Jan. 1633.

The Aberdeen assembly had placed the choice of bursars in 'the Bishops of the Dyocies', but in practice most of the appointments seem to have been made by presbyteries or synods. The synod of Fife allowed its presbyteries to nominate their own bursars, and in Aberdeen each presbytery sent commissioners to a meeting in Aberdeen 'for tryall and admissioun of the bursers of divinitie'. Bursars in Moray were chosen by the synod.[8]

Before admission a bursar not only had to complete his arts course but also might be required to demonstrate his competence in the arts. In Moray a bursar was admitted provided he 'give a prooffe of his Greek and phylosophie befor the brethren of the Presbiterie of Elgin'. A few years later two graduates were tried in 'the humanities, philosophie, and Greek', and the better of the two was awarded a bursary.[9]

Bursars were 'ordained that they live *colegialiter*, that they depairt at no tym from the colledge without express licence from the maisters' and that 'they report to the presbyteries be quhom they wer nominat ane testimonial from the saids maisters of thair diligence and guid behaviour for that yeir'.[10]

In 1641 Alexander Henderson wrote that in most presbyteries:

> there be Students of Divinity whereof some, if they have opportunity of their Studies, do make their abode within the bounds of the Presbytery. . . . Others, who are the greater part, stay at the Universities, and in the time of vacation come home and wait upon the Presbytery.[11]

To establish a bursary system of this extent and effectiveness was a remarkable achievement and was certainly one reason why 'the greater part stay at the Universities'. The support of a substantial number of bursars in divinity was one more sign of the growing stability, prosperity and good order of the Church after 1600.

Having completed his study of theology, a man usually sought admission to a presbytery as an expectant. Usually he was required to deliver an 'addition' or sermon in private before he was admitted.

[8] Fife Synod, 229; Ellon Presb., 13 December 1620; Moray Synod, 65.
[9] Moray Synod, 65, 73.
[10] Fife Synod, 259. For some annual reports of bursars, see Moray Synod, 65.
[11] *Government and Order of the Church of Scotland*, 5-6.

A candidate in the presbytery of Perth was required 'to exercise privatlie this day eight dayis upon the 11 verse 2 Corinthians'. In 1630 the synod of Moray outlined much more extensive examinations for the

> resaving of aney nowis [i.e. new members] upone the exercise: viz. first he sall be tryed on the Catiches, secondlie it salbe tryed quhat he can doe in the Scriptures, 3 on the contraversies, 4 he salbe hard privatly upon a text.

However, extended tests of this sort rarely appear in presbytery records.[12]

Alexander Henderson described the place of expectants in a presbytery after they were admitted:

> It is permitted to the expectants having entered before upon the publick exercise ... to sit by the Ministers and Elders[13] in the meeting of the Presbyterie, and to give their judgment of the doctrine, but they have no voice when matters of doctrine or discipline are debated. And in the handling of some matters which are thought fit to be concealed and kept secret ... they use to be removed.[14]

Expectants were frequently assigned to make an exercise or an addition at presbytery meetings, but their most useful function was as preachers in vacant parishes. A typical example was a request in 1619 by the parishioners of Collace, who

> earnestlie desyrit that the presbyterie will appoynt Mr James Lyoun ane expectant in this presbyterie to teich in the paroche kirk for comforting thame with the preiching of the Word untill thei be provydit of ane minister, being now destitute'.

The request was approved.[15]

If an expectant moved to another presbytery, usually because he had received or hoped to receive a presentation, he was given a testimonial by his own presbytery. A testimonial issued by the presbytery of St Andrews in 1630 showed the care with which expectants were examined and testimonials prepared. The testi-

---

[12] Perth Presb., 1 July 1618; Moray Synod, 46.
[13] Elders were introduced into presbyteries in 1638.
[14] *Government and Order of the Church of Scotland*, 47–8.
[15] Perth Presb., 16 June 1619.

ADMISSION TO THE MINISTRY

monial was addressed 'in speciall to the Right Reverend Fathers in God, the Archbishopes, Bishops and ministeris'. It mentioned 'his tryelles . . . privat and publick both in Latin and Engliss in interpreting the Sacred Scriptours, and in sustaining publick disputes upon the controversies in Religione'. He was urged to 'continow in fervent prayer, diligent reading of the holy Scriptoures and sanctified meditationes'. Each member of the presbytery signed the testimonial.[16]

Between 1600 and 1638 the number of expectants was increasing. No general statistics for expectants exist, but there are many signs that the number was rising. There were not many in 1602. An assembly in that year drew up a list of those 'persons quho are vacand within thair Presbitries, and willing to entir in the Ministrie' and only twenty-four names appeared on the list.[17] When the extant records of the presbytery of Jedburgh began in 1606, that presbytery had no expectants. Nor did it acquire any until two arrived early in 1609; a third came later that year, and a fourth was added in 1611.[18] A similar pattern can be seen in the presbytery of Ellon. The presbytery was established in 1598 and acquired one expectant in 1603. No more arrived until 1610, when three were admitted. A fourth was added in 1612 and a fifth in 1613.[19] By 1623 the presbytery of Dunblane had four expectants and the presbytery of Lanark had five.[20] Synod records also reveal a substantial number of expectants. In 1611 the synod of Fife had twenty-eight expectants, more than the entire church could muster nine years earlier. Nine more were admitted in 1612.[21] The total number of expectants in Scotland in 1638 can only be estimated, but there were probably not less than one hundred and fifty expectants in the church who were waiting for benefices.[22]

[16] Craven Bequest, 33 (28 July, 1630), which is a photostat of the original testimonial.
[17] B.U.K. III, 997-8.
[18] Jedburgh Presb., 18 January, 22 March, 5 July, 1609; 25 September 1611.
[19] Ellon Presb., 21 December 1603; 2 May, 30 May 1604; 31 January, 13 March, 25 April 1610; 1 April 1612; 28 December 1613.
[20] Dunblane Presb., 26 December 1616; Lanark Presb. 26 June, 10 July, 7 August, 21 August, 1623.
[21] Fife Synod, 17, 73-4, 99, 115.
[22] This figure is based on an average of three expectants in fifty presbyteries. The figure may well be too low since there were more than sixty presbyteries, and some presbyteries had more than three expectants.

The Church of Scotland could now enjoy the luxury of having a number of qualified candidates for every vacant post in the ministry.

Some expectants never received a benefice, and many were employed as private tutors or found a place in the growing parochial school system as schoolmasters and readers. Presbytery records often contain such entries as 'Mr James Spens, expectant, pedagog to the Lard of Lundy, maid the exerceis', or 'Mr Alexander Innes, scuillmaister in Auchinaroy, addid'. Mr Samuel Tullidaff, son of Thomas Tullidaff, who was minister at Foveran, was a regular expectant of the presbytery of Ellon. After failing to secure a presentation to Slains in 1618, he became schoolmaster at Ellon.[23]

Patronage continued to be the practice of the church, and those who wished to become ministers sought presentations from patrons. In practice the wishes of the congregation were often taken into account, but the final word was that of the patron. An example of concern for the wishes of a congregation took place when the parish of Kippen was vacant in 1618. Commissioners from that parish were asked by the bishop and presbytery of Dunblane:

> anent thair opinioun and favor to Mr Harrie Livingstoune, quhom they have hard, ... or gif they desyre to heir ony uther young man awaiting upon the ministerie to teach to thame.

The parishioners did ask to hear a second candidate, but finally reported that they preferred Mr Livingston; and in 1619 he became the next minister of Kippen.[24] An even more interesting example of concern for all interested parties took place at Paisley in 1606. The patron of Paisley, 'the ryt noble James, Lord of Abercorn, promeissed ... [to] give over all and haill the benefice ... of Paisley ... to such a qualified pastour as all pairteis quha hes any interest therin could agrie and condiscend upoun to choose', and a new minister was elected by the patron, the Bishop of the Isles (and former minister of Paisley), and commissioners from the kirk session.[25]

However, if a patron insisted upon a candidate his rights were upheld even though that candidate might be unpopular in a

---

[23] Dunblane Presb., 23 October 1617; Ellon Presb., 13 March 1610, 27 October 1618, 22 September 1619, 27 December 1620.
[24] Dunblane Presb., 21 January, 18 March, 1 April, 6 May 1619.
[25] Paisley Presb., 27 March 1606.

ADMISSION TO THE MINISTRY 139

parish. In 1618, Mr John Mercier, the fiery-tempered minister of Methlick, 'obtenit presentatioun from the principall, masters, and memberis of the Kingis Colledge of Aberdeen, patronis of the kirk of Slaynis'. However, the parishioners of Slains, including the Earl of Erroll, thought Mr Mercier 'ane sawer of seditioun, ... ane bissie body, ... ane perturber of the peice, ... and we heir he is ane cauld gospellar'. They urged that young Mr Samuel Tullidaff, who had assisted at Slains for the past seven years, be given the presentation. However, their objections were overruled and by 1619 Mr Mercier was settled at Slains.[26]

Presentations were directed to presbyteries before 1610 and to bishops after that date.[27] In either case a candidate was tried or examined by a presbytery prior to his ordination. In 1641 Alexander Henderson wrote that presbyteries examined candidates in 'Latine, Greek, and Hebrew, in his interpreting of Scripture, in the controversies of Religion, in his gift of exhortation, in the holy and Ecclesiasticall History and Chronologie'.[28] During the previous generation synods had established 'Canones for tryall of ministers' which outlined examinations in Hebrew, Greek, and Latin.[29]

Some other examinations were as extensive,[30] but most were considerably less strenuous. The complete trials of a candidate for Southdean in 1609 and a candidate for Kilmacolme in 1630 consisted of an exercise before the presbytery.[31] In most cases extensive examinations were probably redundant. A candidate had often been an expectant in a presbytery for some years; his abilities and weaknesses would be well-known to the brethren long before he received a presentation. Even if a candidate came from another presbytery, he would arrive with a carefully prepared testimonial from a presbytery that did know him well. Further extensive examinations were hardly necessary for most men.

After passing his trials a candidate was expected to have an edict

[26] Ellon Presb., 27 October 1618, 22 September 1619.
[27] See above, 24–5.
[28] *Government and Order if the Church of Scotland*, 7.
[29] Calderwood, VII, 155 (Synod of Lothian); Ellon Presb., 23 July 1623 (Synod of Aberdeen); Fife Synod, 269–70.
[30] Ellon Presb., 23 July, 6 August, 20 August, 1 October, 15 October, 1623.
[31] Jedburgh Presb., 12 July, 23 August, 6 September, 13 September, 7 December 1609; Paisley Presb., 25 February, 11 March 1630.

served at the parish to which he was presented, informing the parishioners of his appointment and giving them an opportunity to object. Serving an edict was an old reformation tradition and went back to the earliest service book or Book of Common Order. After Mr James Fisher was approved by the presbytery of Jedburgh in 1626 he:

> reported that he had caused serve ane edict at the Kirk of Sudan in name and behalff of the Archbishop of Glasgow warning the Parochiners of that congregatioun to compeir befor the Presbyterie of Jedburgh this day, and to object if anything they had against the admission of the said Mr James ... and being called upon commissioner for the rest George Eliphiston did deliver thair consent, objecting nothing.[32]

Any investigation of Scottish ordinations in the seventeenth century must take account of the fact that the word 'ordination' did not have the precise meaning which it now has. Prior to 1610 the most common terms were either 'inauguration' or 'admission'.[33] Furthermore, the word 'ordination' might mean an ordination in the twentieth-century sense of the word,[34] but it equally could mean an 'institution'. As late as 1620 some parishioners of Collace protested that 'Mr Andro Forrester be not ordained minister at thair kirk speciallie because he being a minister of befoir bringes not ane testimoniall from his presbyterie'. Mr Forrester had been a minister since 1588 and had served at Glencorse, Corstorphine and Dunfermline. The protest of the parishioners was disallowed by the presbytery of Perth, who ordered one of their members 'to give him institutioun' and charged the parishioners 'to be present at the said ordinatioun'.[35] Because terminology was varied, it is unwise in studying particular cases to place much reliance upon the presence or absence of words like 'ordination', 'admission' or 'inauguration'.

Difference of opinion also existed in the sixteenth century about

---

[32] Jedburgh Presb., 28 June 1626.

[33] Cf. Duncan Shaw, 'The Inauguration of Ministers in Scotland', 35–37. Shaw argues that 'admission' meant 'induction', but I have found a number of examples where 'admission' was used in place of 'ordination' (e.g. Ellon Presb., 3 May 1598; Edinburgh Presb., 1 June 1603).

[34] The second Book of Discipline spoke of 'the ceremonies of ordinatioun' (*B.U.K.* II, 493 [Calderwood, III, 534]).

[35] Perth Presb., 9 February 1620; *Fasti*, IV, 199; VIII, 3.

ADMISSION TO THE MINISTRY

the practice of the laying on of hands. The first Book of Discipline rejected that action.

Other ceremony than the public approbation of the people, and declaration of the chief minister, ... we cannot approve; for albeit the Apostles used the imposition of hands, yet seeing the miracle is ceased, the using of the ceremony we judge is not necessary.[36]

However, the second Book of Discipline favoured the practice. 'The ceremonies of ordinatioun ar fasting, ernest prayer, and impositioun of handis of the elderschip'.[37] James insisted upon imposition of hands, and required Robert Bruce of Edinburgh to receive the laying on of hands before admission to the ministry there. In 1597 an assembly ordered 'that there be an uniformitie in the ordinatioun of the Ministrie throughout the haill countrey, impositioun of hands'.[38]

What happened when a candidate was ordained or admitted to the ministry between 1600 and 1610? Unfortunately, evidence is too slight to allow more than tentative conclusions on several points. Presbyteries continued to ordain, normally with the addition of commissioners from surrounding presbyteries.[39] Only rarely did a presbytery record describe an ordination sufficiently to indicate whether the laying on of hands was used or not. The presbytery of Paisley ordained a man in 1605 *per impositionem manuum presbyteratus*, but the following year they apparently only gave another candidate *dexteras societatis*'.[40] To generalise from these two cases would be unwise, but probably the use of imposition was increasing.

[36] Knox, *History of the Reformation* (Dickinson), II, 286. W. McMillan and others have proposed alternative interpretations. However, their explanations have, I think, been decisively answered by Duncan Shaw, who argues that the reformers meant exactly what they wrote – the 'ceremony ... is not necessary' (W. McMillan, *The Worship of the Scottish Reformed Church*, 343; Duncan Shaw, 'The Inauguration of Ministers in Scotland', 39–46).

[37] *B.U.K.* II, 493 (Calderwood, III, 534).

[38] Calderwood, V. 721–3; *B.U.K.* III, 925 (Calderwood, V. 642).

[39] E.g. Ellon Presb., 3 May 1598; Edinburgh Presb., 1 June 1603; Paisley Presb., 1 March 1604; Jedburgh Presb., 24 August, 5 October 1608, 21 December 1609. Occasionally no commissioners were present (Paisley Presb., 3 January 1605).

[40] Paisley Presb., 3 January 1605, 31 July 1606.

By 1600 the Church of Scotland had two rites for admission of a candidate to the ministry: (1) 'Of the Ministers and Their Election', first printed in *The forme of prayers and ministration of the Sacraments, &c., used in the Englische Congregation at Geneva*, 1556, and used in Scotland since 1560; and (2) *The Form and Order of the Election of the Superintendent which may serve in election of all other ministers*, 1569. Probably both of these rites were used for the admission of ministers in the late sixteenth and early seventeenth centuries, with the second rite probably gaining in popularity and frequency of usage.[41]

[41] This conclusion has been sharply challenged by Dr Duncan Shaw who argues that use of *The Form and Order* for admission of ministers was precluded by a general assembly act in 1570 and 'could not be used for the admission of ministers other than superintendents'. And since no superintendents were appointed after 1561, 'it is extremely doubtful whether this order of service was used again during the remainder of the sixteenth century'. Perhaps, but several questions are unanswered by Shaw's interpretation. The act to which Shaw refers was passed in July 1570. Its primary purpose was to prevent ministers from abandoning their ministry. 'Because some, who had once accepted the office and charge of preaching the word, had deserted their calling, the Assembly ordained, That all and sundry Ministers, who hereafter shall accept the said office, shall be inaugurate publickly, *conform to the order appointed in the end of the Booke of Excommunicatione*'. (*B.U.K.* I, 176 [Calderwood, III, 2], italics added.)

Shaw argues that the 'Booke of Excommunication' refers to a sentence in the 1556 rite, 'Of the Ministers and Their Election': 'If so be the Congregation upon just cause agree to excommunicate, then it belongeth to the Minister, according to their generall determination, to pronounce the sentence'. Therefore only the 1556 rite was authorized, and *The Form and Order* could not be used for the admission of ministers other than superintendents. Perhaps, but the sentence in the 1556 rite is simply a reference to excommunication; and the assembly act spoke of the 'order appointed in the end of the Booke of Excommunication'. (Calderwood's copy of the act had 'the treatise of excommunicatioun'.)

What was the 'Booke [or Treatise] of Excommunication'? A year earlier, in July 1569, an assembly ordered the printing of 'the form of excommunication with the inauguration of the superintendents and ministers' (*B.U.K.* I, 155 [Calderwood, II, 493]). Later that year these services were printed in Edinburgh by Robert Lekprevik, a leading Scottish reformed printer. The title page of that edition read *The Ordoure of Excommunicatioun and of Publict Repentance*, but the edition included (as the assembly had ordered) not only *The Ordoure of Excommuncatioun* but also *The Form and Order of the Election of the Superintendent which may serve in election of all other ministers*. Therefore the simplest explana-

ADMISSION TO THE MINISTRY 143

tion of the assembly's action in 1570 was that 'the Order appointed in the end of the Booke of Excommunication' meant *The Form and Order of the Election of the Superintendent* ... This was the form which came immediately after the 'Booke of Excommunication', and since the title page of Lekprevik's edition referred only to *The Ordoure of Excommunicatioun*, the 1569 admission rite was literally 'in the end of the Booke of Excommunication'. In other words, the assembly of 1570, far from precluding use of *The Form and Order* for the admission of ministers, was in fact encouraging its use. And it is no surprise that the next edition of the Book of Common Order, in 1571, included for the first time *The Order of Excommunication* and *The Form and Order of the Election of the Superintendent* ... Both services continued to be included regularly in subsequent editions.

Shaw's interpretation also assumes that an ambiguous reference in one assembly act would prevent use of a service which continued to be printed and available to all ministers. If the general assembly really wanted an action enforced, they found it necessary to insist on the point again and again. It does not seem likely that presbyteries would avoid using a printed and available service because of an ambiguous reference in the unprinted acts of one general assembly.

Furthermore, *The Form and Order* had impeccable Reformation credentials. It was first used at the admission of Mr John Spottiswood as Superintendent of Lothian 'at Edinburgh the 9th of March 1560 [/61], John Knox being Minister'. And *The Form and Order* had one great advantage over the earlier rite since it included a large number of searching questions which were put to the candidate and to which he must publicly respond. And, like the earlier rite, *The Form and Order* did not include the laying on of hands.

Possibly late sixteenth-century church court records may have some additional evidence, but at present I think it likely that *The Form and Order* was used – and probably increasingly used – in the late sixteenth and early seventeenth century for the admission of ministers. (Duncan Shaw, 'The Inauguration of Ministers in Scotland', 46–48. *Of the Ministers and Their Election* was included in many editions of the Book of Common Order. The 1556 version is reprinted in William D. Maxwell, *The Liturgical Portions of the Genevan Service Book*, Oliver and Boyd, 1931, 165–8. *The Form and Order of the Election of the Superintendent* was also included in many editions of the Book of Common Order after 1570 and was reprinted in Knox, *History of the Reformation in Scotland* [Dickinson], II, 273–9. An original copy of the Lekprevik edition of *The Ordoure of Excommunicatioun* is in the Lambeth Palace Library. It is described by Robert Dickson and John Philip Edmond, *Annals of Scottish Printing*, MacMillan & Bowes, 1890, 239–40; the title page of that edition is reproduced in Knox, *Works* [Laing], VI, 447. Also see W. Cowan, *A Bibliography of the Book of Common Order and Psalm Book of the Church of Scotland, 1556–1644*, Edinburgh, 1931, p. 66 and Nos. 11, 16, 17, 19, 21, 24, 27, 31, 33, 53, 57.)

144   THE CHURCH BEFORE THE COVENANTS

The Glasgow assembly of 1610 made no change in the admission or ordination rite although that assembly did require a bishop to be the chief minister at an ordination.[42] In the same year James sent instructions that ordination was to be by imposition of hands 'and to that end an uniform order may be kept in the admission of ministers, that a form thereof may be imprinted and precisely followed of every bishop'.[43] Ten years passed before that form was printed. Row declared that shortly after 1610 ordinations by bishops began in 'a new and uncouth forme'.[44] Unfortunately, he does not elaborate; but his statement (if true) probably did not refer to the English Ordinal. References to that Ordinal appear around the end of the period but not in the years immediately after 1610. The most readily available services would be the two printed in the *Book of Common Order*. In 1618 Calderwood was able to attack the Perth Articles by appealing to one of the questions in *The Form and Order of the Election of the Superintendent* which, he declared, was used by 'the ministers of this church . . . at their admissions'.[45]

Fortunately, a series of ordinations held by Archbishop Gladstanes between 1611 and 1614 were recorded in greater detail than was customary. Nine ordinations were held and all followed the same basic pattern. One of the first was the ordination of Mr Ninian Drummond to the Kirk of Kinnoull on 19 April 1611:

> The quhilk day the ryt reverend Father in God Georg, Archbishop of St Androis, and with his Lordship, Mr William Coupar, the Bishop of Dunblane, Mr Arthur Futhie [and three other ministers], . . . being convenit at the said kirk together with the gentlemen, eldaris, and deaconis and parochinaris of Kinnoull for plantatioun of Mr Ninian Drummond in the ministrie thairof. After incalling of Godis holy name and exhortation maid be the said ryt reverend father, the edict for the effect forsaid wes giffen in executt upon the saboth preceiding.

No objections were made to the ordination:

> And thairfor the said ryt reverend father proceidit to the

---
[42] *B.U.K.* III, 1096 (Calderwood, VII, 100); also see below, 151-3.
[43] Spottiswood, *History*, III, 211.
[44] Row, *History*, 302.
[45] Calderwood, VII, 330.

ADMISSION TO THE MINISTRY 145

plantatione foirsaid, posed the said Mr Ninian upon his consciens anent his sinceritie in entrie to the holy ministrie and constant resolutioun to glorifie God thairin, with uther ordinar questiounes, took his oath of obediens to the King his majestie and to his ordinar, And thairefter with prayer and impositioun of handis of the said ryt reverend father and brethren of the ministrie abovenamed wes resavit and admitted to the ministrie of the said Kirk with power to preach the word, minister the sacraments and exerce the haill partes of the ministrie, ffinallie wes resavit be [eight] . . . eldaris in name of the haill parochinairs, and the brethren gaiff to him *dextram societatis*. Thanks giffen to God the meiting ceased.[46]

Subsequent ordinations by the archbishop sometimes used slightly different questions. At Kennoway a candidate was asked:

anent his sinceritie in the entrie to the holy ministrie, . . . soundnes in the professioun of the trew religoun as it is presentlie taucht and avowed in this kirk and kingdome of Scotland, with sum uther ordinar questiouns.

And ordinands were often admitted 'to the holy ministrie with power to preache the word, minister the holy sacraments and exerceis discipline'.[47]

The service used by Archbishop Gladstanes was influenced by both *The Form and Order of the Election of the Superintendent* and the English Ordinal, but it was not a copy of either. In fact, the nearest Scottish parallel to these ordinations was the Scottish Ordinal of 1620.

The 1620 Ordinal seems to have been as little known in its own day as in ours.[48] The only contemporary reference is in a letter sent by Archbishop Laud to Bishop Wedderburn of Dunblane in 1636. Only one copy of the Ordinal is known to be extant.[49] It is likely, therefore, that the Scottish Ordinal was not itself widely

[46] Fife Synod, 29.
[47] *Ibid.* 33, 37, 53.
[48] The Ordinal ws reprinted in *The Miscellany of the Wodrow Society*, I, 597–615, and in G. W. Sprott, *Scottish Liturgies of the Reign of James VI* (William Blackwood and Sons, Edinburgh, 1901), 111–131.
[49] *The Forme and Maner of Ordaining Ministers and Consecrating of Arch-bishops and Bishops, used in the Church of Scotland* Thomas Finlason, 1620, Edinburgh. National Library of Scotland, Edinburgh: STC 16605 (Aldis 549).

used, and it probably had little influence in determining the tradition of Scottish ordinations. However, the reverse may well be true, for contemporary Scottish practice appears to have determined to a considerable extent the material which went into the 1620 Ordinal.

The 1620 *Forme and Maner of Ordaining Ministers* took its structure and much of its text from *The Form and Order of the Election of the Superintendent*. However, material from the English Ordinal was inserted into the Scottish structure in the first half of the service. A comparison of *The Form and Order* with the 1620 Scottish Ordinal makes this point clear.

The Form and Order ... (*Book of Common Order*)	1620 Ordinal[50]
Edict previously served	Edict previously served
Sermon	Sermon
	Presentation (English text)
Challenge to people	Challenge to people (English text)
Election and promise of obedience by people	
	Oath of Supremacy (English text)
	Exhortation (English text)
Questions to candidate	Questions to candidate (English text)
Questions to congregation	
Charge to nobility	Charge to people (Scottish text)
Prayer for candidate	Prayer for candidate (Scottish text)
Our Father	Our Father
	Laying on of Hands (Scottish text from Benediction)
	Delivery of Bible
Right hand of fellowship	Right hand of fellowship
Benediction	
Final exhortation	Final exhortation (Scottish text)

[50] The text of the 1620 rite and its sources are compared in my thesis, 'Ecclesiastical Administration in Scotland: 1600–1638', (Edinburgh, 1963), 376–401. The English structure for the Ordination of Priests is quite different: exhortation, collect for purity, epistle from Acts or Timothy, gospel from Matthew or John, Veni Creator, presentation, challenge to people, litany, collect, oath of supremacy, exhortation to candidates, questions to candidates, silent prayer, prayer, laying on of hands, delivery of Bible, creed, English communion service, final prayer (post-communion), blessing.

Psalm 23   Psalm 23
              Prayer and Benediction (English and
              Scottish texts)

The preface to the Ordinal began with an appeal to Scottish Reformation history – the edicts of the general assembly of 1570[51] – and closed with the ambiguous statement that this form 'hereafter shall be observed by these that have power to ordaine or consecrate'. Thereafter the Ordinal largely followed the Scottish structure but introduced considerable material from the English Ordinal in the early part of the service. The main English borrowings are in the Oath of Supremacy, the Exhortation, and the Questions to the Candidate. The latter half of the service comes almost entirely from *The Form and Order of the Election of the Superintendent*. Moreover, important elements in the English rite were ignored in 1620; the service was not set within the framework of the Holy Communion, and neither the Litany nor the Veni Creator was included.[52]

Even when English material was borrowed, it was often altered to fit the Scottish situation. Everywhere the English assumption that several men were to be ordained at the same time was altered to the more usual Scottish practice of ordaining men individually.[53] The word 'priest' was regularly changed to 'minister'; unpopular English congregational responses (such as the Litany) were not introduced; short English collects were not retained in their collect form but were inserted into longer Scottish prayers. The episcopal 'we' was changed to a simpler 'I' in some cases, but not all; and Scottish egalitarianism (as well as the language of the Book of Common Order) may well be reflected when both the archdeacon and the bishop address the candidate as 'Brother'.

The 1620 Ordinal can hardly be called a very original composition, but it may well have been typical of the general tradition of ordinations in Scotland between 1610 and 1635. There are some interesting parallels between the 1620 Ordinal and the ordinations held by Archbishop Gladstanes. The structure of the rite used by

[51] Dr Shaw points out that the Preface incorrectly dated the assembly as March instead of July, 1570 (Duncan Shaw, 'The Inauguration of Ministers in Scotland', 47).
[52] The Veni Creator was in the Scottish Psalm Book.
[53] 'These persons' became 'this Brother'; 'the persouns' became 'this person'; 'your selves' was altered to 'your selfe', etc.

the archbishop, in so far as it can be determined, was almost identical with the 1620 rite. An edict was served, often on the previous Sunday. The ordination began with prayers and a sermon. A challenge to the congregation was followed by the oath of supremacy and questions to the candidate. After prayers, the candidate was ordained with imposition of hands by the archbishop and ministers present and was then received by his elders with the right hand of fellowship. The service concluded with a final thanksgiving.

The questions asked by Gladstanes varied somewhat from service to service and may have been extemporary ones. However, there was one striking parallel between the text used by Gladstanes and the 1620 Ordinal.

Archbishop Gladstanes

And wes with prayer and impositioun of the handis of the said ryt reverend father and brethren of the ministrie admitted to the holy ministrie with *power to preach the word, minister* the *holy sacraments, and exerceis discipline.*[54]

1620 Ordinal

The BISHOPE, with the MINISTERS that are present, shall lay their hands upon the head of him that is to be admitted ... and the BISHOPE shall say, – In the name of God ... wee give unto thee *power* and authoritie *to preach the Word* of God, *to minister* his *holie Sacraments, and exercise Discipline.*

Subsequent ordinations by other bishops usually record only the use of prayers and the imposition of hands. Probably imposition was normal, although it may not have been universal, since the Aberdeen assembly in 1616 found it necessary to order 'that none teache in pulpit publictly before the people, but these that have received imposition of hands; and whosoever does otherways be incapable of the Ministry'.[55] The evidence is meagre, but a tentative conclusion is that a generally conservative tradition was followed by Scottish bishops between 1610 and 1635. The major influence was *The Form and Order of the Election of the Superintendent* which was familiar and widely used before 1610. Imposition

---
[54] Fife Synod, 33.
[55] *B.U.K.* III, 1124 (Calderwood, VI, 230).

ADMISSION TO THE MINISTRY

of hands was probably normal and represented one of the major additions to *The Form and Order*. Some prayers and questions may have been extemporary, but the general structure of the rite followed *The Form and Order*, perhaps with the insertion of some texts from the English Ordinal. The 1620 Ordinal was in this general tradition.

Near the end of the period, references to use of the English Ordinal are found for the first time. James Gordon, who wrote after the Restoration, declared that 'the Bishopps, whilst they gave Orders to Ministers, did use the English Service Booke'. *The Large Declaration*, which was printed in 1639, was more cautious. 'The Bishops *or some of them* never gave Orders . . . but they used the English Service-book'.[56]

A new Scottish Ordinal was being considered in 1635. A draft copy was included in the manuscript liturgy produced in Scotland in 1635 and sent to Charles in April of that year. Although the contents of this draft liturgy are not precisely known, Charles referred to the ordinal in his reply:

> We have sene and approved of the Liturgie sent by yow to us, with the book of Canons [and] the forme and maner of making and consecrating of bischops, presbiteris and deacones. . . . We recommend that all be furthwith printed.[57]

Nothing was printed immediately, however, and a year later the 1620 Ordinal was still being considered. In April 1636 Archbishop Laud sent a significant letter to James Wedderburn, the new Bishop of Dunblane:

> By these last Letters of yours, I find that you are consecrated; God give you joy. And whereas you desire a Coppy of our Booke of Ordination, I have heere sent you one. And I have acquainted his Majesty with the two great reasons that you give,[58] why the

[56] J. Gordon, *History of Scots Affairs*, I, 6; *Large Declaration*, 20 (italics added). *The Large Declaration* was attributed to Charles I but was probably written by Dr Balcanquhall, perhaps with the assistance of Archbishop Spottiswood and Bishop Maxwell. It may well describe the practice of the 'Canterburian bishops'. (Baillie, *Letters and Journals*, I, 140, 175, 208.)

[57] Charles Rogers, *The Earl of Stirling's Register of Royal Letters*, II, 856; Gordon Donaldson, *The Making of the Prayer Book of 1637*, 48.

[58] 'That you give' certainly implies that these criticisms of the Scottish Ordinal originated with the Bishop of Dunblane and not with Archbishop Laud. Undoubtedly Laud would have agreed.

Booke which you had in K. Iames his time is short and insufficient At first, that the order of Deacons is made but as a Lay Office at least, as that Booke may be understood.[59] And secondly, that in the admission to Priesthood, the very essentiall words of conferring Orders are left out. At which, his Majesty was much troubled, . . . [and] he hath commanded me to write, *that either you doe admit of our booke of Ordination, or else that you amend your owne in these two grosse oversights . . . and then see the Booke reprinted.*[60]

A Scottish Ordinal was probably printed later that year, although its contents are unknown and no copy is known to be extant. However, there are a number of references to its publication. Row declared, 'In the yeare 1636, the Bishops caused print a Book of Ordination'. The Glasgow Assembly of 1638 also referred to the new Ordinal:

> Then there was a large and learned Treatise red by these reverend brethren . . . descryving the Idolatrie and Superstition of the Service book, the tyrannie and usurpation of the Booke of Cannons and Ordination, and the unlawfulness of the High Commission.

And in the discussion which followed, Mr Andrew Cant declared, 'I think that Booke of Ordination like the beast in the Revelation'.[61]

Further evidence of the increasing influence of English practice can be seen in the ordination of at least one man as a 'preaching deacon' in 1637. In that year Mr John Trotter became minister of Dirleton. A year later some of his parishioners registered a large bill of complaints against him, including the fact that he 'did befor his admission to that calling receave the ordour of a preaching deacon, quhilk office [was] never heard of in this kirk till of lait'. Mr Trotter replied that 'as for the receaving the ordour of deacon-

[59] This is a surprising statement since there is no mention of the diaconate in the surviving 1620 Ordinal. Dr Sprott conjectured that a subsequent edition may have been issued with more definite provisions for the diaconate as an order of the ministry (G. W. Sprott, *Scottish Liturgies* [1871], lviii).

[60] W. Prynne, *Hidden Works of Darkness*, 152–3, italics added. The last lines of this letter imply that the English Ordinal was not recognised as authoritative in Scotland. Even copies of the Ordinal were not readily available.

[61] Row, *History*, 391; A Peterkin, *Records of the Kirk*, 163–4; cf. J. Gordon, *Scots Affairs*, II, 92–3.

ADMISSION TO THE MINISTRY 151

shipe, treuly I grant I did receave that ordour, bot presentlie efter the order of ane presbyter'. There may have been other cases. The 1638 Assembly took care to include 'Preaching-deacons' among those titles such as 'Abbots, Pryors, Deans, Arch-deacons' which were to be 'banished out of this reformed Kirk'.[62]

If there is uncertainty about the rite used in admission of ministers between 1600 and 1638, there is less doubt about the presiding minister at ordinations. The greatest change which the assembly of 1610 introduced into the practice of admission was the requirement that a bishop be the invariable presiding minister at an ordination. Each bishop 'being assisted be such of the Ministrie of the bounds quher he is to serve, as he will assume to himselfe . . . [is] to perfyte the haill act of ordinatioun'.[63] This practice was widely and (as nearly as I can discover) universally followed between 1610 and 1637. Although it has often been asserted that presbyteries occasionally ordained ministers by themselves, evidence for such ordinations is singularly slight. In some cases an ordination has been confused with an institution.[64] Other exceptions have assumed that a man who refused to take an oath of conformity to obey the Perth Articles was therefore ordained only by a presbytery.[65]

The two best known examples of men who may have been non-

[62] Haddington Presb., 18 April, 2 May 1638; A. Peterkin, *Records of the Kirk*, 37.

[63] *B.U.K.* III, 1096 (Calderwood, VII, 100).

[64] Thus, Mr William Forbes was not ordained 'to one of the town charges of Aberdeen by the laying-on of the hands of three ministers' in 1616 (W. G. S. Snow, *Patrick Forbes*, 156). Forbes was minister of Alford in 1614 and was moved to Monymusk in 1615. The general assembly of 1616 'transportis' Mr Forbes to Aberdeen and in October two ministers 'admittit and resaved Mr Willieame Forbes, minister at Monymusk, ane of the ordinar ministers of this burgh . . . with full and uniforme consent and applause of the haill congregatioun, and with earnest prayeris to God for a blessing on his travellis, and with all uther solemnitie requisitt' (*Selections from the Ecclesiastical Records of Aberdeen*, 85; *Fasti*, VI, 118, 175).

[65] Thus we do not 'read of ministers being admitted to their office without any semblance of episcopal ordination' (W. G. S. Snow, *Patrick Forbes*, 156). This assertion is based on a statement by John Livingston who attempted to secure the parish of Torphichen in 1626. 'But Mr John Spotswood, the pretended Bishop of St Andrews, stopped all because of my unconformity; and when the Earle of Lithgow, and Lord Tarphichen, and some others, dealt with him upon my behalf, for *even at*

episcopally ordained were John Forbes of Corse and Samuel Rutherford of Anwoth. John Forbes has often been said to have been 'ordained by a Dutch presbytery' in 1619. Dr Henderson has examined the evidence in some detail and concluded that 'what precisely happened is not completely evident, but certainly this statement is wrong'. His conclusion is based mainly on the facts that two of the five 'ordaining' presbyters were not members of the presbytery of Walcheren, nor is there any evidence in the minutes of that presbytery of any ordination of Mr Forbes.[66]

Samuel Rutherford is also said to have been 'ordained according to the Presbyterian form to the parish of Anworth'. The evidence for this conclusion is a statement by the editor of *Mr Rutherfoord's Letters* which were published in 1664:

> Of his being called thence to the Ministry in *Anworth* (to which charge he entered, by the means of that worthy Noble-man my Lord Kenmur, *without giving any engagement to the Bishop*) where he laboured night & day with great success.

The term 'engagement' was not in common use in 1627. This statement may mean that Rutherford was ordained by the presbytery of Kirkcudbright, but it more probably means that Rutherford was one of several ministers who were admitted after 1625 without giving an oath of obedience to his bishop that he would conform to the Perth Articles.[67] In any case, evidence that either of these men received non-episcopal ordination is hardly conclusive.

[66] G. D. Henderson, 'The Ordination of John Forbes of Corse', 33–5.
[67] W. G. S. Snow, *Patrick Forbes*, 156; *Historical Papers of the Christian Unity Association*, 139; S. Rutherford, *Joshua Redivius, or Mr Rutherfoord's Letters*, Preface, 82r. Cf. John Row's statement that Mr Rutherford was confined in Aberdeen for his book against Arminianism and his 'want of conformitie' (Row, *History*, 396).

---

that time some few by moyen were suffered to enter the ministrie without conformity, he pretended that, *nothwithstanding of my unconformity*, he should not hinder my entrance in some other place' (Wodrow, *Select Biographies*, 2, 136, italics added). After 1618 'conformity' was a common term and always referred to conformity to the Perth Articles. Some men were ordained without taking an oath of conformity, especially in the early years of the reign of Charles I; and Charles found it necessary to threaten bishops with deposition if they continued to ordain men without first requiring a 'band of conformitie' (Balfour, *Works*, II, 143–4). There is no evidence of any connection between refusal to take an oath of conformity and ordination by a presbytery.

ADMISSION TO THE MINISTRY 153

Ordinations by presbyteries did begin in 1638. On 11 April the presbytery of Haddington ordained Mr Robert Ker at Prestonpans. 'By impositione of hands of the presbiterie and earnest prayer to God, he was admitted to the ministerie thair'. Two weeks later the presbytery of Kirkcaldy, 'having the power of ordinatioun and admissioun *jure divino*,' did the same, as did the presbytery of Lanark in May.[68] These ordinations were part of the growing revolt against episcopal authority in 1638, but there is no convincing evidence that similar ordinations took place between 1610 and 1637.

Following his ordination, a minister received collation, either from a presbytery before 1610 or from his bishop after that date. He was then instituted into his parish, usually by one or two members of his presbytery. In 1609 a member of the presbytery of Jedburgh reported that 'he had given institution to Mr Thomas Thompsoun upon his presentation to the kirk as wes ordaineit and that the people of Hopkirk had verie lovinglie imbraced the said Mr Thomas'. A collation granted by the Bishop of Moray in 1615 to a new minister at Farnua required the moderator of the presbytery of Inverness to go to the parish kirk on Sunday and 'enter him to the reall possession of the saids personage and viccarage . . . be delyvering the buik of God in his hands'.[69]

One of the more significant facts about the ministers of the church is that their number was increasing. In 1596 an assembly declared that there were still 'above foure hundreth paroch kirks destitute of the ministrie of the word' and this figure did not include vacancies in Argyll and the Isles. Their complaint is corroborated by the Register of Assignation and Modification of Stipends which (omitting Argyll and the Isles) lists only five hundred and thirty-nine ministers as having received stipends in 1596.[70]

An assembly in 1608 still complained about 'the want of Preschers

[68] Haddington Presb., 11 April 1638; *Kirkcaldy Presb.*, 130; Lanark Presb., 31 May 1638.
[69] Jedburgh Presb., 3 May 1609; Bught Papers, D/3 (30 November 1615 [23 February 1682]).
[70] *B.U.K.* III, 876 (Calderwood, V, 416); Register of Assignation and Modification of Stipends, 1596–7. There were about nine hundred parishes in Scotland if those in Argyll and the Isles are not included.

in many congregatiouns in this land', but its report showed that some progress had been made. 'In ane province thretie ane Kirks are to be found vakand, and in uthers some 17 as in Nithesdaill, and in uthers 28 as in Annerdaill, and sicklyke throughout many uther parts of this land'. In 1610 Patrick Forbes of Corse wrote to James that he lived in 'pairtes wheir, within the precinct of two Presbiteries at leist, twentie and one churches lay unplaunted'. The same year the general assembly declared that 'through sundrie parts within this realme, as well in the highlands and borders as in the mid countrey ... there be many Kirks lying destitute of a Pastor'.[71]

However, subsequent assemblies did not renew complaints about large numbers of vacant parishes. Annandale and Nithsdale, which in 1596 had been described as 'destitute of Pastors', had progressed sufficiently to have three new presbyteries erected around 1625.[72] Ministers were settled at Ruthwell (1605), Kirkbean (1608), Kirkpatrick-Juxta (1612), Dornock (1612), Dryfesdale (1612), Hutton and Corrie (1615), Johnstone (1615), Mouswald (1615), Middlebie (1615), New Abbey (1618), etc.[73]

In 1621 Archbishop Spottiswood referred to the 'nyn hundreth or thairabout of Ministeris' in Scotland,[74] and it would appear that by the death of James VI the ministry of word, sacraments and discipline under qualified and reformed ministers was to be found widely throughout the parishes of Scotland.

During the early seventeenth century ministers continued to be admitted to their benefices by an ordered and lengthy process. After 1610 this process included an ordination at which a bishop was invariably the chief minister, although no attempt was made to reordain men who had received presbyterial ordination earlier. Much of the ordination or admission rite was a traditional one and reflected earlier reformation practice. No church and no process of admission has ever been able to exclude all unqualified and unworthy ministers. However, by 1638 the ministry of the reformed

[71] *B.U.K.* III, 1053, 1101 (Calderwood, V2, 765, VIII, 83); *O.L.* I, 227
[72] *B.U.K.* III, 862. The three presbyteries were Penpont, Lochmaben, and Middlebie (Annan). See above, 86.
[73] *Fasti*, II, 254, 277, 211, 244, 203, 205, 207, 218, 252, 293.
[74] *O.L.* II, 644.

Church of Scotland was certainly larger in number and probably included a higher proportion of men who had been trained in arts and divinity than at any time in the sixteenth century. And that ministry was successfully established and supported in most of the parishes of Scotland. That which had seemed only an ideal in 1560 had to a remarkable degree been realised.

CHAPTER EIGHT

A Constant Platt Achieved: Provision for the Ministry

A parish ministry established throughout the country depended to a considerable degree upon the provision of a regular and sufficient stipend or other income. An assembly in 1616 declared that 'the laik of competent maintainance of Ministers is the cheefe cause' of the evils facing the church.[1] Not all churchmen took such a completely economic view of the church's problems, but few would deny the importance of a satisfactory financial settlement. The framers of both Books of Discipline had given much thought to the financial support of the reformed kirk. Many general assemblies had urged that at least a 'constant platt' or common plan for adequate support of reformed ministers be established.[2] An assembly in 1596 was probably not exaggerating when it declared 'that in many places of the countrey, for lake of provision of sufficient stipends for provision of Pastors, the peiple lyis altogether ignorant of thair salvatioun'.[3]

An example of this situation was Lenzie, where the annual stipend in 1596 was only 'fourtie aucht lib. with the vicarage worth tuentie merkis'. No competent minister could be secured for this sum, and in 1598 the presbytery of Glasgow 'fund that the parochin of Leinyae is dissolute and gevin to all kind of impietie for laik of exercise of the word of God . . . and of all gud ordour in discipline'. Shortly thereafter the presbytery wrote 'the Abbot of Cambuskynett . . . schawing to him that for laik of stipend thair is apperandlie na service to be maid in the ministerie at the kirk of Leinyae . . . for it is ane miserabill congregatioun at this present'.[4]

[1] *B.U.K.* III, 1,125 (Calderwood, VIII, 102).
[2] Knox, *History of the Reformation* (Dickinson), II, 288–91, 300–306; *B.U.K.* II, 501–2, 635, 726, 778, III, 849–51, 927–8, 932, 940–1, 942–3, 969, 982, 988–9, 999, 1067.
[3] *B.U.K.* III, 876 (Calderwood, V, 416).
[4] *Maitland Misc.* I, 79, 92–3.

By 1600 a cumbersome but workable system of stipends had developed.[5] A minister usually received income from several different sources: the vicarage of his parish, perhaps the parsonage, an assignation from the thirds, and perhaps a pension or chaplaincy. The minister of Pittenweem drew a stipend from the priory of Pittenweem, the priory of St Andrews, the bishopric of St Andrews, and the abbey of Jedburgh; and the minister of Kilconquhar received a much smaller stipend from the priory of North Berwick and the bishopric of St Andrews.[6]

Not all stipends were inadequate. About five hundred merks[7] would have been a satisfactory minimum stipend in 1600. The stipends assigned in three areas in 1601 give some indication of the income to which ministers were entitled at the beginning of the century.[8]

ST. ANDREWS

Pittenweem	Mr Nichol Dalgleish	1822 m.
St Andrews	Mr George Gladstanes	1150 m.
Dunino	Mr William Erskine	800 m.
Abercrombie	Mr Alexander Forsyth	738 m.
Kilrenny	Mr James Melville	690 m.
Anstruther	Mr Robert Durie	675 m.
Newburne	Mr John Carmichael	653 m.
Forgan	Mr William Marche	650 m.
Crail	Mr Andrew Duncan	550 m.
St Andrews	Mr David Lindsay	500 m.
Carnbee	Mr David Mearns	313 m.
Kilconquhar	Mr John Rutherford	285 m.
St Leonards	Mr Robert Wilkie	200 m.
Largo	Mr John Auchenleck	91 m.

[5] For the history of stipends before 1600, see Gordon Donaldson, *Accounts of the Collectors of Thirds of Benefices; Scottish Reformation*, 63-4, 93-5; *R.P.C.* (Second Series), I, cvii–clxxvi.
[6] Reg. Assig. Stipends, 1601, Pittenweem, Kilconquhar (St Andrews).
[7] A merk was two-thirds of a pound. Thus five hundred merks equalled £333 6s. 8d.
[8] Compiled from Reg. Assig. Stipends, 1601, St Andrews, Paisley, and Deer.

PAISLEY

Renfrew	Mr John Hay	1990 m.
Paisley	Mr Andrew Knox	900 m.
Killellan	Mr George Sempill	460 m.
Mearns	George Maxwell	420 m.
Kilmacoln	Mr Daniel Cunningham	416 m.
Neilston	Mr Andrew Law	400 m. and vicarage
Inverkip	Mr Thomas Younger	400 m.
Lochwinnoch	Mr Patrick Hamilton	400 m. and vicarage
Houston	Mr John Cunningham	320 m.
Greenock	Mr John Laing	317 m.
Kilbarchan	Mr Robert Stirling	300 m.
Erskine	Mr William Brisbane	260 m.
Inchinnan	Mr Gabriel Maxwell	210 m.

DEER

Deer	Mr Abraham Sibbald	500 m.
Peterhead	Mr Thomas Bissett	460 m.
Rathven	Mr Duncan Davidson	250 m.
Cruden	Mr David Rattray	226 m.
Aberdour	David Howeson	220 m.
Ellon	Mr John Heriot	195 m.
Crimond	Mr John Gordon	150 m.
Fraserburgh	Mr Charles Ferme	130 m.
Slains	Mr Alexander Bruce	120 m. and vicarage
Tyrie	Mr John Howeson	90 m.
St Fergus	Mr David Robertson	60 m. and vicarage

St Andrews was an old and strong centre of the reformed Church. Ten out of fourteen ministers were assigned a stipend of five hundred merks or more. In Paisley only two stipends exceeded five hundred merks, although over half of the stipends reached four hundred merks. In northern Deer, on the other hand, nine out of eleven stipends were two hundred and fifty merks or less. Clearly, the immediate problem was to increase low stipends in some parishes, as well as to provide adequate stipends for parishes which were as yet 'unplanted'.

In 1596 James declared that it was:

> our good will to have all the kirks of Scotland plantit with Ministers, and sufficient livings appointed to them. . . . Therfor

we thought good to sett fordwart ane ordour for local stipends, founded upon this ground, that all the kirks of Scotland would have Ministers, and all Ministers stipends within thair awin paroches, of sick valour as ... might be obtainit from the taksmen of teinds, present possessours of the said rent.

And he added:

> We and our Counsell is most willing that the haill kirks be plantit, and the rents of the Ministers augmentit, so farre as lawfullie may be obtainit with consent of our Nobilitie, and uthers taksmen of teinds, whose rights, but [i.e. without] ordour of law, We cannot impare.[9]

James was not dissembling; his subsequent policies showed that he had honestly stated his intentions. He was prepared to support the augmentation of low stipends, provided this did not mean ignoring the legal rights of the nobility and other tacksmen and thereby alienating them.

The first significant step was taken in 1606. In that year parliament completed the restoration of temporalities of bishoprics and also erected many abbeys into temporal lordships. The latter action, which secured the legal claim of the nobility to their abbey lands, was accompanied by the appointment of a commission of bishops, ministers and noblemen 'to set doun and conclude ane sufficient and reasonable stipend for the minister of ilk kirk that salbe conteined in any of the creations quhilk salbe past in this present Parliament'. Moreover, the erections were not to pass the seals until 'the Ministeris sufficient and competent stipends be first modefeit, decernit and declarit'. In spite of some initial opposition in the Articles, the act was approved.[10] In exchange for secure rights to their lands, the lords were expected to guarantee an adequate stipend to the ministers dependent upon them.

Meetings of the appointed commissioners were held in subsequent years, and bishops vigorously maintained their right to an equal voice with laymen on the commission lest they should be forced 'to content so mony Churchis with a smal provisioun'.[11]

One hundred and thirty-three parishes are known to have had

[9] *B.U.K.* III, 867–8 (Calderwood, V, 412–3).
[10] *R.P.C.* VII, 222–3; *A.P.S.* IV, 299–300.
[11] *R.P.C.* VII, 232–3, 249, 402–3, 427; *A.P.S.* IV, 372–3, 431; *O.L.* I, 101.

stipends assigned '*secundum modificationem dominorem commissionariorum*',[12] and these stipends were cited in subsequent presentations. The commissioners did not always raise low stipends, but a number was given substantial increases. At Ellon the stipend was raised from 195 merks to 550 merks, at Clackmannan from 150 merks to 550 merks, at Lenzie from 253 merks to 600 merks, at Lauder from 338 merks to 600 merks, at Pettinain from 150 merks to 300 merks, at Carluke from 132 merks to 600 merks, at Tranent from 195 merks to 500 merks, and at Eckford from 300 merks to 500 merks.[13]

Not all stipends assigned by the commissioners were as high as these. Parliament set no minimum stipend, and some were left at a low figure. Some indication of the scope of the stipends assigned by the commissioners can be seen in the following table:

Stipends assigned to parishes annexed to erected abbeys[14]

Less than 150 merks	3
150 m. to 299 m.	33
300 m. to 399 m.	16
400 m. to 499 m.	19
500 m. to 599 m.	32
600 m. to 699 m.	19
700 m. and over	11
Total	133

Sixty-two of these parishes, or 46 per cent of the total, were assigned 500 merks or more. Thirty-six of them, or 27 per cent, could expect less than 300 merks.

To assign a stipend to a parish did not necessarily mean that a minister would receive the total amount assigned. Stipends were a matter for endless litigation, as can be seen in almost any volume of the Acts and Decreets of the Court of Session. Between February and July 1612 the court heard nine cases involving unpaid stipends.

[12] *R.M.S.* VI, 2,001, 2,002, 2,003, 2,004, 2,074, 2,075, 2,138, VII, 9 35, 139, 290, 1,222; Reg. Pres. IV, 37–40, 43–8, 52–6, 59–60.
[13] Reg. Assig. Stipends, Deer, 1601 (*R.M.S.* VI, 2074), Stirling, 1601 (*R.M.S.* VII, 1,222), Glasgow, 1601 (*R.M.S.* VII, 1,222), Melrose, 1601 (*R.M.S.* VII, 1,222), Lanark, 1601 (*R.M.S.* VII, 1,222; VI, 2003), Haddington, 1601 (*R.M.S.* VI, 2,004), Jedburgh, 1601 (*R.M.S.* VII, 290).
[14] Compiled from the charters of erections.

In one case the son of a deceased minister sought to recover stipends due his father, and in two cases augmentations granted by the 1606 commissioners were in dispute.[15] Moreover, the testaments of many ministers record large amounts of unpaid stipends and reveal the universal difficulty of collecting them. However, to assign a stipend was a first step and the work of the commissioners appointed in 1606 must have helped to improve the income of a number of ministers.

The 1606 commissioners could only assign stipends to that limited group of parishes affected by the erection of abbey lands, nor were the commissioners required to establish any minimum stipend. After 1610 some individual stipends were raised by those who possessed the teinds, and the 'bischopis and lords of platt' continued to meet as late as 1616 in an effort to improve stipends. However, the commissioners had no authority to raise stipends which did not fall under the provisions of the 1606 act, and when they attempted to do so at Udny in 1615, they were forced to acknowledge that 'be thair travells the minister or his provisioun wes litill or nathing betterit'.[16]

By 1616 the question of adequate stipends was again being debated. At James's request the assembly at Aberdeen appointed a large commission to consider 'the lack of the competent manteinance to Ministers'.[17] When parliament assembled the next year, there was much debate over the 'choosing of the Lords of the Articles. The noblemen . . . feared a prejudice to their estate, and namelie, touching the dissolution of the erectiouns, and of the right they had to the tythes'.[18] However, James had no intention of alienating the nobility by challenging 'the right they had to the tythes', and the Act passed by Parliament 'anent the Plantatioun of Kirkis'[18] illustrated once again the government's skill at finding a compromise solution. The act authorised a commission whose powers lasted for a year. The commission was composed of the chancellor and thirty-two members: bishops, noblemen, barons,

[15] Register of the Acts and Decreets of the Court of Session, CCLXXII, 21, 83–4, 84–5, 90–1, 120–1, 152–3, 188–9, 238–9, 245–6.
[16] In 1613 the Earl of Mar raised a minister's stipend 'out of pitie and for a support to him' (Airlie Muniments, 47/35). In 1614 the Earl of Kinghorn raised a tack of the teinds of Belhelvie from 260 merks to 500 merks (Dalhousie Muniments, 13/33, 14/2392). Ellon Presb., 8 May 1616.
[17] B.U.K. III, 1131–2 (Calderwood, VIII, 109–11).
[18] Calderwood, History, VII, 250; A.P.S. IV, 531–4.

and commissioners from burghs. They were authorised to consider any parish whose stipend was less than 500 merks and to assign a stipend from the teinds of the parish of not less than 500 nor more than 1,000 merks. Tacksmen and others who possessed the teinds were not only confirmed in their tacks; but as a compensation for the increased stipends which would be taken from the teinds, 'reasoun and equitie' demanded that the tacksmen be given a further extension of their tacks 'efter the expyring of the present takis'.

The commission was soon at work, hearing cases and issuing decrees. The copies of many decrees have been lost and the exact number issued is unknown. But the number must have been considerable. Copies of thirty-two decrees are extant, and there are many references in these decrees to other actions of the commissioners.[19] Usually a stipend of 500 to 600 merks was assigned, and a long extension was added to the existing tack as compensation to the tacksman. In many cases the new stipend was a considerable increase over previous stipends. Anwoth, which in 1601 was assigned a stipend of only 163 merks, was now given a stipend of 520 merks, and the tacks were extended for ninety-five years. In 1601 the minister of Stow could expect 226 merks. In 1618 this figure was raised to 600 merks, and the tacks were extended for seventy-three years.

Other evidence of the work of the 1617 commissioners can be found in burgh records. On 10 December 1617 the council of Edinburgh sent four commissioners to meet with 'the commissioneris appoyntit in parliament to tak ordour with modeficatione of ministeris stipendis'. A week later the council 'consentis that the stipend of the ministeris serving the cure at the Kirk of Currie salbe in all tyme cuming the soume of sex hundreth merks ... conforme to the act of the commissioneris appoyntit be his Majestie'. Later the council raised the stipend of Mr William

---

[19] Registers of Old Decreets Recorded in the Books of the Commission on Teinds (later referred to as Old Decreets). Summaries of many of these decrees are given in Connell, *Tithes*, II, Appendix, 44–5. In addition to thirty-two complete decrees, a number of decrees are extant which deal with only a portion of the teinds of a parish. Also decrees which were further revised by the Commission on Teinds after 1627 have disappeared from the extant records of the 1617 Commission (Connell, *Tithes*, I, 345n). For Anwoth and Stow, see Old Decreets, II, 999, I (2), 91.

A CONSTANT PLATT ACHIEVED 163

Black, minister at Dumbarny, Pottie and Moncrieff, from 400 merks (and vicarage) to 570 merks (and vicarage) by virtue of an agreement between the 'commissioners appointed for the modification of ministers' stipends' and the 'provost, bailies and council'.[20] Nor was it true that only ministers who favoured episcopacy received augmentations. One staunch opponent of episcopacy was Mr William Row, minister of Forgandenny. He had signed a protest against episcopacy in 1606 and the following year was imprisoned in Blackness Castle for his opposition to 'constant moderators'. Later he was warded in his parish, and even after his release in 1614 he refused to attend meetings of the presbytery of Perth, presumably because Bishop Lindsay was moderator.[21] According to a report in 1627, the stipend at Forgandenny was '40 bolls, 1 firlot victual, . . . togidder with the soume of 500 lib. assignit to the Minister be the Lordis Commissionaris in anno 1618 yeiris'.[22] In other words the augmented stipend at Forgandenny was just over 1,000 merks.

As with many compromises, none of the parties was completely satisfied with the decisions of the commissioners. Archbishop Spottiswood complained of the extension of tacks, whereby the church was 'more damnified than bettered'. However, James was not prepared to ignore the legal rights of tacksmen, and several assemblies in the past had proposed an extension of tacks as the best solution of a difficult problem.[23]

Calderwood accused the commissioners of uniting benefices 'to the number of two hundreth or thereby' and added that bishops were bribed to gain their consent. In the extant decrees of 1618 some parishes, such as Logie and Coldstone (Aberdeenshire),

[20] *Extracts from the Records of the Burgh of Edinburgh, 1604–26*, 171, 128, 172. Stipends in Edinburgh itself were steadily rising: 1596, 500 merks; 1605, 800 merks; 1614, 1000, 1616, 1200 merks, 1635, 2000 merks. Edinburgh had considerable difficulty in securing good ministers, which may in part account for their high stipends. (*Extracts, 1604–26*, 8, 10, 117, 139, 223, 230, 262; *1626–41*, xl, xliv; cf. *Spottiswood Miscellany*, II, 292, 295, 298).
[21] *Fasti*, IV, 209; *R.P.C.* VII, 385–91, 522, VIII, 434, X, 258; Perth Presb. *passim*. Mr Row's son, who became assistant minister at Forgandenny in 1624, regularly attended presbytery meetings.
[22] *Reports on the State of Certain Parishes in Scotland*, 166–7. After 1624 this stipend had to support two ministers, Mr Row and his son.
[23] Spottiswood, *History*, III, 252; *B.U.K.* III, 940–1, 988, 1026 (Calderwood, V, 687–8, VI, 178, 612).

were united.[24] However, if the commissioners did unite two hundred benefices, they must have issued a remarkable number of decrees. Nor was the proposal to provide a satisfactory stipend by the union of benefices a new one. Both Books of Discipline had recommended the practice, and an assembly in 1581 (when episcopacy was almost negligible) actually proposed a drastic series of unions which would have left only six hundred parishes in Scotland outside of Argyll and the Isles.[25]

No comprehensive settlement was intended or achieved by the 1617 commission, but its achievements did not go unnoticed in England. In 1628 Sir Benjamin Rudyerd reminded the English parliament that many English vicars received only £5 a year, while James had settled ministers 'through all Scotland, the Highland and the Borders' with stipends of £30 sterling (540 merks Scots).[26]

A second commission was authorised by parliament in 1621. No minimum or maximum stipend was specified by parliament, and little is known about the work of this commission. Some of its decrees were in existence in 1830.[27] In 1622 the synod of Fife ordered ministers who did not yet have 'local stipends, according to the rate of the lait platt' to appear before the commissioners at a meeting in November. The presbytery of Jedburgh sent commissioners the same year to appear 'befoir the Lords off the plat'.[28] Probably both commissions issued similar decrees, although the second one was not required to establish a minimum stipend of 500 merks and may not have done so in some cases.

At James's death in 1625 much progress had already been made towards providing satisfactory minimum stipends for ministers. No comprehensive settlement was attempted, but many individual stipends had been raised substantially. Presbytery records show a striking contrast between the frequent complaints made about

---

[24] Calderwood, VII, 302–3; Old Decreets, I (1), 10. A stipend of 650 merks was assigned to the combined parish. Temple was also united to Clerkington and Moorfoot in 1618. A stipend of 500 merks was assigned to the 'thrie vnited paroches' (*Reports on the State of Certain Parishes in Scotland*, 93–4).
[25] Knox, *History of the Reformation* (Dickinson), II, 310; *B.U.K.* II, 508, 480 (Calderwood, III, 550, 520).
[26] Benjamin Rudyerd, *His Speech in Behalf of the Clergie*, 3–4. Cf. *Calendar of State Papers, Domestic, 1628–29*, 164.
[27] *A.P.S.* IV, 605–9; Connell, *Tithes*, I, 120.
[28] Fife Synod, 251; Jedburgh Presb., 8 May, 12 June 1622.

inadequate stipends before 1610 and the virtual disappearance of those complaints by 1625.

Shortly after his accession Charles I issued his first act of revocation. This was the first of a series of acts, proclamations, letters, and eventually acts of parliament by which Charles sought to carry through a comprehensive reorganisation of ecclesiastical finance.[29] Although Charles's legislation had little real effect upon temporalities or ecclesiastical lands which had passed into the hands of the nobility, his scheme did establish machinery for the valuation and commutation of teinds and for the provision of adequate stipends from teinds which endured to the twentieth century. Probably no government could have carried through this comprehensive plan without alienating powerful groups, but the king's secretiveness and emphasis upon principle tended to increase opposition further. Sir James Balfour's explanation of the 1638 revolution was probably too simple, but he believed that the act of revocation 'was the ground stone of all the mischeiffe that folloued after, bothe to this kinges gouerniment and family'.[30]

A study of Charles's complex legislation, which affected the income of farmers, tacksmen and lords of erection, as well as of ministers, is beyond the scope of this study. The immediate question is the effect of this legislation upon the stipends of ministers.[31]

In February 1627 a commission of teinds was appointed by the King.[32] Among its other duties the Commission was to provide 'ministers with sufficient locall stipends and fies'. The next month the commissioners ordered 'the lowest minister's stipend to be eight chalders of victuall, or proportional in silver duties', that is 800 merks. Between 1630 and 1633 the commissioners assigned stipends to a few parishes. However, the commissioners appear to have been uncertain of their authority. They had been appointed only by the king, and no parliament had met to confirm their appointment. Some of their early augmentations were not to go into effect until 'ratified in parliament'.[33]

[29] *Source Book of Scottish History*, III, 66–77.
[30] Balfour, *Works*, II, 128.
[31] Much of the following discussion is based upon Connell, *Tithes*, I, Book IV, Chapter One. Many important documents are printed in the Appendix to this work.
[32] *R.P.C.* (Second Series), I, 509–16.
[33] Connell, *Tithes*, II, Appendix, 78, I, 339–44.

Until the parliament of 1633 many of the bishops and clergy were also uncertain whether they would benefit from Charles's scheme. In 1627 the bishops wrote to Charles, 'shewinng that quhat was intendit be his Majesty for a helpe to the churche, was lykly to prove the utter undowing thereof', and three years later the synod of Fife 'with one comoun voice, did heavelie regrait the apparant detriment and hurt quhilk is liklie to cum upon the estait of the Kirk, by occasion of the present cours of valuation of the gryt and small tythes quhilk is in hand.,[34] Charles tried to reassure them, and his first Scottish parliament passed acts which would eventually affect the majority of parishes in Scotland. Parliament appointed a new set of commissioners who were authorised 'effir the chosing and allowance of ilk kirk and parochin of the valuatione thairof, to appoint, modifie, and sett downe a constant and locall stipend and maintenance to ilk minister, to be payit out of the teinds of ilk parochine'. Parliament also approved the action of the 1627 commissioners:

> whairby it is fund meit and expedient that the lowest proportione for maintenance of ministers sall be aucht chalder of victuall or aucht hundreth markes proportionallie except such particular kirks occure whairin thair sall be a just, reassonable and expedient caus to goe beneath the forsaid quantitie.[35]

No maximum stipend was stipulated.

Between 1634 and 1636 the commissioners augmented a number of stipends. Eighteenth-century copies of twenty-seven decrees are extant,[36] and in these some considerable augmentations were made. Thus a stipend at Cockburnspath of 900 merks was augmented by 150 merks, and a stipend at Eccles of 800 merks was increased to 1,000 merks.[37] Stipends could only be augmented 'eftir the ... valuatione' of local teinds, and the teinds in many parishes had not been valued by 1636. However, Charles's legislation achieved two objects. In some parishes augmentations of

---

[34] Balfour, *Works*, II, 156; Fife Synod, 318–9.
[35] *A.P.S.* V, 35–9.
[36] A summary of their contents is in Connell, *Tithes*, II, Appendix, 279–80. One original decree in 1634 raised the stipend of the minister of Arbirlot from 600 m. to 700 m. (Dalhousie Muniments, 13/3).
[37] Old Decreets, III, 619, II, 938.

stipends were actually made. More important, Charles provided machinery whereby the whole of the teinds was potentially available for the use of the church. His plan was essentially that of the first Book of Discipline, which implicitly recognised that monastic lands were permanently alienated from the church, but demanded the whole of the spirituality for the use of the church.[38] That reform of ecclesiastical finance which in England did not begin until the nineteenth century had in Scotland started two centuries earlier.

Unfortunately, to augment a stipend did not mean that a minister would necessarily receive that augmentation. Stipends were not always easy to collect. In 1630 the synod of Moray asked the minister of Inverkeithney why he 'did not yeirlie exact his stipend as it was modified by the Lords of the Platt'. The minister 'answered that he had givin a Band [bond] to the Laird of Frendrocht that he suld seik no moire of him then he hed befoire'.[39] Assignments of stipends must therefore be used with caution in attempting to assess the actual income of ministers, and a more accurate index of their real income can be found in the testaments they left. The testaments of eighty-one ministers who died between 1600 and 1638 were filed in the Commissariot Courts of Edinburgh, Brechin, and Dunblane.[40] The average figures for each of the first four decades show a clear upward trend.

	Total number of testaments	Average value of movables	Average net assets
1600–1609	29	£282	£1,244
1610–1619	16	£271	£1,529
1620–1619	17	£751	£3,777
1630–1638	19	£597	£2,160

In these testaments the value of movables left by ministers had doubled between 1600 and 1638. Both testaments and stipends indicate that the income of ministers was rising. Moreover, this

---

[38] Gordon Donaldson, *Scottish Reformation*, 95.
[39] Moray Synod, 36.
[40] Compiled from the Edinburgh, Brechin, and Dunblane Testaments. Detailed references are in my thesis, 'Ecclesiastical Administration in Scotland', University of Edinburgh, 407–14.

increase represented a genuine advance in the prosperity of the clergy, for the inflationary movement of the late sixteenth century was beginning to subside by 1600 and prices remained relatively stable thereafter.[41]

The largest testaments were left by the ministers of Edinburgh, whose wealth often exceeded that of bishops. Mr Patrick Galloway, a prominent minister in Edinburgh, left net assets of almost £11,000 including a library worth 4,000 merks and 4,000 merks 'in reddie money'. Mr William Struthers, the dean of Edinburgh who died in 1633, left an estate of almost £16,000. He bequeathed 6,000 merks for the support of four 'students in divinitie by the spaice of four yeires'.[42]

Outside the major burghs a minister often had much of his wealth in victuals and livestock. Mr George Inglis, minister at Bathgate from 1575 to 1617, left in his estate 'tua naigis ... thrie meirs ... fyve oxin ... seven ky[cows] ... ten auld scheip' as well as oats and bear.[43] He had net assets of almost £1,400. Even more impressive was the testament left by Mr James Mitchell, minister at Stow. At his death in 1626 he owned livestock and crops worth more than £1,000, including 110 hogs. His total assets exceeded £4,300.[44] At the other end of the scale was Mr James Hepburn, minister of Finhaven (now Cathlaw, Angus). At his death in 1595 his net assets were £38 including 'an auld quhoit naig, price 10 merks'.[45]

Probably most ministers possessed a few books and many had substantial libraries. Almost half of the ministers listed above had libraries large enough to be listed separately in their inventory. These libraries ranged in value from 15 merks to 4000. Most of the larger ones were left by men who died after 1616.[46]

Ministers, like bishops, often had large sums due them at their

---

[41] 'Much of the upsurge of Scottish prices took place in the last quarter of the sixteenth century ... But by about 1600 the upward rush was slackening, so that, for the last twenty-five years of James VI's reign, the overall rise was everywhere slight and, for some commodities, negligible' (S. G. E. Lythe, *The Economy of Scotland*, 110).

[42] Edinburgh Testaments, 18 May 1626, 8 August, 1635.

[43] Barley of a hardy but inferior quality.

[44] Edinburgh Testaments, 27 August 1617, 19 July 1626.

[45] Brechin Testaments, 24 December 1599.

[46] Before 1616 only one library of the ministers studied exceeded 200 merks. After that date there were ten libraries worth more than 200 merks.

death, much of the debt in unpaid stipend. Mr Andrew Strachan, minister of Dun, was an extreme example. His testament of over £13,000 consisted almost entirely of debts due to him, much of it in unpaid stipend and tacks extending from 1604 to 1622. More typical was the case of Mr John Duncanson who died in 1601. Some of his stipend had been unpaid since 1598.[47]

However, not all of the debts due to ministers were unpaid stipend, and in some cases ministers were prosperous enough to lend money at interest. In 1611-12 about three hundred and fifty persons were summoned by the privy council for 'ockery', that is, usury or changing more than 10 per cent interest on loans. Among the persons summoned were eight ministers.[48] In 1641 Mr Gilbert Power, minister of Stoneykirk, was tried on a number of charges by the presbytery of Stranraer. Among other charges he was accused of lending money at excessive interest. A witness declared that in 1613 or 1614 he 'did borrow a 100 merks from him [i.e. Mr Power] and had it about 9 years'. The witness paid an annual rent of 10 merks with the option of paying 'a bol meal', an option he sometimes used. Since Mr Power had not received more than 10 per cent, the charge was dismissed.[50]

Ministers were entitled to a glebe of four acres of kirkland which was to be free of teinds. By the early seventeenth century most ministers appear to have had a glebe or to acquire one shortly thereafter. In 1611 fourteen out of ninety-nine ministers in the synod of Fife had no glebe. A year later the number had dropped from fourteen to nine. By 1629 only four parishes in the synod were said to have no glebe.[51] In 1600 only four of the eight parishes in the presbytery of Ellon had glebes. In 1605 glebes were designed at Slains and Cruden. In 1607 'Mr Peter Blakburne, bischop of Aberdene' and the presbytery of Ellon assigned a full glebe for Ellon. The eighth parish, Logie-Buchan, however, did not receive a glebe until a visitation by Bishop Patrick Forbes in 1620.[52] At a visitation in 1611 Archbishop Gladstanes 'be delyverie of the earth

[47] Brechin Testaments, 4 December 1622, 31 January 1624; Edinburgh Testaments, 8 February 1602.
[48] *R.P.C.* IX, 385, 387, 412, 425.
[49] Stranraer Presb., 3 November 1641.
[50] *A.P.S.* III, 73, 98, IV, 17, 285-6, 612.
[51] Fife Synod, 63, 70-2, 98-9, 114, 313.
[52] Ellon Presb., 23 May, 17 July 1605, 25 November 1607, 6 September 1617, 5 September 1620.

and stane as use is gave reall and actuall possessione' of a glebe to a minister.[53]

A minister was also entitled to a manse, although expenses for repairs or additions to the manse often had to be paid by the minister himself. According to an act of parliament in 1612, expenses up to 500 merks which a minister had spent on his manse were to be repaid by his successor.[54] Repairs made to manses were carefully valued and entered in presbytery books.[55] As a result, most ministers had a large sum to pay as soon as they entered a new parish. Mr William Weir, the new minister at Hobkirk in 1626, had to pay the widow of the former minister. The presbytery of Jedburgh appointed 'arbiters for the accord quhat satisfaction the said Mr William suld give to the said relick [i.e. widow] in contentment for the manse of the kirk built and repaired by hir and her unquhile husband'.[56] In 1616 the new minister of Kilspindie was not resident 'because the relick of the laitt minister possessis the mans and will not remove thairfra until she was reimbursed for expenses spent on the manse.[57] Yet most ministers appear to have possessed manses. In 1611 only two ministers in the synod of Fife were reported to have no manse.[58] Of the twenty-two ministers in the presbytery of Lanark, one had no manse in 1627.[59]

In 1611 the synod of Fife proposed an alternative arrangement for the construction and improvement of manses.

> Forsamikle as gryt lossis comes to the intrant ministeris through the payment of soumes for the mansis, quhilk still remaine for the use of the parochine, It is thoght meitt, that at the first Parliament ane suitt be maid for ane act to be granted, that the parochineris may bigg the manses to thair kirkes, quhair as yet their ar not bigget, and refound the expenssis bestowed on such as ar bigget already.[60]

To assign responsibility for building a manse to heritors was obviously preferable, at least as far as ministers were concerned.

[53] Fife Synod, 30.
[54] *A.P.S.* IV, 472.
[55] *Kirkcaldy Presb.*, 7–8, 38, 102–4, 118–9.
[56] Jedburgh Presb., 24 May 1626.
[57] Fife Synod, 194.
[58] At Scoonie and Kinnaird (Fife Synod, 71).
[59] Lanark Presb., 19 April 1627.
[60] Fife Synod, 63.

However, this provision was not approved by parliament until 1649,[61] and more prosperous ministers made their own additions to their manses. In 1630 the minister of Kinglassie spent £341 in repairing his manse and in building 'ane stabill, and ane barn, and ane brewhouss'. The manse appears to have consisted of a large hall with a chamber on either side, two rooms above, and a kitchen at the back.[62]

The church also took some responsibility for widows and orphans of ministers. In 1612 the synod of Fife agreed to collect 450 merks for the widow of the minister of Kennoway. When Mr Samuel Cockburn, minister of Minto, died in 1623 the members of his presbytery ordered 'for the support of Mr Samuell Cokburne his bairne everie brother suld pay fourtie shillings in the yeir'. A few years later the kirk session of Trinity College also contributed to the 'sustentatioun of the bairnes of unquhill Mr Samuell Cockburne sumtyme minister at Minto'.[63] The same session gave money in 1633 to 'ane preicher seik both in bodie and memorie namet Mr Colene Caldwell'.[64] In 1626 the synod of Moray established a small pension fund to enable an old minister to retire, but this arrangement was unusual.[65]

To conclude that satisfactory financial arrangements had been established for all ministers by 1638 would be an exaggeration. Ministers could not take advantage of Charles I's legislation until the teinds had been valued, and this was not done in many parishes. Some ministers who died in the 1630s left small testaments, and any improvements in church finance which had been made probably meant little to them.[66] However, an observer in 1641 wrote that Scottish ministers

beside their Gleab and Manse, are all provided to certaine, and the most part, to competent stipends, which are paid either in

[61] *A.P.S.* VI (II), 287–8; VII, 472–3; cf. my *Bishop and Presbytery*, 111.
[62] *Kirkcaldy Presb.*, 7–8, 38.
[63] Fife Synod, 92; Jedburgh Presb., 8 October 1623; Trinity College Kirk Session, 6 August 1629.
[64] Trinity College K. S. 4 July 1633. He was the son of Mr James Caldwell, former minister at Falkirk.
[65] Moray Synod, 19.
[66] E.g. Edinburgh Testaments, 5 April 1636, 8 March 1637; Brechin Testaments, 24 November 1640.

victuall or moneys, or in both: And if the charge of their family be great, and their children put to Schooles or Colledges, they are helped, and supplied by the charity of the people, which useth also to be extended, if need be, toward their widows and Orphanes.[67]

Almost endless negotiations and plans were necessary before that statement could be made, and the achievement which it summarised was one of the major accomplishments of the Church of Scotland before 1638.

[67] *Government and Order of the Church of Scotland*, 32.

CHAPTER NINE

Parish Life in Scotland

I

The first Book of Discipline urged that 'churches ... be with expedition repaired in doors, windows, thatch'. Even though the resources of the church were very limited in the sixteenth century, repair of churches was not overlooked and by 1610 considerable progress had been made.[1] The visitation reports of Archbishop Gladstanes (1611–14) provide a revealing picture of the state of church buildings in the northern half of the diocese of St Andrews. Nineteen of his visitations contained reports on church buildings. Repairs were needed in five parishes, usually to the church roof. The other fourteen were all found as at Forgan 'in reasonable gude estate'.[2] In other words, no major repairs were needed in almost 75 per cent of the churches on which reports were made. A similar picture of the churches in Aberdeenshire was contained in the visitation reports of the presbytery of Ellon. Two of the eight parishes in that presbytery needed church roofs repaired in 1607. When the presbytery next reported on church buildings ten years later they had 'no ruynous kirks. ... They have all bells bot not bears [i.e. biers]'.[3]

Repairs were the responsibility of the heritors who were taxed by the church for necessary repairs. At Culross the church was badly damaged in a storm in 1633. Repairs were estimated to cost

[1] Knox, *History of the Reformation* (Dickinson), II, 320–1; Gordon Donaldson, *Scottish Reformation*, 99–100.
[2] Fife Synod. The churches which needed repair were Fettercairn (34), Falkland (45–6), Kennoway (53), Kilspindie (128), and Mains (133–4). Those in good repair were Perth (26), Rescobie (32), Kilmany (36), Linlithgow (39), Slamannan (40), Ferry-Port-on-Craig (48), Forgan (51), Abdie (54), Inverkeillor (78), Kinfauns (127), Kinnaird (130), Liff, Invergowrie, and Logie (131), Murroes (135), and Monifieth (136).
[3] Ellon Presb., 16 July, 23 July 1607, 6 September 1617.

500 merks. 'Therfor it was concluded that an impost must needs be stented and imposed upon all paroshineris in toun and land able to pay', A year later the treasurer had collected only fifty pounds 'in taxatione silver for the thacking of the kirk'. However, other funds were also used, and that year the session spent £204 19s. 4d. for repair of the church.[4]

The reformed Church was able to build few new churches in the sixteenth century, the unusual square church at Burntisland in 1592 being a notable exception.[5] However, by the second decade of the seventeenth century a number of new churches were under construction. The most notable examples were Greyfriars, Edinburgh (1612–20), Dirleton (1612 and after), Dairsie (1621), Auchterhouse (1630), South Queensferry (1633) and Anstruther Easter (1634).[6] At least five churches were built in the diocese of Aberdeen during the episcopate of Bishop Patrick Forbes. A new church was also completed at Kiltarlity in the Diocese of Moray, and repairs were carried out on a number of other churches in the diocese.[7]

The new churches were built in traditional rectangular shape, usually with a tower and belfry at the west end. In larger churches the east end or chancel was often set aside as a Communion Aisle and formed a railed off enclosure. The pulpit was the dominant feature. It was usually a panelled enclosure with a reader's desk in the centre.[8] Special lofts were often built by the crafts for their own use, and heritors built permanent desks or enclosed pews for themselves and their families. Other parishioners were expected to use movable 'brods' or stools, and the kirk session of Elgin found

[4] Culross K. S., 10, 17 February 1633, accounts at back, 6 May 1634. For other examples of taxation, see Ellon Presb., 16 July, 23 July 1607.

[5] *Ancient and Historical Monuments of Scotland*, Fife, No. 68, Edinburgh, 1933.

[6] Gordon Donaldson, 'Post-Reformation Church at Whithorn: Historical Notes', *Proceedings of the Society of Antiquaries of Scotland*, LXXXV, 127.

[7] W. G. S. Snow, *Patrick Forbes*, 112–3. Struggles to build a new church at Udny between 1597 and 1605 can be traced in the records of the presbytery of Ellon, 29 May 1600, 18 November 1602, 12 July 1603, 30 May 1605. Moray Synod, 16–18, 21, 23, 27, 29, 30, 33, 34, 39, 75.

[8] Gordon Donaldson, 'Post-Reformation Church at Whithorn: Historical Notes', 126–8; George Hay, 'Scottish Post-Reformation Church Furniture', *Proceedings of the Society of Antiquaries of Scotland*, LXXXVIII, 48–9.

it necessary to order 'all the fixit wemen stuillis in the kirk ... removitt'.[9] Instructions issued by the presbytery of Lanark in 1627 were typical. 'Na man sall have within any of our kirks a daske or proper seat peculiar to himself, his wyff or bairnes bot they onlie that hes heritablie lands or few within the paroche'. Others were to use the 'common seates or formes appoynted be the session for that effect'.[10]

An English visitor in 1629 was quite impressed with the churches he visited. At Selkirk 'they have a very pretty church, where the Hammermen and other Tradesmen have several [i.e. separate] seats ... the women sit in the high end of the church, with us in the choir'. Leith had 'two fairer churches for in-work than any I saw in London'. At Perth, which was as far north as he went, 'every Trade sitteth in the church by themselves. There be two churches in the town, the one called St John's Church having seven great bells, four little, and chimes, the finest in Scotland. The Church is hung with many candlesticks'.[11]

The latter part of the period also saw considerable emphasis upon securing vessels for baptism and the holy communion. The liturgical programme of James, which culminated in the Perth Articles, the greater liturgical interests of his son, and the growing prosperity of the church were probably all reasons for this interest. Parliament in 1617 (the year before the Perth Articles were passed) required

> that all the paroche kirkis within this kingdome be prowydit off Basines and Lavoiris for the Ministratioun of the sacrament of Baptisme and of Couppes tablis and table Clothes for the ministratioun of the holie Communione.[12]

The session at Elgin began at once to collect money for communion vessels. By March 1619 the minister had 'receavit ane hundredthe pundis from the toun for ther pairt to furneis weschellis to the kirk for celebratting the sacramentis', and vessels were secured shortly thereafter. The elders at Ellon were ordered by

---

[9] Culross K. S., 1 June 1634; *Elgin K. S.* 79.
[10] Lanark Presb., ?8 February 1627.
[11] Agnes Mure MacKenzie, *Scottish Pageant, 1625–1707*, Oliver and Boyd, Edinburgh, 1949, 100.
[12] *A.P.S.* IV, 534.

their presbytery to secure communion vessels in 1620, and some had been acquired at least by 1634.[13] An outstanding set was obtained by Trinity College, Edinburgh. In 1633 a merchant gave 'ane silvir basein . . . frielie for the sacrament of baptisme' and another merchant 'giftit also frielie ane silvir laver for that same use'. They were acquired just before Charles's visit to Edinburgh. Later that year the session authorised a voluntary collection for communion vessels. Almost £1400 was collected and communion vessels were purchased. A handsome silver cup, two silver flagons, and a bread plate 20 inches in diameter still exist. In 1636 the same Session spent almost £150 for linen cloths, including four 'communion cloathis' thirty-seven feet long, and 'tua schort cloathes' which were about fifteen feet long.[14]

Communion vessels still exist for forty-two parishes which were either made or acquired during the early seventeenth century. This figure is all the more remarkable since many vessels were destroyed after an act in 1640 requiring all silver and gold work in Scotland to be given in to the revolutionary government. Mr Burns' conclusion is certainly warranted: 'By the year 1638 . . . the sacramental plate in the service of the Church must have been very considerable'.[15]

Scotland was a poor country in the early seventeenth century, and its church buildings cannot begin to compare in splendour and wealth with those of richer nations. Given the resources of the country, however, the state of churches in 1638 would probably have pleased earlier reformers. New churches had been built, innumerable repairs had been carried out, new equipment had been added. The impression is of a church enjoying a growing measure of prosperity and of support from many of the monied and landed people of Scotland.

[13] *Elgin K. S.*, 158–9, 225; Ellon Presb., 27 December 1620; Thomas Burns, *Old Scottish Communion Plate*, 427–9. One cup is now in the National Museum of Antiquities of Scotland, Edinburgh.
[14] Trinity College K. S., 14 February, 26 September 1633, 1 December 1636; Thomas Burns, *Old Scottish Communion Plate*, 223–4, 520–1.
[15] Thomas Burns, *Old Scottish Communion Plate*, 143. Forty-one of the communion sets are described in this book. Colmonell also has some silver cups dated 1617–19 (Letter from the Rev. James Brown, former minister at Colmonell). For the act confiscating silver and gold work and its implementation, see Burns, 143–8.

II

One of the more distinctive features of the church's worship was a widespread attempt to maintain daily services, especially in burgh churches. At Elgin the bell was to be 'roung ilk day at four efternoone to the evenyng prayers' and every winter (when it would be dark at four) the session provided a four penny candle 'ilk nycht to the evening prayeris'. At Culross, where the church was almost a mile from the centre of the town, the session 'ordained se[ats?] to be seit up in the Tolbuith and the prayers to be [rea]d thair upon Wednesday and Fryday in the morning twixt 8 and 9 hours'. Even in the more remote village of Tarves (Aberdeenshire) the minister 'reids the prayers ilk oulk day at sax hours in the morning or thairby'. A minute in the records of the kirk session of St Andrews described the beginning of the practice in that place. In 1598 commissioners from the town council 'desyrit of the sessioun that commoun prayaris may be publiclie red in the kirk ilk day mornyng and evinyng . . . as in uther townis of this realme'. The session agreed and ordered their reader

> to reid every day, morn and evin . . . ane chaptour of the New Testament and ane uther of the Auld befoir none . . . with ane prayer befoir and eftir; and evining, sum Psalmes with ane prayer befoir and eftir'.[16]

Even a weekday sermon was maintained in some prominent parishes. The session of St Andrews ordered 'the sermone in tyme cuming [to] begyn at viij houris on Weddinsday and Friday, and to be endit be nyne houris, prayaris and all'. For many years a sermon was held at Elgin on Tuesday or Wednesday.[17]

In spite of these attempts, daily services were probably largely unknown in most parishes. Weekday services where they existed were difficult to maintain, attendance was often poor, and visitation records suggest that most parishes had little public instruction during the week except during pre-communion examinations.

The great service of the week was that on Sunday morning. The service was marked by three bells: the first to call the people to

---
[16] *Elgin K. S.*, 64, 71, 100, 130, 136; Culross K. S., ? February 1630; Ellon Presb., 6 August 1617, 14 June 1621; *St Andrews K. S.* II, 829–30.
[17] *St Andrews K. S.* II, 828–9; Elgin K. S. *passim*.

church (essential at a time when most people did not have watches), the second to mark the beginning of the reader's service, and the third to announce the arrival of the minister into the pulpit. One of the best descriptions of the whole service was written by William Cowper, the moderate and pious Bishop of Galloway.

> [At the beginning the people] bow themselves before the Lord to make an humble confession of their sinnes ... which you will heare openly read out by the publike Reader. ... [Next, the people prepare] their Psalmebooke, that all of them, with one heart and mouth, may sing unto the Lord. There is the Psalme which the Reader hath proclaimed. [Next, the reader opens] the Bible: you will heare him read some portion of holie Scripture. ... [After the arrival of the minister] he will conceive a Prayer ... thereafter he reads his Text of holy Scripture ... then hee falls to the preaching, which some heare with their heads covered, some otherwise. ... He concludes all with a thanksgiving, after which there is a Psalme sung by the whole Congregation, and then the Minister blesseth the people in the name of the Lord, and so dimits them.[18]

There are many references in church records to the reading of prayers, both at weekday and at Sunday services.[19] In fact that church officer known as a reader read not only lessons from Scripture but also prayers. In this as other matters, readers often had to be rebuked for attempting to act like a minister and use extemporaneous prayer. In 1624 the synod of Fife ordered

> readers in al Congregations ... tyed to read in the publict audience of the peopl only such prayers as ar printed in the commoun psalme buik [*The Book of Common Order*] and ordained be the Kirk of Scotland to be red publictlie.[20]

But the practice of reading prayers *per se* was not an issue at this time. Even in 1640, when read prayers were under attack, the presbytery of Perth was prepared to challenge a candidate for ordination if he opposed this widespread custom. The candidate

> was posed befor the presbytrie whether it was lawful to reid

---

[18] William Cowper, *Works*, 680, 682.
[19] E.g. Jedburgh Presb., 5 December 1610; Fife Synod, 133.
[20] Fife Synod, 271.

prayers because ther went a report of him that he distained reading of prayers altogether. He declared he was never of that mynd bot thought them lawfull tho to conceive was better.[21]

The whole Sunday morning service was expected to take about two hours, and ministers were sometimes warned not to preach too long. The kirk session of Elgin actually threatened to fine its minister 6s. 8d. unless 'the prayeris, psalme and preitching be all endit within the hour'. All parishioners were expected to attend and might be punished if they did not. Parishes which had schools often expected pupils to attend in a body. At St Andrews the 'maister of the sang schole' was ordered 'to caus the best of his scholaris sitt besyid himself, about the pulpeit, to help to sing the Psalmes'.[22]

Sermons were sometimes preached on Sunday afternoon as well, but instruction in the catechism was more common. Ministers were often charged to begin the morning 'sermone precislie at ten houres, thaireafter hold thair sessioun and catechise ane part of the parochine in the efternoon'.[23] During the summer, this practice was quite general.

Although the Lord's Prayer and the Apostles' Creed (or 'the Belief') were not regularly used every Sunday, they were accepted and common standards which every churchman was expected to know. In 1608 an assembly

> of new inactit, that all Ministers examine young children of the age of sixe yeirs, and try that they have the Lords Prayer, the Articles of Beliefe, and the Commandements; in the quhilk thair parents salbe haldin to instruct them.

At Aberdeen the people were ordered to repeat the Creed after their reader so that 'be the oft repeting' they could memorise it. At Elgin some ignorant parishioners were ordered 'to learne the crede and the Lords prayer betuix and Whitsonday nixt under the pain of 20s.' Many kirk sessions required couples to know the Creed, the Lord's Prayer and the Ten Commandments before they could be married, and sermons were preached on 'the Beleeff'.[24]

---

[21] Perth Presb., 12 August 1640.
[22] *Elgin K. S.*; Belhelvie K. S., 8 May 1631; *St Andrews K. S.* II, 908.
[23] Fife Synod, 128. For other examples, see 31, 35, 40, 47.
[24] *B.U.K.* III, 1052; *Aberdeen K. S.* 38; *Elgin K. S.* 88; Belhelvie K. S. 8 May 1631.

One other practice which affected the ordinary lives of parishioners was the proclamation of a fast. A fast could be kept on either a weekday or a Sunday and might be enjoined by a general assembly, a synod, the privy council or a diocesan bishop.[25] In 1627 the presbytery of Lanark received 'ane letter from the Bischop injoyning thame to keep ane fast the eight of August being Weddnisday and the Sabbath nixt thereafter'. Among other causes, the fast was kept for 'the reformed kirkes of Bohemia . . . whose blood is spilt by war into the streits . . . for prospering the kinges armies . . . [and] becaus of the extraordinarie raines threatning famnyn'. According to Alexander Henderson 'the dayes of the fast from morning to evening, are kept holy unto the Lord in the nature of an Extraordinary Sabbath, with abstinence from meat and drink'. And kirk sessions summoned those who had eaten 'beif and uther meit . . . that day of publict Fast' or even those who had been 'at breid and cheis'.[26]

The worship of the church, especially the great parish service on Sunday morning, was central to the life and being of the reformed kirk. Here was the largest public gathering of the week in most places, here the gospel was proclaimed and the people renewed their faith. The Sunday morning service was the most visible and immediate symbol of the power and spiritual authority of the church. And the many injunctions requiring parishioners to come inside the church on time suggest that a good deal of business and visiting took place before and perhaps after the service as well.

Professor Cheyne has wisely reminded historians that at every period in Scottish Reformation history there has been variety and change in the worship of the church.[27] There was certainly variety in the early seventeenth century, variety because of local traditions because ministers had different abilities and convictions, because Scotland was in contact with the rest of Europe, especially England. And, as Mr Cheyne points out, variety was allowed by the Book of Common Order. But there was also at this time a wide and broadly

---

[25] *B.U.K.* III, 966 (Calderwood, VI, 116), Paisley Presb., 16 Sept. 1602; Perth Presb., 7 May 1628; Belhelvie K. S., 3 July 1636.

[26] Lanark Presb., 2 August 1627. A similar fast was kept by the presbytery of Dunblane (Dunblane Presb. 1 August 1627). *Government and Order of the Church of Scotland*, 25–6; Dundonald K. S. 73.

[27] A. C. Cheyne, 'Worship in the Kirk: Knox, Westminster and the 1940 Book', *Reformation and Revolution*, edited by Duncan Shaw, The Saint Andrew Press, 1967, 71.

accepted common tradition of worship, acknowledged by all and hardly questioned. The great Sunday service of psalms, Scripture, prayer and sermon was the most public, enduring, and splendid symbol of the reality of the Reformation in Scotland.

III

The Perth Articles were a different matter.[28] The Five Articles passed by the assembly at Perth in 1618 were the high point of James's policy of introducing some English traditions into Scottish worship. An interest in conformity with England did not begin when James moved his residence to London, but the union of the crowns greatly increased the likelihood that uniformity might be sought in other matters as well. A contemporary wrote that James first

> gained an uniformity in government betwixt the churches of the two nations; which being atchieved [sic] his majesty went on to press that there might be an uniformity also in worship betwixt them: for which end he recommended to the bishops the introduction of some English customs into this church.[29]

To alter the worship of a church was to affect the life of every parish in a far more intimate and direct way than to change church government. James never insisted on altering the regular Sunday worship of the church; but the changes which he did introduce threatened his whole religious settlement, and the liturgical policy of his son (which would have affected regular weekly worship) was completely disastrous.

James' first major liturgical innovation was introduced by an act of council in 1614 which required all persons to communicate at their own parish church on 24 April, although the act did not mention the fact that this day was Pasch or Easter. No equivocation was used the following year when an act ordered all ministers to celebrate the Communion 'in all tyme heirefter . . . upoun ane day yeirlie, to witt, Pasche day'.[30] James was urged by his bishops to use church courts rather than civil courts to introduce liturgical changes, and James did take the more difficult route of securing approval from general assemblies. An assembly at Aberdeen in

[28] See Ian B. Cowan, 'The Five Articles of Perth'.
[29] Guthrie, *Memoirs*, 7–8.
[30] *R.P.C.* X, 215–7, 316–7.

1616 agreed to order the communion to be 'at the terme of Easter yeirlie', and to authorize the examination of children by bishops on their visitations, which might be considered a modified form of confirmation.[31]

During James' visit to Scotland in 1617 he apparently decided on a much more extensive liturgical policy. The major points of this policy were first introduced at the synod of Lothian in June. They were 'kneeling in the act of receiving the sacramentall elements of breade and wine at the Communion; observation of some holie dayes dedicate to Christ [Yule, Good Friday, Pasch, Ascension, Whit Sunday]; episcopall Confirmation or bishoping; private Baptisme, and private Communion'.[32] That synod declared that only a general assembly could pass this programme, and an assembly was hurriedly summoned to meet at St Andrews in November. Opposition to the articles was immediate and strong. Little was passed before it became necessary to dissolve the Assembly. James threatened his bishops with 'the anger of a King,'[33] and more careful plans were made for the next assembly which met at Perth in August 1618.

Surprisingly, James did not resort to his earlier practice of packing the Perth assembly with nominated commissioners, and elections were held in many presbyteries, including those where opposition was strongest.[34] But if elections were free, those commissioners who arrived at Perth were made to feel the weight of royal authority. Debate was limited, royal letters were read and reread, and the five articles were presented as one motion to be accepted or rejected as a whole. As David Lindsay, later Bishop of Brechin, put it, 'To avert the King's wrath, he thought it best to yield'.[35] The Articles passed by a vote of about eighty-six to forty, and were confirmed by James and the privy council within months.[36]

[31] *B.U.K.* III, 1127-8 (Calderwood, VII, 228-9); *O.L.* II, 512. For confirmation, see above, 57
[32] Calderwood, VII, 249.
[33] Cf. Spottiswood, *History*, III, 249 (Bannatyne Club).
[34] See above, 124-5, James was accused of trying to influence the choice of commissioners by manipulating stipends (Calderwood, VII, 304).
[35] Calderwood, VII, 331.
[36] *B.U.K.* III, 1143-67 (Calderwood, VII, 304-332); *R.P.C.* XI, 454-6. Ian B. Cowan's 'The Five Articles of Perth' contains a convenient account of the proceedings at Perth.

How widely were the Perth Articles observed? David Calderwood, the seventeenth-century historian, argued that they were generally resisted or ignored in the south but were observed by many in the north; and his view has been generally accepted. Opposition was stronger in the south than in the north, but church records suggest that the response in both north and south was a good deal more varied and complex than the simple pattern presented by Calderwood.

Some of the articles were almost a dead letter from the start. Episcopal confirmation never developed. Private baptism and private communion for the sick may have raised some theological issues, but the practices were apparently never widespread.

One of the more widely observed articles was the injunction, first introduced four years before the Perth assembly, to celebrate the Holy Communion at Pasch. This practice did not begin everywhere at once, but it appears to have spread not only in the north but over much of the rest of the country as well. A survey of the archbishopric of St Andrews, which included nine dioceses, revealed that in 1614 'some ministeris hes nocht celebrate the communioun . . . becaus it wes Easterday', but most did.[37] The next year the kirk session at Perth,

> the Bishop of Galloway [Mr William Cowper] and the haill Elders present, . . . ordain the Communion to be celebrated at this burgh on the 9th and 16th days of April . . . but Mr John Malcolm, Minister, dissented therefrom, alleging the celebrathereof on the said 9th day of April, which is Pasch Sunday, to be contrary to the Acts of Assembly.[38]

However, by 1621 members of the presbytery of Perth regularly celebrated the Communion at Pasch. Suspected papists were ordered 'to communicat at Pashe nixt' and meetings were postponed before Easter 'becaus of the preparatioun to the communioun on Pashe day'.[39] In 1617 the members of the presbytery of Ellon were asked 'quhat tyme the communioun wes given. It wes ansserred at Pasch last'.[40] At Elgin the Communion was celebrated in 1615 on Passion Sunday and Palm Sunday. By 1616 the celebrations took place on Easter Day and the following Sunday,

[37] Fife Synod, 166 (Provincial Assembly of St Andrews).
[38] *Spottiswood Misc.* II, 287.
[39] Perth Presb., 7 March, 21 March 1621.
[40] Ellon Presb., 6 September 1617.

and this practice continued until 1638.[41] In the synod of Fife in 1623 'the Communion is fund to have been celebrat be the haill brethren almost at the ordinarie prescryved tyme.[42] At Belvelvie the Communion was regularly celebrated at Easter, although Palm Sunday was more frequently the day of celebration at Culross.[43] At Trinity College, Edinburgh, the Communion was usually given on Easter and the following Sunday in 1626 and perhaps earlier.[44] In 1633 the Communion was probably celebrated on Easter Day at Lanark. And at Aberdeen in 1642 'na communion givin on good-frydday nor this Pashday as wes usit befoir. Marvallous in Abirdene to sie no Marcat, foule or flesche to be sold on Pash-evin'.[45]

However, the Communion was not celebrated in all churches at Easter. At Forgandenny in 1629 the minister was 'giving of communion to his parochiners' a month after Easter, and the previous year the people at Kilspindie had their communion on Whit-Sunday.[46] In 1634 the Presbytery of Jedburgh received a letter 'from the Archbishop of Glasgow for teiching on Good Fryday and giving the communion Pasche Sonday. The brethren for shortnes of tyme could not convenientlie give the communion that day'.[47]

Extant church records are too fragmentary to make any statistical survey of the whole country; but if those records which have survived are typical, the communion was widely although not universally celebrated at Pasch in the parishes of Scotland after about 1620.

The Perth Articles also required observance of Yule (or Christmas), Good Friday, Ascension Day and Whit-Sunday. Ascension

---

[41] Elgin K. S., 2 April 1615; 31 March, 7 April 1616; 13, 20, 27 April 1617; 5, 12 April 1614; 28 March, 4, 11 April 1619, etc.
[42] Fife Synod, 255.
[43] Belhelvie K. S., 21, 27 March 1630; 3, 10 April, 1631; 1 April 1632; 14, 21 Agril 1633, etc. Culross K. S., accounts at back, 18, 25 March 1632; 7, 14 April 1633; 16, 23 March 1634; 15, 22 March 1635, etc.
[44] Trinity College K. S., 9, 16 April 1626; 25 March, 1 April 1627; 28 March, 4 April 1630; 10, 17 April 1631, etc.
[45] Lanark Presb., 25 April 1633; Spalding, *History of the Troubles*, II, 30.
[46] Perth Presb., 20 May 1629, 28 May 1628.
[47] Jedburgh Presb., 19 March 1634; cf. Johnston of Wariston, *Diary*, I, 250, 256, 261, 269, 272.

Day and Whit-Sunday appear to have been largely ignored. Presbyteries which met on Thursday continued to do so on Ascension Day, and the day always passed without comment in presbytery or kirk session records. Whitsunday was often mentioned as a legal term and a well-known time of year (as were Michaelmas and Lammas), but there is no evidence in church records that special religious observances took place on that Sunday. Moreover, neither bishops nor the government issued any injunctions after 1618 requiring observance of Ascension Day or Whit-Sunday.

Services were held at Christmas in some places although observance was far from general. Sermons were preached in Edinburgh on 25 December 1618 and thereafter, although congregations were said to be small.[48] Bishop Alexander Lindsay, moderator of the presbytery of Perth in 1618, warned the ministers of that presbytery 'to teich in thair particular kirks the xxv day of December', but few did so that year. After Christmas Archbishop Spottiswood learned that 'divers [in the presbytery of Perth] hes disobeyit, and not onlie forburne to [preach at Christmas] . . . bot also . . . soicht occasionis to condemn the proceidingis of the assemblie'. The presbytery received similar charges in subsequent years, and at least by 1622 Yule was observed in some parishes of that presbytery.[49] References to 'Youll' first appear in the records of the Kirk Session of Elgin in 1620 and at Belhelvie in 1629. By 1640 the observance of Yule at Aberdeen was an old tradition. However, even in the north, Christmas was not universally observed, and the synod of Moray in 1634 had to warn 'some of the brethren [who] have not teached upon the day of the nativitie'.[50]

Good Friday was even less widely observed than Yule. In 1619 the presbytery of Dunblane held a special meeting on Good Friday and the bishop preached a 'sermone upon the passioune of Christ'. The first reference at Elgin to 'Gud Fryday' was in 1626, although the day was observed every year thereafter until 1639. Sermons were held in two Edinburgh churches on Good Friday 1621,

[48] Calderwood, VII, 341–2, 410, 454, 518–9; *O.L.* II, 643.
[49] Perth Presb., 16 December 1618; 10 March, 1 December 1619; 20 December 1620; 12 December 1621; 18 December 1622.
[50] Elgin K. S., 22 December 1620. Also in subsequent years from 1623 to 1638; Belhelvie K. S., 25 December 1629; Spalding, *History of the Troubles*, I, 179–80; Moray Synod, 68.

although the day does not appear to have been observed at Trinity College until 1637.[51] Most kirk session records contain no evidence that services were held or collections taken on Good Friday.

The most debatable of the Perth Articles was the one requiring 'kneeling in the act of receiving the sacramentall elements of breade and wine' during the Holy Communion.[52] That article aroused more debate at the Perth assembly than any other, and James was particularly insistent that it be enforced. Bishops were given the unwelcome task of enforcing the injunction. Archbishop Spottiswood wrote to the presbytery of Perth two weeks before Easter in 1619 informing them that the bishops had met at Edinburgh and decided that

> warning suld be gevin be everie bishop to the exercises [i.e. presbyteries] within his diocise for a precis keiping of the said actis . . . speciallie for gevin communioun upone Easter Day in the forme prescryvit of kneilling.

And he added, 'We are commandit be his Majestie to suffer na man bruik [i.e. enjoy] the ministrie that dois not obey'. In 1620 the presbytery of Dunblane received a letter signed 'be the Bischopis of S. Androis, Glasgow, Galloway, Dumblane and Brechine' warning them to conform. Financial pressure was also used. The bishops asked James 'to send expresse command . . . not to give owt letters to any Minister upon the late modifications . . . unless the Ministers produce their Bischop's testimoniall of their conformitie to the Actis of the late Assemblie', and an appropriate command was issued by the king.[53]

Opposition to kneeling communion was immediate and strong in and near Edinburgh. According to Calderwood, scandalous scenes took place in the capital. At Easter in 1619 'the inhabitants of the toun went out at the ports in hundreths and thousands, to the nixt adjacent kirks. . . . Cold and graceless were the Communions'. There was similar trouble the next year. According to the Earl of Melrose

[51] Dunblane Presb., 26 March 1619; Elgin K. S., 7 April 1626, 23 March 1627, 12 April 1628, etc.; Calderwood, VII, 457; Trinity College K. S., 30 March 1637.
[52] Calderwood, VII, 332.
[53] Perth Presb., 10 March 1619; Dunblane Presb., 22 June 1620; O.L. II, 586.

The nomber of communicants [at Edinburgh on Easter 1620] wes small . . . few of the townes people of good sort. The greatest part received kneeling . . . but sindrie of the base sort, and some wemen, not of the best, did sit. In the Colledge Church, I heare . . . that, the nomber of communicants far exceiding that of the Hie Church, verie few of them kneeled.

Spottiswood noted that there was trouble in Edinburgh at every Easter including the one in 1624 when his narrative stops. In fact, in that year an ominous new development began when 'mutinous people, who, separating themselves from the public assemblies, kept private conventicles', and later that year the Council found it necessary to condemn those who 'haif assembit them selffis in privat houssis in Edinburgh and otheris placeis to hear from intruding ministeris'.[54]

The mood of those who opposed kneeling communion was reflected in a letter sent by Mr William Bowie from Haddington in 1619.

I wott nocht how your ministeris of Ergyll . . . wilbe handlit with your Bischopis, bot all the honest men of the ministrie heir luikis for nothing bot the werst . . . for everie honest minister in all our eist partis will rather leave thair ministrie or they yield in one jot to the Bischopis. God mak your ministeris thair honest and constant men, for we heir thair is mony slim amongis thame.[55]

However, as Mr Bowie suggested in his closing lines, opposition was not universal throughout the country. Even in the east most ministers did not choose to leave their ministry before they 'yielded in one jot' to the bishops. Both the extent and persistence of nonconformity have often been exaggerated.

A careful inquiry was made in the synod of Fife in 1619 of those ministers who had not conformed at Easter of that year. Over eighty ministers were present. Thirty-two from Fife and two from Angus had not conformed. In addition seventeen ministers were absent from this synod, and probably many of the absentees had also not conformed. In other words, about half of the ministers

[54] Calderwood, VII, 359; *Melrose Papers*, II, *637; Spottiswood, *History*, III, 257, 259, 268; *R.P.C.* XIII, 520.
[55] *The Black Book of Taymouth*, Bannatyne Club, Edinburgh, 1855, 442–3.

of the synod of Fife had failed to minister the communion in 1619 according to the manner prescribed by the Perth assembly. Nonconformity was largely in Fife itself.[56]

Conformity was widespread in the north. The bishop of Moray wrote after Easter 1619 that the ministers of his diocese 'without exceptioun ... have all given obedience at this last Easter', and the extant minutes of the synod of Moray (which begin in 1623) show that nonconformity was no problem there.[57]

James was determined to suppress existing nonconformity. After Easter 1619 an act of council charged ministers to conform under threat of severe punishment, and the most vocal of the nonconforming ministers were summoned to the council or the high commission and either warned or more severely punished.[58]

These repressive measures were effective. Opposition almost collapsed in Fife. At Easter 1620 only nine ministers in that synod failed to conform. A commission was appointed to try them, and two cases were heard in July. One of the ministers promised obedience. The other, Mr David Michell of Garvock, was given an extension of time. In October Mr Michell sent a letter to the archbishop in which he not only agreed to conform but stated the reasons which led him to this difficult decision. His reasons must have been shared by many who became unwilling conformists.

> I have taken pains be reading and conference with learned men to find reasons and warrant for conformitie, bot of al this one s[t]riketh deepest with me, that I must else suffer my mouth to be shutt from preaching the gospel whereunto I find myself in conscience to be called ... being assured of that woe, if I desert my charge rashlie and without a weightie and violent cause. Thairfoir finding these ceremonies (though in themselfs unexpedient ...) not of such moment as that I dare to venture to shut myself out of the service of God and his church ... I wil rather give your Lordship contentment in theis things, and pray God to turn al to the guid of his church.[59]

The introducing of kneeling communions in the town of Perth

---

[56] Fife Synod, 220–24. Usually slightly over one hundred ministers attended meetings of the Synod of Fife.
[57] *O.L.* II, 616–7; Moray Synod, *passim*.
[58] *R.P.C.* XI, 579–81; Calderwood, VII, 352–5, 370–78.
[59] Fife Synod, 232, 236–7.

was an interesting example of conformity where the minister at least could hardly have welcomed them. The minister, Mr John Malcolm, was a prominent leader of the opposition. In 1606 he had signed a protest against episcopacy. In 1615 he opposed the observance of Easter Day and was also admonished by the high commission for support given to some banished ministers. However, before Easter 1619 the matter of conformity was considered by the kirk session of Perth.

Present Mr John Malcolm and Mr John Guthry, Ministers, the Elders and other members. . . . Proposition being made if they will agree . . . that the Lord's Supper be celebrate at this burgh conform to the prescription of the Act of the Generall Assembly . . . viz. that the Ministers give the bread and wine with their own hands to the communicants, and that they be humbled on their knees, . . . all agreed in one that the celebration thereof be made according to the said Act.[60]

Conformity did not necessarily mean agreement, and some conformity was clearly reluctant and imposed. Vigorous enforcement continued to be necessary. After Easter 1620 the council renewed its edict requiring conformity and severe fines were authorised as well. In all, at least thirty-nine ministers and six Edinburgh laymen were summoned before the high commission or the privy council for nonconformity and were warned or punished. The bishops held a formal conference as well as informal ones with nonconformists. Eventually about a dozen ministers were deprived.[61] In 1621 opposition even emerged in a usually subservient parliament. The Perth Articles were confirmed by a majority of only twenty-seven after James promised that he 'should not in his days press any more change or alteration in matters of that kind without their own consents'. Opposition was especially strong among burgh representatives, and nonconformity was probably highest in the burghs.[62]

Strict enforcement of the Articles continued for about a year

[60] *Fasti*, IV, 230; *Spottiswood Misc.* II, 287, 289. Mr Guthry, the assistant minister, probably favoured conformity. He later became the Bishop of Moray.
[61] *R.P.C.* XII, lx-lxvi, 279-81.
[62] *A.P.S.* IV, 596-7; Calderwood, VII, 496-504; *O.L.* II, 661; Spottiswood, *History*, 263.

after parliament met. However, after about July 1622 fewer efforts were made to enforce conformity. Only occasionally did the privy council try offenders for nonconformity after that time. The high commission appears to have heard no case after 1622 against ministers accused of nonconformity to the Perth Articles. Archbishop Spottiswood was never enthusiastic about the Articles and sometimes used his influence to soften enforcement. According to Calderwood, Archbishop Spottiswood 'held a diocesan synod in St Androes' in April 1622:

> He rebuked some ministers that urged kneeling too much upon the people. It was reported that the Bishop of Canterburie [George Abbott] had written to him, and desired him not to urge the ceremonies now when weightier affairs were in hand.

A year later Calderwood also heard a report that a meeting of bishops had 'agreed that noe minister sould be urged heerafter with obedience to the Five Articles'.[63] Inquiries into the conformity of ministers ceased in the synod of Fife after 1622.

James did not intend to drop the Articles. Conventicles were condemned in 1624 and occasional cases continued to be heard by the council. But continuous efforts to discover and punish nonconformity did not continue in the final years of James's reign.

Nor were they revived by Charles I. At the beginning of his reign, Charles found it wise to declare publicly that he had no intention of altering the 'government and pollicie of the kirk alredy established'. That policy included 'the observance of the Actis concludit at Perth'.[64] However, no special attempts were made to enforce the Articles, and the first few years of the new reign actually saw the development of an accommodation scheme which allowed those ministers who had been ordained before the Perth assembly to ignore the Articles:

> provyding they utter no doctrine publickly against our authority, the church government, nor canons thereof ... [and] dissuade no uthers nather privately nor publickly from the obedience thereof.

The accommodation also provided 'that the brethrin that are banished have libertie to returne, and be placed at churches

[63] Calderwood, VII, 397–8, 547–8, 571; *O.L.* II, 627, 773.
[64] *R.P.C.* (Second Series), I, 91–2.

PARISH LIFE IN SCOTLAND 191

againe; and the brethreen confynned or suspendit for their disconformity, be inlarged, and placed againe in the ministry' if they agreed to the above conditions. Although Charles's accommodation specified that all new candidates must sign a 'band of conformitie' before their admission to the ministry, even a few new ordinands 'were suffered to enter the ministrie without conformity'.[65] The success of the accommodation scheme is unknown, but its very existence is evidence that nonconformity had never disappeared and the Perth Articles had never been universally enforced.

The privy council did not concern itself with the Articles until 1634. In that year the council condemned those who 'runnes to seeke the communion at the hands of suche ministers as they know to be disconforme to all good order', and parishioners were ordered to communicate yearly at their own parish church.[66] But no further action was taken by the council.

Charles was not really interested in the Perth Articles as such; he had more extensive and thorough plans for the reordering of Scottish worship. Discussion of a new Scottish liturgy began as early as 1629. Charles's chief liturgical concern in the parliament of 1633 was expressed in an act which (by a somewhat devious route)

[65] Balfour, *Works*, II, 142–3; cf. Charles Rogers, *The Earl of Stirling's Register of Royal Letters*, I, 63–4; Wodrow, *Select Biographies*, I, 136. Also see above, 151–2.

[66] *R.P.C.* (Second Series), V, 421–2. That act may be the reason why a sudden inquiry into conformity was held at the synod of Moray in 1635. The investigation discovered that six ministers in the diocese had not 'given the communion [at Easter] out of thair own hands unto thair people sitting reverently upon thair knees'. By the following Easter only one minister in the diocese had not conformed. (Moray Synod, 75–81).

It has been argued that an act of council in 1629 requiring all major government officers to communicate yearly in the Chapel Royal and also requiring all subjects to communicate once a year in their own parish church was intended to enforce the Articles. This interpretation is doubtful. 1629 was the high point of the government's attempts to repress Roman Catholicism in Scotland. Over twenty-five per cent of the entries in the *Register of the Privy Council* for 1629 and 1630 concern Roman Catholics. Charles was probably not dissembling when he declared in this act that an annual communion was intended as a test for discovering papists. The act mentioned neither communion at Pasch nor the matter of kneeling. (George B. Burnet, *The Holy Communion in the Reformed Church of Scotland*, 90; *R.P.C.* [Second Series], III, xi–xviii, 186–8.)

required a bishop to wear a rockhet and chimere and 'inferior clergy... [to] weare there surplices' when they ministered the Holy Communion. Thereafter, bishops especially were urged to be 'in their Whites'.[67] Charles also required the English Prayer Book to be used in his Chapel Royal in 1633 with a Communion on 'the first Sunday of every month'. Thereafter events moved swiftly. A new code of canons and an ordinal were introduced in 1636, and the following year the ill-fated Prayer Book was imposed by royal authority. The Glasgow assembly of 1638 did take care to condemn the Perth Articles, but by then those Articles were only a small part of their grievances.

The real significance of the Perth Articles lies in the fact that they made possible the creation of a permanent nonconforming party. Earlier attempts to create an active and continuous anti-episcopal party had largely failed. But the Perth Articles, and especially the article requiring kneeling at communion, affected the whole church in a much more direct way than had the revival of episcopacy. These Articles touched the worship of every lay adult at a particularly intimate and sacred moment. Opposition was far from universal, but it was strong enough to form a permanent party of nonconformists who could not be suppressed. Those who preferred to go to conventicles 'in Edinburgh and otheris placeis' in 1624 did not know the future course of events in Scotland, but a later historian might well agree with Archbishop Spottiswood that the Articles were 'new and uncouth'.[68]

IV

Apart from the minister, elders and deacons, the most important church officials in a typical parish were a reader and schoolmaster. Frequently one person held both offices. Unsuccessful attempts were made in the sixteenth century to suppress the office of reader. An assembly in 1580 concluded 'after long reasoning, that... [the office of reader] is no ordinar office within the Kirk of God', and ordered readers who were unable to 'be pastors and preach the

[67] Gordon Donaldson, *The Making of the Scottish Prayer Book of 1637*, 41; *A.P.S.* V, 20–1; John Rushworth, *Historical Collections*, II, 205.
[68] *Spottiswood Miscellany*, I, 65–6. Cf. Gordon Donaldson, *Scotland: James V to James VII*, 209; Ian B. Cowan, 'The Five Articles of Perth', 177.

word' to be 'deposit from the reiding'.[69] However, the shortage of ministers made it impossible to suppress the office of reader, and the number of readers steadily grew. In 1596 stipends were assigned to 129 readers.[70] By the early seventeenth century readers had a well-established place in the church; parishes which had settled ministers often had readers as well.

There was uneasiness about readers who baptised children or solemnised marriages. In 1589 the presbytery of Edinburgh deposed a reader who 'had baptized thrie barns', although the presbytery of St Andrews in 1592 authorised a reader 'to solemnise the bannes of mariage'.[71] An assembly in 1597 tried to regulate the practice, but did not condemn it. The assembly 'ordaines that no Reidar minister the sacrament of baptisme ... and that they presume not to celebrate the bands of marriage without speciall command of the Minister of the Kirk; and in cace ther be no Minister therat, of the Presbytrie'. According to Calderwood, this act was designed to prevent 'the abuse of readers baptising childrein gottin in adulterie and fornicatioun ... and celebrating unlawfull mariages',[72] and cases involving irregular ministrations by readers continued to come before presbyteries. In 1602 the presbytery of Paisley considered a marriage which had been solemnised in Kilmarnock without proclamation of banns by 'Hew P[ ] bering the office of ane redar in the kirk and having pe[rmission?] of the kirk to celebrat mariadges'.[73] However, references to marriages or baptisms conducted by readers soon disappeared from church records, and evidently these rites ceased to be administered by readers.

Readers were admitted by presbyteries, usually upon a recommendation of a local minister and kirk session. Their chief duty was to conduct the first part of the Sunday service. In addition they were sometimes expected to read daily services or to catechise. A reader at Udny was ordered to 'read the Word and publick prayers' every Sunday, and a reader at Ellon was 'authorised to reid and catechise at Ellon'. The parish of Dundonald engaged a reader to assist at the chapel of Corsbie. His duties were 'reding at

[69] *B.U.K.* II, 455–7 (Calderwood, III, 471).
[70] This figure was compiled from the Register of Assignation and Modification of Stipends, 1596.
[71] Edinburgh Presb., 3 June 1589; *St Andrews K. S.* II, 742.
[72] *B.U.K.* III, 927 (Calderwood, V, 646–7).
[73] Paisley Presb., 16 September 1602.

Corsbie and teiching the bairnes at the Kirk'. The reader at Aberdeen was given a new Psalm Book in 1611, and in 1621 he was ordered to catechise the poor on Monday afternoon.[74] The position of reader was often combined with other offices. Sometimes a reader was also a kirk officer, that is an officer of the session who delivered formal summonses to offenders or witnesses. More frequently, a reader was also a clerk of session and was responsible for keeping the session minutes. Parishes which had schools usually expected one man to be both schoolmaster and reader. At Jedburgh in 1609 a man was admitted 'reidar to the Kirk of Jedburgh, and to be doctor [i.e. assistant schoolmaster] in the grammar school and to teitch a musik scholl'. At Belhelvie in 1628 'Mr Robert Thomsoun be mutuall consent of the minister, gentlemen and eldares of the parochin was admittit Clark, Reader, and schoulmaster to the churche and parochin of Balhelvie'.[75]

Readers received small stipends for their services. At Belhelvie a reader was given ten merks a year 'for his reading and service making', but the readers at Elgin and Trinity College, Edinburgh each received twenty pounds a year.[76]

Schools were established in most burghs by 1600. They were supported by town councils and sometimes by kirk sessions as well. The stipends of schoolmasters in burghs steadily rose. At Ayr the master of the grammar school received £40 in 1590, but by 1608 his stipend had doubled. The schoolmaster at Lanark received only five merks in 1570 but £60 in 1615. At Stirling the schoolmaster received 100 merks in 1602 but four times that amount in 1662.[77] Burgh schools were not divorced from church discipline; presbyteries jealously maintained their right to examine and admit burgh schoolmasters, and pupils in burgh schools were often ordered to attend church in a body or even to assist in singing the psalms on Sunday.[78]

[74] Ellon Presb., 29 May, 6 February 1600; *Dundonald K. S.* 121; *Aberdeen K. S.* 77, 97-8.

[75] Ellon Presb., 23 July 1607, 14 August 1611; *Extracts from the Records of the Burgh of Edinburgh, 1604-26*, 10; Jedburgh Presb., 3 October, 8 November 1609; Belhelvie K. S., 30 December 1628.

[76] Belhelvie K. S., 7 October 1627; *Elgin K. S.* 164; Trinity College K. S., 15 April 1630.

[77] George S. Pryde, *Ayr Burgh Accounts*, lxiii-lxv.

[78] *Records of Elgin* (New Spalding Club), II, 401-2; *St Ancrews K. S.* 908; *Maitland Misc.* I, 89-90. Also see above, 107-8.

Schools developed more slowly in rural parishes. The legal basis for the establishment of rural schools was an act of privy council in 1616 which ordered the establishment of a school 'in everie parroche of this kingdome whair convenient meanes may be had', and an act of parliament in 1633 which allowed bishops, with or without the consent of heritors, to 'set downe ane stent [i.e. a tax] ... for maintenance and establisching of the saids schooles'.[79] However, establishment of rural schools began long before 1616. The process was long and often difficult. The records of two very different presbyteries, namely Ellon and Jedburgh, reveal the way in which schools developed in the early seventeenth century.

There were eight parishes in the presbytery of Ellon. A school may have been established at Ellon before 1600, but one was certainly in existence by 1605. At times the school was maintained with difficulty and even ceased to operate for a while. In 1616 the 'parochiners and heritors war unwilling to contribut' and the presbytery regretted 'the want of a scole in Ellen'. However, a schoolmaster was being sought by the session at Ellon in 1617, and the school was again in operation at least by 1620.[80]

A school was established at Slains at least by 1608, when a schoolmaster was admitted reader.[81] At a visitation at Foveran in 1605 the elders 'thocht it convenient that thair suld be ane grammar scuill' at Foveran. By 1609 a man was admitted by the presbytery 'to teich ane scuill in the toun of Newburgh' (in the parish of Foveran); and, shortly after the 1616 act, Bishop Alexander Forbes met with the elders of Foveran and agreed upon a regular stipend, 'viz. 13s. 4d. or ane firlot meill of ilk pleuch for mantenance of the scuillmaster'.[82]

By 1614 'ane Inglis scole' was organised at Udny. The reader there was also schoolmaster between 1614 and 1620. The first

---

[79] *R.P.C.* X, 671-2; *A.P.S.* V, 21-2. For an account of the development of schools in East Lothian, see D. J. Withrington, 'Schools in the Presbytery of Haddington in the 17th Century' in *Transactions of the East Lothian Antiquarian and Field Naturalists' Society*, IX, 90-111.

[80] Ellon Presb., 18 September 1605, 19 June 1616, 26 March 1617, 27 December 1620.

[81] Ellon Presb., 30 March 1608. For subsequent references to the school at Slains, see 19 July 1610, 25 July 1627, 29 June 1640.

[82] Ellon Presb., 26 August 1605, 8 February 1609, 9 October 1617. An unlicensed school existed in Newburgh in 1605 but it was closed by the presbytery (Ellon Presb., 26 August, 27 August 1605).

evidence of a school at Methlick was in 1614, when a schoolmaster was admitted.[83] Plans were made in 1621 to establish a school at Tarves. The following year Bishop Patrick Forbes tried to persuade the heritors and elders at Tarves to establish a school. 'Efter lang contestatioun with sum of the gentillmen and elders . . . and finding na conformitie on thair pairt', the bishop ordered the minister at Tarves to 'rais letters' in Edinburgh to force the heritors to contribute toward a school. In 1623 the first schoolmaster was admitted at Tarves.[84]

Apparently no school was established at Cruden. In 1605 Cruden was described as a place which 'wantit ane scuill for education', but only readers were ever admitted at Cruden and a school was first mentioned in visitation reports in 1640. Nor is there any evidence of a school at Logie-Buchan.[85]

By 1638 six of the eight parishes in the Presbytery of Ellon had some kind of school. Five of these six were probably established between 1600 and 1625.

There were seventeen parishes in the presbytery of Jedburgh. When the extant presbytery records begin in 1606 the school at Jedburgh was well established, and a schoolmaster had been at work in Hawick since 1592. In 1608 a schoolmaster at Eckford was teaching 'a common school their without licens . . . of the presbitery', but the school was probably soon closed. There was a 'scholmaister at Baderwill' (Bedrule) in 1608, and the following year the 'scholemaister at Howname' was allowed to 'read some chapteris before preaching'.[86] Disciplinary cases involved schoolmasters at Minto in 1616, at Hobkirk in 1619, and at Suden (Southdean) in 1620.[87]

Records of the presbytery of Jedburgh are less complete than

[83] Udny: Ellon Presb., 14 September 1620. Methlick: Ellon Presb., 6 April 1614, 6 September 1617.

[84] Ellon Presb., 14 June 1621, 24 April, 25 July 1622, 23 July 1623, 29 May 1627.

[85] Cruden: Ellon Presb., 17 July 1605, 17 July 1633, 26 May 1640. Logie-Buchan: No school was mentioned in visitation reports in 1635 or in 1640. (Ellon Presb., 14 July 1634, 29 May 1640.)

[86] Jedburgh: Jedburgh Presb., 20 November 1606, 3 May 1609, 6 November 1616; Hawick: Jedburgh Presb., 8 January 1607, 13, 20 November 1616; Eckford: Jedburgh Presb., 21 December 1608; Bedrule and Howman: Jedburgh Presb., 28 December 1608, 27 September 1609.

[87] Jedburgh Presb., 9 October 1616, 5 May 1619, 14 June 1620; cf. 8 May 1622.

those of Ellon, nor were the brethren at Jedburgh as assiduous in carrying out regular visitations. Schools probably were in existence in some of the other parishes of the presbytery. However, there is no evidence in church records that schools existed before 1638 at Ancrum, Cavers, Crailing and Nisbet, Abbotrule, Kirkton, Langnewton, Hassendean, or Oxnam. In other words, at least seven of the sixteen parishes in the presbytery had established some kind of local school before 1638.

The main problem was financial support, and many complaints were made by schoolmasters about their meagre stipends. Reports sent in by parishes in 1627 certainly wanted to emphasise the poverty of their schools, but the complaint was real enough. There had been a school at Cockpen 'bot for fault of maintenance it is deserted', and a similar report was received from Killin. The report from Kirknewton declared that their school was 'lyikelie to dissolve the nixt terme for want of maintenance'.[88] Many reports complained about the lack of 'fundation' for a school.[89]

The 1633 act allowed a bishop to establish a formal tax for support of schools, with or without the consent of heritors; and advantage was taken of this act in some areas. In 1636 the presbytery of Kirkcaldy received a special licence from Archbishop Spottiswood to conduct visitations, and twelve parishes were visited that summer. The main purpose of these visitations was to establish a regular income for parish schools. At Kinghorn, for example,

> the commissioun direct from my Lord of St Androis being read, with the act of Secret Counsell for establishing of scholes and appoynting ane sufficient maintenance for the schoolemaster, ... all heretors and elders thinks it verie meit and expedient that thair be ane schoole.

The presbytery first asked the heritors 'to make ane voluntar offer of a sufficient mantenance for ane scholemaster' but they 'wold offer nothing'. The presbytery then concluded that 'thrie hundreth merks is little enough for the yearlie maintenance of ane scholemaster in Kingorne' and ordered this sum to be paid 'yeirlie in all tyme comeing – the half thairof to be payit be the towne, and the other half be the heretors of the paroshe according as they stent

[88] *Reports on the State of Certain Parishes in Scotland*, 46, 180, 84.
[89] *Ibid.* 21, 22, 23, 27, 70, 110, 167.

themselfs'.[90] Similar actions were being taken in Moray. When the synod of Moray learned in 1634 that the schoolmaster of Kiltarlity had 'no mantinance ... the synod orders that they raise letters for mantinance'.[91]

Considerable progress was made toward the establishment of schools between 1600 and 1638. The acts of 1616 and 1633 gave legal support to this movement, but equally important were the persistent efforts of presbyteries, synods and bishops[92] to establish schools in every parish. A report on Mordington in 1627 declared that 'theire is an greit necessatie of ane skule for not ane of the paroche can reid nor wryt except the Minister'.[93] No church could be complacent about this situation if it believed, as did the Church of Scotland, that schools were 'necessar instruments to come to the true meaning and sense of the will of God revealed in his Word'.[94]

[90] *Kirkcaldy Presb.* 97.
[91] Moray Synod, 63.
[92] See, for example, the efforts of the Archbishop of St Andrews in Fife (Fife Synod, 51, 127, 129, 131).
[93] *Reports on the State of Certain Parishes in Scotland,* 22.
[94] *B.U.K.* II, 723 (Calderwood, IV, 665).

CHAPTER TEN

Conclusions

Generally speaking, two different systems of supervision developed in the Church of Scotland during the sixteenth century – oversight administered individually by bishops, superintendents and commissioners, and oversight by presbyteries collectively. In the early seventeenth century a compromise settlement was effected which embraced many of the features of both these systems. This Jacobean compromise or settlement was probably not expected by many. As late as 1610 Archbishop Spottiswood hoped to see presbyteries soon 'evanische'.[1] Nor did writers try to defend its inclusive terms, either before or after 1610. The settlement was based less upon doctrinaire considerations than upon the practical need to reconcile the conflicting interests of various forces – the crown, the nobility, landholders, and different parties within the ministry. Although the compromise may have seemed an unlikely one, it was not only one which worked, but one which worked surprisingly well.

The ordinary functioning of kirk session was not altered by this settlement. They continued to exercise much the same authority after 1610 as they had before that date. They did, indeed, lose their jurisdiction in adultery cases to presbyteries by 1625, although there appears to have been no formal order transferring this function. The change was due more likely to the growing power and stability of presbyteries than to the introduction of episcopacy. Otherwise, jurisdiction exercised by kirk sessions underwent little change. Both bishops and presbyteries used their influence to establish kirk sessions where none existed, and many new sessions were organised between 1610 and 1638. The establishment of a new kirk session was closely related to the 'planting' of a new minister, and the two developments probably took place together.

Kirk sessions were of enormous importance in the administrative

[1] *O.L.* I, 235.

life of the church. All of the special funds which presbyteries, synods or assemblies might seek to raise, whether for poor relief, support of bursars in divinity, or building a bridge, ultimately depended upon the efficiency of kirk sessions for their collection. To administer discipline in a parish was almost impossible without an effective session, and most of the spiritual penalties imposed by both presbyteries and synods had to be enforced by kirk sessions. These sessions brought many laymen into intimate contact with the work of the church and gave them a share in the church's cure of souls as well as in its administration of finances and properties. The reformed Church of Scotland, as it existed in the sixteenth and seventeenth centuries, would have been impossible without the work of kirk sessions. General Assemblies, bishops, even presbyteries might come and go, but kirk sessions remained one unchanging element in the administration of the church.

The first four decades of the seventeenth century also saw progress made in the repair and furnishing of churches as well as in the building of new churches. A large number of schools were established, although there were still many parishes in which satisfactory provision for schoolmasters had probably not been achieved by 1638.

Ordinary Sunday worship was not affected by the Perth Articles, and the great Sunday morning service of prayer and psalm, Scripture and sermon remained the most significant moment in the weekly rhythm of the church's life. Here the spiritual power, authority and corporate character of the kirk were most vividly expressed.

However, some new and controversial elements were introduced into the yearly pattern of the church's worship. Not only was the time for the celebration of the annual Communion Service changed, but the manner of celebration was also altered at a particularly intimate and sensitive place – the communion of the people. The requirement of the Perth Articles that communicants should kneel affected ordinary churchmen far more directly than did the introduction of episcopacy, and disagreement about worship was more divisive than changes in church government. While large areas of the Church observed the most important Articles and continued to observe them even when enforcement was lax, a significant minority of ministers and parishes refused to obey any of the Articles and formed a continuing party of non-

CONCLUSIONS 201

conformists. Response to the Perth Articles was a significant portent of that schism which developed in the Church in the 1640s.

Although the activity of kirk sessions and local parishes was scarcely touched by the 1610 settlement, the jurisdiction of presbyteries was altered; and they no longer exercised an almost exclusive authority over excommunications and admissions to the ministry as they had done since about 1590. Nevertheless, even in these matters presbyteries still had considerable authority. All preliminary trials involving excommunication were heard by presbyteries. Also the examination of ordinands and the institution of ministers into their benefices were usually assigned to presbyteries, often by warrant from bishops. Apart from these two matters the ordinary work of presbyterial discipline as well as the older work of exercising continued without interruption. The number of presbyteries substantially increased during the period, and bishops used their inflence both to establish new presbyteries and to support the actions of presbyteries.

Synods were more directly affected by the revival of episcopacy than either of the two lower courts. Although little change took place after 1610 in the actual work which synods did in the examination of presbyteries, major disciplinary cases, and important administrative decisions, yet after 1610 the bishop's voice was an important and probably a dominant factor in the decisions reached by any synod.

General Assemblies were even more profoundly altered after 1596. Not only did they meet less regularly than before, but also delegates to some crucial assemblies were nominated and no assembly at all met between 1618 and 1638. But the greatest change was the establishment of the principle that 'the Generall Assembly of a realme has not power to conveene themself, but upon a great and weightie occasioun, intimat to the prince, and licence graunted thereto'.[2] Although James tried to manipulate assemblies and succeeded in doing so, he never ignored them. Indeed, prior to the Canons of 1636 no major ecclesiastical change was introduced into the church without at least the nominal assent of an assembly. And much of the routine disciplinary work which had been handled by assemblies was

[2] This was one of the proposals made by Archbishop Adamson in 1584 (Calderwood, IV, 54).

continued either by synods, provincial assemblies, or the Courts of High Commission.

The achievements of the reformed ministry in Scotland between 1600 and 1638 were impressive. By 1638 a university education was standard for all ministers, and rare indeed was the minister who was not a university graduate. A bursary system developed in the church after 1616 and was in full operation within a few years. This system made it financially possible for many candidates to have some years of theological study after their regular arts course. After completing his theological study, a man usually spent further years as an expectant before securing a benefice. During this apprenticeship he would become intimately acquainted with the homiletical and disciplinary work of a presbytery and would often assist in a parish as well. It was a long process, and only the best – or the best-connected – candidates finally entered the ministry.

This period also saw the appointment of ministers in almost every parish, and the extension of the discipline of kirk sessions throughout the lowlands. Probably most cures which had inadequate incomes in 1600 had received substantial increases by 1638; and if financial issues were not settled, at least the 'constant platt' demanded by many general assemblies had been determined upon and in part put into effect. The first Book of Discipline had urged that every parish in Scotland should have a godly and learned minister provided with a competent maintenance. Between 1600 and 1638 the Church came closer to achieving that ideal than at any previous time in Scottish church history.

That bishops as well as presbyteries were both vigorous agents within the church after 1610 is obvious. To what extent, however, was episcopacy really integrated into the life of the church? Were bishops merely a superficial imposition of the crown, easily eliminated when the opportunity arose? The extent of royal authority over bishops is undeniable. Indeed, much of the opposition to episcopacy was due to its association with royal authority. Bishops were spiritual lords and had important positions in parliament, in the committee of the articles, and to a lesser degree in the privy council.

However, bishops were much more than civil officers used to control the church. The word 'bishop' had never been secularised in Scotland as had the words 'abbot' and 'prior'. The bishops who were appointed after 1600 were men who had been ministers of the church for some years. They continued to preach, to administer the Lord's Supper, and even on occasion to baptise. They were closely related to many projects designed to increase the church's material resources and they took an active part in providing better stipends for ministers. Their spiritual or pastoral authority within the church was demonstrated in episcopal visitations, in their review of excommunications and other disciplinary cases, and in their supervision of much of the process of admission to the ministry. Some bishops at least took these duties seriously and appear to have discharged them conscientiously and faithfully.

The Church of Scotland between 1610 and 1638 inevitably invites comparison with the Church during the Restoration period. The restoration settlement of 1662 was in many ways a revival of the settlement of 1610, and the basic terms of both settlements were much the same. During both periods the church was governed by kirk sessions, presbyteries, synods, and bishops. Neither in 1610 nor in 1662 did the introduction of episcopacy change the basic doctrine or worship of the church, and Calvinist ideals of faith and worship were unaltered. Bishops invariably presided at ordinations, although ordination of deacons was exceedingly rare, and most men were simply ordained to the ministry. There is no known case of a minister who had been ordained by a presbytery before 1610 being reordained thereafter, although there were probably a few cases of reordination in 1662.

However, no restoration restores everything, and there were some important contrasts between the two periods. The most obvious contrast was the prominence of conventicles after 1662. In the Restoration period schism, which first developed in the 1640s, became a permanent feature of the Scottish Church, for the Restoration settlement was unacceptable to about one-third of the ministry and a significant minority of the laity. There were a few conventicles before 1638, but they were small and insignificant. Forty-two ministers might sign a protest against episcopacy in 1606, but most of them continued to serve in a church governed by bishops and presbyteries. Enforcement of the Perth Articles severely strained the church's unity, but the willingness of non-conformists to continue in the ministry and the reluctance of bishops to prosecute nonconformity prevented open rupture. Indeed, one of the more striking characteristics of the Jacobean church was its largely unspoken but deep commitment to unity.

It was far more medieval than modern in its visible expression of the belief – as the Confession of 1616 put it – that there is 'an [or *ane*, i.e. one] holy Catholick or universal Kirk. . . . This Kirk we believe to be but one'.[3]

Another marked contrast was the extent of royal authority. Royal supremacy was as staunchly upheld in 1610 as in 1662, but it was exercised by James VI and even by Charles I with more restraint than Restoration monarchs showed. James might threaten in 1617 to have parliament pass an act asserting his right to determine all 'matters of external policy' in the church, but he withdrew this proposal after opposition developed.[4] No act before 1638 ever asserted royal supremacy in as sweeping terms as did the Assertory Act of 1669, nor was anything like the oath required by the Test Act of 1681 imposed upon ministers or bishops by James VI or his son. No bishop was deposed by the crown before 1638, but during the Restoration two archbishops and two bishops were summarily dismissed from their posts, one of them because he supported a movement to call a national Synod of the Church.[5] Only on the subject of worship was the government of Charles II more conservative than that of his father and grandfather. Changes in traditional Scottish worship had been difficult for James VI and disastrous for Charles I. After the Restoration, bishops were forbidden to introduce canons and a liturgy 'lest such things should provoke to a new Rebellion'.[6]

Recently, Professor A. C. Cheyne has made some valuable observations about the worship of the church which are applicable to the whole of Scottish reformation history. He wrote:

> In worship, as in government and doctrine, the Church of Scotland has seldom presented a uniform and unchanging pattern; and there are strong grounds for contending that the principles whereby conformity or non-conformity with 'essential Presbyterianism' may be determined are not deducible from history itself but must rather be brought to it from elsewhere.

---

[3] From the 1616 Confession of Faith (B.U.K. III, 1138 [Calderwood, VII, 240]). Cf. Gordon Donaldson, 'The Emergence of Schism in Seventeenth-Century Scotland'.

[4] Spottiswood, *History*, III. 241.

[5] R. E. Head, *Royal Supremacy and the Trials of Bishops*, chapters V, VI.

[6] *Miscellany of the Scottish History Society*, II, 354n.

And he concluded:

Only a very bold or a very bigoted man would claim the unerring ability to detect, in all the welter of divergent views and changing practices, the essential or characteristic tradition of Scottish Presbyterian worship.[7]

The comprehensive settlement which developed in Scotland in the early seventeenth century can hardly claim to be *the* authentic Scottish Reformation tradition. But it was *an* authentic tradition; the integrity and good faith of those who built up this settlement should not be lightly dismissed. To concentrate on opposition in Edinburgh and dismiss the conforming north (where at least half the population lived) as simply swayed by 'erastian Aberdeen' is a one-sided and shallow view. The Aberdeen professor who defended kneeling at communion believed himself to be as authentically Christian and Scots as did the Edinburgh citizen who opposed that practice.

The search for a comprehensive settlement is not as dramatic an approach as the proclamation of an *Athanasius contra mundum*. If less doctrinaire, that search can be as difficult, can command the allegiance of as qualified and noble Christians, and can have its own rewards. To build up a comprehensive settlement meant that the interests and convictions of many different groups would have to be considered and partly reconciled – kings and tacksmen, noblemen and farmers, ministers and lairds. And when significant interests of some national groups began to be ignored in the 1630s, the settlement disintegrated. Yet for over a generation that settlement was effective; the kirk made remarkable progress towards meeting its own goals of a reformed, educated and financially secure ministry as well as a disciplined parish and nation. Moreover, the settlement was unique, combining elements in a way and on a scale that could be found nowhere else. In a sense the combination of kirk session, presbytery, and bishop was a Scottish discovery. The 1610 settlement should be neither ignored nor dismissed as somehow unauthentic. It remains a genuine and valuable part of Scottish Reformation history. Surely the experiences, successes, and failures of the many Christians who lived within that settlement can provide some very useful perspective for those who are considering similar comprehensive schemes today.

[7] A. C. Cheyne, 'Worship in the Kirk: Knox, Westminster, and the 1940 Book', 71, 81.

Bibliography

I

MANUSCRIPT SOURCES

(All manuscripts are in the Scottish Record Office, Edinburgh, unless otherwise noted.)

General Works:
Aberdeen Parish Register, 168a (12). New Register House, Edinburgh.
Canongate Parish Register, 685[3] (12), New Register House,
Court Book of the Bishopric of Orkney, 1614–38.
Dunfermline Parish Register, 424 (1), 424 (2), New Register House.
Hope, Norman Victor, 'Ministerial Stipends in the Church of Scotland from 1560 to 1633', Ph.D. thesis, New College, University of Edinburgh, 1944.
Hopkirk, D. S. 'A Study of Accommodation Movements between Presbytery and Episcopacy', Ph.D. thesis, New College, University of Edinburgh, 1946.
Inverness Parish Register, 98 (1), New Register House.
Perry, John, 'John Spottiswoode, Archbishop and Chancellor', Ph.D. thesis, New College, University of Edinburgh, 1905.
Prugh, John Wiley, 'The Theory and Practice of Discipline in the Scottish Reformation', Ph.D. thesis, New College, University of Edinburgh, 1958.
Records of Testaments, Commissariot Court of Brechin.
Records of Testaments, Commissariot Court of Dunblane.
Records of Testaments, Commissariot Court of Edinburgh.
Records of Testaments, Commissariot Court of Glasgow.
Records of Testaments, Commissariot Court of Hamilton and Campsie.
Records of Testaments, Commissariot Court of St Andrews.
Register of the Acts and Decreets of the Court of Session, CCLXXII.
Registers of Old Decreets Recorded in the Books of the Commission on Teinds, I–IV, Teind Office, New Register House.
Register of Assignation and Modification of Stipends, 1596–7, 1599–1601, 1607–8.
Registrum Secreti Sigilli
Register of Presentations to Benefices.
Shaw, Duncan, 'The Origin and Development of the General Assembly

of the Church of Scotland, 1560–1600', Ph.D. thesis, University of Edinburgh, 1862.
Wadsworth, C. C. 'The General Assembly of 1610', Ph.D. thesis, New College, University of Edinburgh, 1930.

Synod Records:
Records of the Synod of Fife, 1610–36 (CH2/154/1).
Records of the Synod of Lothian and Tweeddale, 1589–96 (CH2/252/1).
Records of the Synod of Moray, 1623–44 (CH2/271/1).

Presbytery Records:
Records of the Presbytery of Aberdeen, 1598–1610 (CH2/1/1).
Records of the Presbytery of Dunblane, 1616–28. These records are in the possession of the Presbytery of Stirling and Dunblane.
Records of the Presbytery of Edinburgh, 1586–1593 (CH/2/121/1), 1601–7 (CH2/121/3).
Records of the Presbytery of Ellon, 1597–1607 (CH2/146/1), 1607–28 (CH2/146/2), 1634–43 (CH2/146/3).
Records of the Presbytery of Haddington, 1627–39 (CH2/185/4).
Records of the Presbytery of Jedburgh, 1606–21 (CH2/198/1), 1522–44 (CH2/198/2).
Records of the Presbytery of Lanark, 1623–57 (CH2/234/1).
Records of the Presbytery of Paisley, 1602–7 (CH2/294/1), 1626–47 (CH2/294/2).
Records of the Presbytery of Melrose (or Selkirk), 1607–19 (CH2/327/1).
Records of the Presbytery of Perth, 1618–47 (CH2/299/1).

Kirk Session Records:
Records of the Kirk Session of Belhelvie, 1623–41 (CH2/32/1).
Records of the Kirk Session of Culross, 1630–46 (CH2/77/1).
Records of the Kirk Session of Elgin, 1598–1605 (CH2/145/2), 1613–22 (CH2/115/3), 1622–29 (CH2/145/4), 1629–40 (CH2/145/5).
Records of the Kirk Session of Trinity College, Edinburgh, 1626–38 (CH2/141/1).

Family Papers:
Airlie Muniments
Breadalbane Letters
Barclay Allardie Papers
Bught Papers
Cardross Writs
Clerk of Penicuk Muniments
Craven Bequest
Cunninghame Graham Muniments
Dalhousie Muniments
Dunecht Writs
Duntreath Muniments
Lord Forbes Collection
Morton Papers
Newbattle Collection
Reay Papers

II
PRINTED WORKS

Acts and proceedings of the General Assemblies of the Kirk of Scotlan d Maitland and Bannatyne Clubs, Edinburgh, 1845. Cited as *B.U.K.*

Acts of the Parliaments of Scotland, III (1814), IV (1816), edited by T. Thomson, V (1870), edited by C. Innes. Cited as *A.P.S.*

Aldis, Harry G. *A List of Books Printed in Scotland before 1700* Edinburgh Bibliographical Society, 1904.

Anton, A. E. 'Handfasting in Scotland', *Scottish Historical Review,* October, 1958.

Ayr Burgh Records, 1534–1624, edited by George S. Pryde, Scottish History Society, Edinburgh, 1937.

Balfour, Sir James, *Historical Works,* Edinburgh, 1824.

Barclay, Robert S. editor, *The Court Book of Orkney and Shetland, 1612–1613,* The Kirkwall Press, 1962.

Birrell, Robert, *Diary,* printed in Sir John Graham Dalyell, *Fragments of Scottish History,* Edinburgh, 1798.

Bonar, Horatius, *Catechisms of the Scottish Reformation,* James Nisbet and Co. London, 1866.

Botfield, Beriah, editor, *Original Letters Relating to the Ecclesiastical Affairs of Scotland from 1603 to 1625,* Bannatyne Club, Edinburgh, 1851. Cited as *O.L.*

Brereton, Sir William, *Travels in Holland, the United Provinces, England, Scotland, and Ireland,* Chetham Society, 1844.

Brunton, George, and Haig, David, *Senators of the College of Justice,* Thomas Clark, Edinburgh, 1832.

Burnet, George B. *The Holy Communion in the Reformed Church of Scotland,* Oliver and Boyd, Edinburgh and London, 1960.

Burnet, Gilbert, 'Preface' in *The Life of William Bedell,* John Southby, 1685.

Burns, Thomas, *Church Property, The Benefice Lectures,* George A. Morton, Edinburgh, 1905.

Burns, Thomas, *Old Scottish Communion Plate,* R. and R. Clark, Edinburgh, 1892.

Calderwood, David, *History of the Kirk of Scotland,* I – VIII, edited by the Rev. Thomas Thomson, Wodrow Society, Edinburgh, 1844. Cited as Calderwood.

Calendar of the State Papers Relating to Scotland, XII, edited by M. S. Giuseppi, H.M.S.O. 1952, XIII (1), edited by Professor J. D. Mackie, 1964.

Campbell, William A. 'Robert Boyd of Trochrigg', *Records of the Scottish Church History Society*, XII (1958), 220-34.
Campbell, William A. *The Triumph of Presbyterianism*, Saint Andrew Press, Edinburgh, 1958.
Canons and Constitutions Ecclesiastical . . . for the Government of the Church of Scotland, Edward Raban, Aberdeen, 1636 (Aldis 868).
Charles I, *A Large Declaration*, probably written by Walter Balcanquhall, Robert Young, London, 1639.
Cheney, C. R. *Handbook of Dates*, Royal Historical Society, London, 1955.
Constitutions and Canons Ecclesiastical, Treated upon by the Bishop of London, Robert Barker, London, 1612.
Chronicle of Perth, Maitland Club, Edinburgh, 1831.
Connell, Sir John, *A Treatise on the Law of Scotland Respecting Tithes*, I, II, Thomas Clark, Edinburgh, 1830.
Cowan, Ian B. 'The Five Articles of Perth' in *Reformation and Revolution* edited by Duncan Shaw, The Saint Andrew Press, 1967, 160-77.
Cowan, William, *A Bibliography of the Book of Common Order and Psalm Book of the Church of Scotland, 1556-1644*, privately printed, Edinburgh, 1913.
Cowper, William, *Works*, London, 1629.
Craven, J. B. *History of the Church in Orkney, 1558-1662*, William Peace & Son, Kirkwall, 1897.
——, *A History of the Episcopal Church in the Diocese of Caithness*, William Peace & Son, Kirkwall, 1908.
Detailed List of the Old Parochial Registers of Scotland, Murray and Gibb, Edinburgh, 1872, annotated copy, Scottish Record Office.
Donaldson, Gordon, 'The Church Courts', *Introduction to Scottish Legal History*, Stair Society, Edinburgh, 1958, 363-73.
——, editor, *Accounts of the Collectors of Thirds of Benefices, 1561-72*, Scottish History Society, Edinburgh, 1949.
——, 'David Lindsay', *Fathers of the Kirk*, edited by R. S. Wright, Oxford, London, 1960, 27-37.
——, 'The Emergence of Schism in Seventeenth-Century Scotland', *Studies in Church History, Volume 9, Schism, Heresy, and Religious Protest*, edited by Derek Baker, Cambridge, 1972, pp, 277-293.
——, *The Making of the Scottish Prayer Book of 1637*, University Press, Edinburgh, 1954.
——, *Scotland; James V to James VII*, Oliver and Boyd, Edinburgh, 1965.
——, 'Scotland's Conservative North in the Sixteenth and Seventeenth Centuries', *Transactions of the Royal Historical Society*, 5th Series, Vol. 26, 1966, pp. 65-79.
——, *The Scottish Reformation*, Cambridge, 1960.

BIBLIOGRAPHY

——, *Shetland Life under Earl Patrick*, Oliver and Boyd, Edinburgh, 1958.
Dunlop, A. Ian, 'The Polity of the Scottish Church, 1600-37' *Records of the Scottish Church History Society*, XII (1958), 161-184.
Extracts from the Council Register of the Burgh of Aberdeen, 1625-42, Scottish Burgh Records Society, Edinburgh, 1871.
Extracts from the Presbytery Book of Strathbogie, 1631-54, Spalding Club, Aberdeen, 1843.
Extracts from the Records of the Burgh of Edinburgh, 1604-26, 1626-41, edited by Marguerite Wood, Oliver and Boyd, Edinburgh, 1931, 1936.
Extracts from the Records of the Burgh of Glasgow, 1573-42, Scottish Record Burgh Society, 1876.
Forbes, William, *Considerations modestae et pacificae*, Library of Anglo-Catholic Theology, 1850-56.
Form and Maner of Ordaining Ministers and Consecrating of Archbishops and Bishops, used in the Church of Scotland, Thomas Finlason, 1620, Edinburgh (Aldis 549).
Foster, W. R. *Bishop and Presbytery*, S.P.C.K. 1958.
Fraser, James, *Chronicles of the Frasers*, edited by William Mackay, Scottish History Society, Edinburgh, 1905.
Fraser, William, *The Chiefs of Grant*, II, Edinburgh, 1883.
——, *Memoirs of the Maxwells of Pollok*, II, Edinburgh, 1863.
——, *Memorials of the Earls of Haddington*, II, Edinburgh, 1889.
Gordon, James, *History of Scots Affairs*, I, Spalding Club, Aberdeen, 1841.
Graeme, L. G. editor, 'Some Letters and Correspondence of George Graeme, Bishop of Dunblane and of Orkney', *Miscellany of the Scottish History Society*, II, 1904, 231-67.
Guthrie, Henry, *Memoirs*, Glasgow, 1748.
Handbook of British Chronology, edited by Sir F. Maurice Powicke and E. B. Fryde, Royal Historical Society, London, 1961.
Head, R. E. *Royal Supremacy and the Trials of Bishops*, S.P.C.K. London, 1962.
[Henderson, Alexander], *Government and Order of the Church of Scotland*, Edinburgh, 1641.
Henderson, G. D. *Religious Life in Seventeenth Century Scotland*, Cambridge, 1937.
——, 'The Exercise', *Records of the Scottish Church History Society*, VII (1941), 13-29.
——, 'The Ordination of John Forbes of Corse', *Scottish Notes and Queries*, Third Series, X, March, 1932, 33-4.
Heylyn, Peter, *Aerius Redivivus, or The History of the Presbyterians from ... 1536 to ... 1647*, Oxford, 1670.

Historical Papers Submitted to the Christian Unity Association of Scotland, T. and A. Constable, 1914.
James VI, *The Basilicon Doron*, I, edited by James Craigie, Scottish Text Society, Edinburgh, 1944.
Johnston, Sir Archibald, of Wariston, *Diary, 1632–39*, Scottish History Society, Edinburgh, 1911.
Keith, Robert, *An Historical Catalogue of the Scottish Bishops*, Edinburgh, 1824.
Knox, John, *History of the Reformation in Scotland*, edited by William Croft Dickinson, Thomas Nelson & Sons, Ltd. London, 1949.
Lamb, John A. 'The Kalendar of the Book of Common Order, 1564–1644', *Records of the Scottish Church History Society*, XII (1958), 15–28.
Lythe, S. G. E. *The Economy of Scotland in its European Setting*, Oliver and Boyd, Edinburgh, 1960.
Mair, Thomas, *Narratives and Extracts from the Records of the Presbytery of Ellon*, W. Jolly & Sons, Aberdeen, 1898.
Maitland Club Miscellany, I, Edinburgh, 1834.
Makey, W. H., 'The Elders of Stow, Liberton, Canongate and St. Cuthbert's in the Mid-Seventeenth Century', *Records of the Scottish Church History Society*, XVII—Part II (1970), 155–167.
Mathew, David, *Scotland under Charles I*, Eyre & Spottiswoode, London, 1955.
Mathieson, William Law, *Politics and Religion*, James Maclehose and Sons, Glasgow, 1902.
McMahon, George I. R. 'The Scottish Courts of High Commission, 1610–38', *Records of the Scottish Church History Society*, XV—Part III (1965), 193–209.
McMillan, William, *The Worship of the Scottish Reformed Church, 1550–1638*, James Clark & Co. Ltd. London, 1931.
M'Crie, C. G. *The Confessions of the Church of Scotland*, Macniven & Wallace, Edinburgh, 1907.
M'Crie, Thomas, *Life of Andrew Melville*, William Blackwood & Sons, London, 1856.
Melrose Papers, edited by John Hope, Abbotsford Club, Edinburgh, 1837.
Melville, James, *The Autobiography and Diary of Mr James Melville*, edited by Robert Pitcairn, Wodrow Society, Edinburgh, 1842.
Mitchell, Leonel L. 'Episcopal Ordinations in the Church of Scotland: 1610–1688', *Historical Magazine of the Protestant Episcopal Church*, XXXI (June, 1962), 143–59.
Pearson, A. F. Scott, *Church and State*, Cambridge, 1928.
Peterkin, Alexander, editor, *Records of the Kirk of Scotland*, John Sutherland, Edinburgh, 1838.

BIBLIOGRAPHY

Presbytrie Booke of Kirkcaldie, edited by William Stevenson, James Burt, Kirkcaldy, 1900. Cited as *Kirkcaldy K. S.*

Prynne, William, *Hidden Works of Darknes Brought to Publike Light*, London, 1645.

Rait, Robert S. *The Parliaments of Scotland*, Maclehose, Jackson and Co. Glasgow, 1924.

Records of Elgin: 1284–1800, edited by William Cramond, New Spalding Club, Aberdeen, 1908. Cited as *Elgin K. S.*

Records of Old Aberdeen, I, II, edited by Alexander M. Munro, New Spalding Club, Aberdeen, 1899, 1909.

Register of the Ministers, Elders and Deacons of the Christian Congregation of St. Andrews, II, edited by D. H. Fleming, Scottish History Society, Edinburgh, 1890. Cited as *St Andrews K. S.*

Register of the Privy Council of Scotland, V–XIV (First Series), I (Second Series), edited by David Masson, II–VII (Second Series), edited by P. Hume Brown, H.M.S.O. Edinburgh, 1882–1906. Cited as *R.P.C.*

Registrum Magni Sigilli, edited by J. M. Thomson, Edinburgh, 1880, 1892, VI, VII. Cited as *R.M.S.*

Reports on the State of Certain Parishes in Scotland, Maitland Club, Edinburgh, 1835.

Row, John, *The History of the Kirk of Scotland*, Wodrow Society, Edinburgh, 1842.

Row, William, *The Life of Mr Robert Blair . . . with Supplement*, Wodrow Society, Edinburgh, 1848.

Rudierd, Sir Benjamin, *His Speech in Behalf of the Clergie and of Parishes*, Oxford, 1628.

Rushworth, John. *Historical Collections*, London, 1686.

Rutherford, Samuel, *Joshua Redivius, or Mr Rutherfoord's Letters*, 1664.

Scott, Hew, *Fasti Ecclesiae Scoticanae*, I–VIII, Oliver and Boyd, Edinburgh, 1915–50. Cited as *Fasti*.

'Scottish Contributions to the Distressed Church of France in 1622', edited by David H. Fleming, *Miscellany of the Scottish History Society*, III, Edinburgh, 1919, 181–202.

Select Biographies, edited by W. K. Tweedie, Wodrow Society, Edinburgh, 1845

Selections from the Records of the Kirk Session, Presbytery and Synod of Aberdeen, The Spalding Club, Aberdeen, 1846. Cited as *Aberdeen K. S.*

Session Book of Dundonald, 1602–1731, edited by Henry Paton, printed privately, 1936.

Shaw, Duncan, *The General Assemblies of the Church of Scotland, 1560–1600*, St. Andrew Press, Edinburgh, 1964.

Snow, W. G. S. *The Times, Life, and Thought of Patrick Forbes*, S.P.C.K. London, 1952.

Source Book of Scottish History, III, edited by W. C. Dickinson and Gordon Donaldson, Thomas Nelson & Sons, London, 1961.

Spalding, John, *The History of the Troubles and Memorable Transactions in Scotland and England*, I, II, Bannatyne Club, Edinburgh, 1828–9.

Spottiswood, John, *History of the Church of Scotland*, III, Spottiswood Society, Edinburgh, 1851.

Spottiswoode Miscellany, I, II, edited by James Maidment, Spottiswood Society, Edinburgh, 1844–5.

Sprott, George W. *Scottish Liturgies of the Reign of James VI*, Edmonston and Douglas, Edinburgh, 1871.

Warrender Papers, II, edited by Annie I. Cameron, Scottish History Society, Edinburgh, 1932.

Whitaker, Ian, 'The Reports on the Parishes of Scotland, 1627' *Scottish Studies*, III, 229–32.

Willson, David Harris, *King James VI and I*, Jonathan Cape, London, 1956.

Wodrow Society Miscellany, edited by David Laing, Edinburgh, 1844.

Wright, Ronald Selby, *The Kirk in the Canongate*, Oliver and Boyd, Edinburgh, 1958.

Index

Act of Revocation: issued by Charles I, 165; discussed by provincial assemblies, 117–18.

Bishops: before 1596, 8–10; civil episcopacy, 15–17; presentations to bishoprics, 16–17; restoration of temporalities, 17–18; consecrated in London, 29; civil duties, 32–9; consecration service, 42–3; income of, 43–5; residence of, 45–7; and Court of High Commission, 47–8; visitations, 49–52; ordination of ministers, 52–3; and discipline, 53–6; administrative and pastoral duties, 56–7; comparison of Jacobean and Caroline, 63–4; jurisdiction over excommunication, 102–4; relations with presbyteries, 53–4; 104–5.

Blackburn, Peter, bishop of Aberdeen: presented by James VI, 16; unsuccessful attempt to exercise office, 19.

Bursars, 133–5.

Canons, Book of, 127.
Catechisms, 130–1.
Christmas, observance of, 185.
Church buildings, 173–5.
Commission for Modification of Stipends: in 1606, 21, 159–61; in 1617, 161–4, in 1621, 164; in 1627, 165; in 1633, 166.
Commissioners: their authority, 10; support for episcopacy, 15.
Communion vessels, 175–6.
Confession of 1616, 128–30.
Confirmation, 57, 182–3.
Consecration of bishops, 29, 42–3

Court of High Commission, 47–9, 188–9.
Cowper, William, bishop of Galloway, 59–60.

Discipline: exercised by kirk sessions, 71–80; exercised by presbyteries, 95–100; exercised by bishops, 53–6.

Edinburgh riot of 1596, 12–13, 121.
Elders: election of, 66–70; and discipline, 72–3; membership in presbyteries, 88–91; membership in synods, 72–4; position after 1638, 136.
Excommunication: and bishops, 102–4; and presbyteries, 100–105.
'Exercise', 93–5.
Expectants, 135–8.

Fasts, 180.
Forbes, Patrick, bishop of Aberdeen, 59.

General assemblies: at Leith in 1571/2, 8; at Perth in 1596/7, 14, 121; at Dundee in 1597, 14, 121–2; at Linlithgow in 1606, 120, 122; at Glasgow in 1610, 25–6, 120, 122–3; at Aberdeen in 1616, 120–1, 124, 126–32; at Perth in 1618, 124–5 182; membership of, 119–21; appointment of representatives, 121–5; and royal influence, 121–6, estimate of, 201–2.

Gladstanes, George, archbishop of St. Andrews, 59; ordains candidates, 144–5, 147–8.

Glebes, 169–70.

High Commission, Court of, 47–9, 188–9.
Holy Communion: vessels for, 175–6; celebrated on Pasch, 181–4; kneeling required, 186–90. Also see Perth Articles.

James VI: rise to power 6; support for episcopacy, 11–12.

Kirk sessions: establishment of, 66–7; membership of, 69–70; exercise of discipline, 71–80; care for poor, 80–3; estimate of, 83–4, 199–200.
Knox, Andrew, bishop of the Isles, 23–4.

Lindsay, David, bishop of Ross, 57–8.

Manses, 170–1.
Melville, Andrew, 4.
Ministers: education of, 133–5; examinations, 139; ordination and admission, 52–3, 139–53; not ordained by presbyteries, 151–3; increase in numbers, 153–5; income, 156–8; testaments of, 167–9; deposition of, 115–16.

Nobility: attitude toward presbyterianism, 27; attitude toward episcopacy, 27–8, 35–8; members of general assemblies, 119–20, 126.

Ordinal of 1620, 145–9.
Ordination of ministers, 52–3, 139–53.

Parish registers, 131.
Patronage system, 138–9.
Perth Articles: Spottiswood's estimate of, 64, 190; and the 1618 assembly, 124, 182; observance of, 183–92, 200–1.
Poor, care of, 80–83.
Prayers, read at services, 178–9.
Presbyteries: establishment of, 85–8; membership of, 88–91; moderators of, 20, 91–3; the exercise, 93–5; discipline, 95–100; excommunication administered by, 53–4, 100–105; visitations, 105–6; other duties, 107–8; estimate of, 108–10, 201.
Presentations to benefices, 24–5.
Provincial assemblies, 117–19.

Readers: expectants as, 138; and worship, 178; admission and duties, 107, 192–4.
Restoration church, contrasted with Jacobean, 62–3, 203–4.

Schools: admission of schoolmasters, 107–8; expectants as schoolmasters, 138; establishment of, 194–7; financial support, 197–8.
Spottiswood, John, archbishop of St. Andrews: warrant to visit churches, 22; judge of Court of Session, 24; estimate of, 58–9.
Stipends, 156–8, 167–9; *see also* Commission for Modification.
Superintendents: in synods, 111–12; in general assemblies, 122; authority and work, 7–8.
Synods, 111–17, 201.

Testaments of bishops, 44; of ministers, 167–9.

Visitations: by bishops, 49–52; by presbyteries, 105–6.

Worship: daily services, 177, 193; Sunday services, 177–81. *Also see* Perth Articles.